Technology, Education—Connections
The TEC Series

Series Editor: Marcia C. Linn
Advisory Board: Robert Bjork, Chris Dede,
Carol Lee, Jim Minstrell, Jonathan Osborne, Mitch Resnick

Digital Teaching Platforms: Customizing Classroom Learning for Each Student
CHRIS DEDE AND JOHN RICHARDS, EDITORS

Leading Technology-Rich Schools: Award-Winning Models for Success
BARBARA B. LEVIN AND LYNNE SCHRUM

The Learning Edge: What Technology Can Do to Educate All Children
ALAN BAIN AND MARK E. WESTON

**Learning in the Cloud:
How (and Why) to Transform Schools with Digital Media**
MARK WARSCHAUER

**Video Games and Learning:
Teaching and Participatory Culture in the Digital Age**
KURT SQUIRE

**Teaching and Learning in Public:
Professional Development Through Shared Inquiry**
STEPHANIE SISK-HILTON

**Rethinking Education in the Age of Technology:
The Digital Revolution and Schooling in America**
ALLAN COLLINS AND RICHARD HALVERSON

**The Computer Clubhouse:
Constructionism and Creativity in Youth Communities**
YASMIN B. KAFAI, KYLIE A. PEPPLER, AND ROBBIN N. CHAPMAN, EDITORS

WISE Science: Web-Based Inquiry in the Classroom
JAMES D. SLOTTA AND MARCIA C. LINN

Creating and Sustaining Online Professional Learning Communities
JONI K. FALK AND BRIAN DRAYTON, EDITORS

**Designing Coherent Science Education:
Implications for Curriculum, Instruction, and Policy**
YAEL KALI, MARCIA C. LINN, AND JO ELLEN ROSEMAN, EDITORS

Data-Driven School Improvement: Linking Data and Learning
ELLEN B. MANDINACH AND MARGARET HONEY, EDITORS

**Electric Worlds in the Classroom:
Teaching and Learning with Role-Based Computer Games**
BRIAN M. SLATOR AND ASSOCIATES

**Meaningful Learning Using Technology:
What Educators Need to Know and Do**
ELIZABETH A. ASHBURN AND ROBERT E. FLODEN, EDITORS

Using Technology Wisely: The Keys to Success in Schools
HAROLD WENGLINSKY

Digital Teaching Platforms

Customizing Classroom Learning for Each Student

Chris Dede &
John Richards
EDITORS

Teachers College, Columbia University
New York and London

Published by Teachers College Press, 1234 Amsterdam Avenue, New York, NY 10027

Library of Congress Cataloging-in-Publication Data

Digital teaching platforms : customizing classroom learning for each student /
  EDITED BY Chris Dede and John Richards.
    pages cm. – (Technology, education--connections)
Includes index.
ISBN 978-0-8077-5316-3 (pbk. : alk. paper) – ISBN 978-0-8077-5317-0 (hardcover
: alk. paper)
    1. Computer-assisted instruction. I. Dede, Christopher. II. Richards, John,
1946-
LB1028.5.D555 2012
371.33'4–dc23   2011052043

ISBN 978-0-8077-5316-3 (paper)
ISBN 978-0-8077-5317-0 (hardcover)

Printed on acid-free paper

Manufactured in the United States of America

19   18   17   16   15   14   13   12   8   7   6   5   4   3   2   1

Contents

Digital Teaching Platforms

Opportunities and Challenges of Digital Teaching Platforms

John Richards
Chris Dede

This book describes the emergence of a new type of learning technology enabled both by advances in research and by modern one-to-one computing infrastructures in school settings. The Digital Teaching Platform (DTP) is a category of products designed to bring interactive technology to teaching and learning in classrooms; in a DTP, each student and the teacher have a laptop, or some equivalent computational device, connected to the network. A DTP is designed to operate in a teacher-led classroom as the major carrier of the curriculum content and to function as the primary instructional environment in today's technology-intensive classrooms.

A full-fledged DTP addresses three major requirements of contemporary classrooms: First, a DTP is a completely realized, networked digital environment that includes interactive interfaces for both teachers and students. Teachers use the administrative tools of this digital environment to create lessons and assignments for students and to manage and evaluate the work the students return. A DTP provides specific tools for assessment: for creating tests, assigning them to students, and reviewing the results. The teacher tools also provide timely reports on student progress or their remedial needs. The administrative tools for students allow them to complete assignments and assessments. More important, these tools allow for both individual and group work. Some students can work independently on individualized assignments, while others can work collaboratively on shared assignments.

Second, a DTP provides the content of the curriculum and assessments for teaching and learning in digital form. This content includes all of the information in the curriculum, the instruction, the exercises, and the assessments. The content also includes interactive elements, manipulative activities, special-purpose applications, and multimedia materials.

Third, a DTP supports real-time, teacher-directed interaction in the classroom. It includes special tools for managing classroom activity; monitoring progress on assignments; displaying student work, demonstrations, and challenges on interactive displays; managing group discussions; and coordinating all large-group and small-group activities.

All of these capabilities of a DTP are designed to function effectively in the give-and-take atmosphere of a traditional classroom. The teacher can shift quickly from large-group demonstrations, to small-group activities, to individualized practice and assessment. Students move seamlessly from using their devices for some of these activities to closing their computers and participating in discussions. The teacher is fully in control of student activities by giving assignments, mentoring individuals, and leading discussions. In DTPs, the pedagogy of the curriculum is designed using principles of guided social constructivism as a theory of learning, and the system provides the support for a transformation of teaching and learning.

This book articulates the current state of design and research on DTPs, sets forth principles for evaluating this type of integrated classroom technology, and sketches the likely evolution of this powerful medium for educational improvement.

The 2010 National Educational Technology Plan (NETP), recently released by the United States Department of Education, articulates the advances in learning, teaching, assessment, and infrastructure that underlie the emergence of DTPs. Chris Dede, one of the editors of this book, served on the 15-person Technical Working Group that developed the draft NETP. This book frames its discussion of DTPs in this larger context of research, policy, and practice.

THE EVOLUTION OF THE DTP

The development of comprehensive curriculum and assessment systems has a 40-year history, dating back to Patrick Suppes in the 1960s with the introduction of Computer Based Training (CBT). In the 1980s, CBT evolved into Integrated Learning Systems (ILSs). These systems are now referred to as Learning Management Systems (LMSs), and we will use this terminology. Throughout this history, there has been the close connection between content delivery and student assessment. The LMS model invoked a constrained curriculum delivery with regular feedback from the assessments for learning, as seen in Figure I.1.

The limitation of these systems is their exclusive dependence on computer diagnostics. The tests that the LMS can deliver and evaluate consist entirely of closed-response items—multiple-choice questions that have a single right answer. Furthermore, individual questions are tied directly to specific aspects of

Figure I.1. The tight linkage between learning and assessment can be richly exploited in computer-based products.

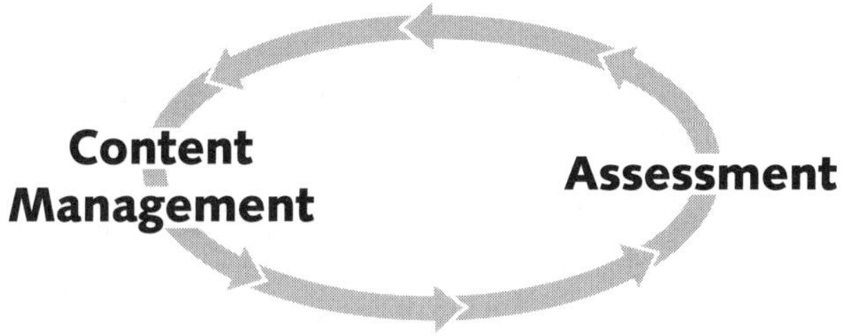

the curriculum. This creates a fairly rigid assessment model with little flexibility in its diagnostics response. These limitations are found in all LMS products.

This design is consistent with behaviorist psychological theory and the programmed learning model that it spawned. But other approaches to learning and development, seen principally in constructivist theories, suggest that deep learning does not transpire in these rigid systems. Constructivist systems require more open response from students, such as writing, project work, brainstorming, problem solving, creativity, invention, and so on. Open responses cannot be effectively evaluated by computer, so a system that supports deep learning requires the diagnostic presence of a teacher in the classroom.

A DTP provides the closed feedback loop and also a second feedback loop that flows through the teacher in typical interactions in a conventional classroom (Figure I.2). The teacher evaluates student responses and makes prescriptive decisions about each student based on that evaluation.

Digital Teaching Platforms are a *disruptive* technology, in contrast to a *sustaining* technology. Sustaining technologies foster improved performance of established products. These innovations are generally incremental and allow for the gradual evolution and improvement of products. In contrast, a disruptive technology is marked by a rapid transition that "brings to market a very different value proposition than had been available previously" (Christianson, 2003, p. xviii ff.). This disruption is an outgrowth of three concurrent paradigm shifts that are about to transform K–20 education: print-to-digital transition, one-to-one computing, and interactive display technologies.

- *Print-to-Digital Transition.* A steady transition is occurring from the print delivery of content to the digital delivery of content. The print-to-digital transition requires that digital content be accessible to students and teachers in the classroom, at home, in the library, and wherever they need access.
- *One-to-One Computing.* The ready availability of powerful, inexpensive computing devices is making ubiquitous computing

a reality in a growing number of classrooms and schools. One-to-one, ubiquitous computing demands that the technology be deeply integrated into the curriculum and pedagogy.

• *Interactive Display Technologies.* The emergence of powerful classroom displays, such as digital whiteboards, is empowering the teacher and changing the nature of classroom interactions.

These transitions, when combined to empower the teacher, are giving rise to radically more effective classrooms.

The Digital Teaching Platform is a disruptive technology that marks a transition in the nature of curriculum and pedagogy, and is in stark contrast to the behavioral beginnings of comprehensive teaching and learning environments. DTPs facilitate the management of groups of students without losing focus on individuals. They free up the teacher for small-group work and individual tutoring. In these ways, the platform respects the current accountability policies for schools by teaching to standards and preparing students for high-stakes tests.

Therefore, the technology of the Digital Teaching Platform supports both uniform mastery and individualized understanding. DTPs are designed to empower the teacher in the classroom, but they also provide anytime, anywhere access to learning. Through the personalization of learning that DTPs enable, this can transform teaching and learning for all students.

Figure I.2. The DTP adds a second loop that flows through the teacher to support open-ended activities.

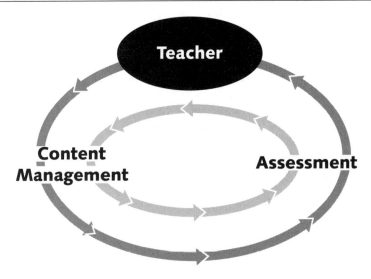

STRUCTURE OF THE BOOK

DTPs have evolved as a result of many research-based solutions to specific issues, as opposed to addressing the full integration of digital content, digital processes, and the realities of 21st-century classrooms. Research projects have provided single-subject interactive environments that challenge the student and support the teacher in the classroom. This book integrates research themes from a variety of fields to show how their synthesis is enabling DTPs.

For the past 2 decades, researchers have been developing innovative solutions to classroom practice that assume the ubiquity of technology in a classroom setting. Their designs have focused on answering questions such as: How can this ever-evolving technology support learning? How can assessment be integrated with classroom practice? What different kinds of experiences can trigger classroom discussions? In what ways can the technology provide scaffolding for the teacher? The concept of a DTP is a product of these research efforts. This book is the result of an invitational conference held in March 2010, at Harvard University, to discuss aspects of Digital Teaching Platforms. The conference was sponsored by Time To Know, Inc., the developer of the first comprehensive, scalable DTP.

Digital Teaching Platforms are a disruptive change in the evolution of technology in the classroom. The design requires new types of interactions between content, assessment, and implementation. Consequently, the book is divided into four parts. Part I, Framing the Innovation, defines DTPs and provides the current context for their evolution. The curriculum content and pedagogy, which are the focus of Part II, and the continuous formative assessment of the student, which is the focus of Part III, are deeply interwoven. Finally, in Part IV, a comprehensive, scalable DTP is examined. The chapters in this part also describe how the practical implementation of this DTP in a school creates both opportunities and challenges in professional development around pedagogy, classroom management, and technology.

Overall, this volume moves the debate about the effectiveness of technology beyond the binary "magic versus useless" debate in order to look at how technology can provide solutions to current classroom challenges. The DTP is designed to provide support for the teacher in curriculum, pedagogy, and assessment; it is developed to address the unique demands of the classroom of the 21st century.

Students, teachers, and administrators live in a digital world outside the school. This external reality is having an impact on what happens within the classroom. States are beginning to allow adoption of digital materials; classrooms are moving to one-to-one computing; interactive whiteboards are becoming ubiquitous—and yet teachers remain the most important element in a child's education. Digital Teaching Platforms are designed to support the teacher and the learner in this evolving digital world. This volume combines 20 years of research and development on how to support learning in a digital environment, synthesizing this with the realities of classroom implementation.

ACKNOWLEDGMENTS

As editors, we gratefully acknowledge the contributions of many people whose assistance was essential in producing this volume. We thank Time To Know, Inc. (in particular, Shmuel Meitar, Yosi Ben-dov, Louise Dube, Catherine Page, and Ziv Carthy) for its corporate vision in championing Digital Teaching Platforms as a method to improve education, and we appreciate the resources the company provided that enabled all the authors to prepare their contributions. We also thank Marcia Linn, Executive Editor of the Teachers College Press TEC series for which this volume was written, and all the staff at Teachers College Press who so ably improved the quality of the manuscript we submitted. We are particularly grateful to the authors, incredibly busy professionals who put precious time and effort into collaborating with one another and developing chapters for us, integrated around the theme of Digital Teaching Platforms. Finally, we thank Kurt Moellering for his assistance in copyediting and in shepherding the manuscript through to completion.

REFERENCES

Christianson, C. (2003). *The innovator's dilemma: The revolutionary book that will change the way you do business.* New York: Harper.

Suppes, P. The uses of computers in education. (1966). *Scientific American, 215,* 206–220.(*doi:10.1038/scientificamerican0966-206*).

U.S. Department of Education, Office of Education Technology. (2010). *National education technology plan 2010: Transforming American education: Learning powered by technology.* Washington, DC: U.S. Government Printing Office.

FRAMING THE INNOVATION

Part I examines the historical and conceptual context for the emergence of Digital Teaching Platforms. Trends in technology use in schools have changed the educational landscape and set the stage for a radical change in learning.

Chapter 1 examines the historical emergence of the DTP as a disruptive technology and the implications of this for the teacher and the classroom. Unlike other comprehensive curriculum and assessment products, a DTP is designed to make the teacher-led classroom the primary carrier of the curriculum content. A DTP supports the teacher with a suite of integrated tools for curriculum planning, classroom management, and student assessment. Chapter 1 places DTPs in the context of other types of comprehensive systems; reviews the research that has guided the design of DTPs from both a technological and a pedagogical perspective; and speculates on the changing 21st-century classroom in light of these three perspectives, leading to a prediction that DTPs will transform teaching practice and student learning.

Chapter 2 examines the continuing trend in technology toward one-to-one computing in schools, and how this leads naturally to the development of DTPs for the classroom. The chapter examines a survey of 1,000 schools conducted by Project RED that highlights potential challenges as well as factors for success, noting that the processes and techniques used to produce high-performing one-to-one schools are not well understood and are often undocumented, yet key implementation factors are central to their success. The author discusses how DTPs are a type of instructional infrastructure that leverages and exploits a one-to-one environment and provides improvements in student achievement. They facilitate the transition of the teacher from sage to mentor and guide. Absent a DTP, the teacher is burdened with significant challenges and additional work to implement an effective one-to-one program. In addition, DTPs can play a crucial role in enabling full personalization and individualization of the student educational experience. This is critical to efforts to improve student performance.

The author posits that we are at a tipping point in the effort to transform schools via the use of technology, and closes with an examination of second-order changes to make the transformation.

CHAPTER 1

Digital Teaching Platforms in the Spectrum of Educational Technologies

John Richards
Joseph Walters

The Digital Teaching Platform (DTP) is a new category of educational product that provides the primary instructional environment in today's technology-intensive classrooms. Unlike prior comprehensive curriculum and assessment products, it is designed for the teacher-led classroom as the primary carrier of the curriculum content. It supports the teacher with a suite of integrated tools for curriculum planning, classroom management, and student assessment. The Time To Know (T2K) product is the first example of a commercial, extensive Digital Teaching Platform operating at scale. Time To Know replaces the textbook as the medium of classroom interaction with a comprehensive, interactive digital curriculum. At the same time, it provides time-saving tools to streamline classroom management, create a smooth flow between group and individual instruction, and support customized activities and multimedia graphic materials.

This chapter first describes the Digital Teaching Platform and illustrates its concrete features with examples using the Time To Know product. The DTP is placed within the context of other comprehensive systems that address the mission of teaching, learning, and assessment in schools, both as a historical emergence and as a categorically different enterprise. The chapter then reviews the research that guided the design of one instance of a DTP, from the perspectives of the technology, the teacher, and the pedagogy.

The last section of the chapter speculates on the changing 21st-century classroom in light of the mutually supportive transitions to one-to-one computing, digital materials, and dynamic interactive displays. The DTP has the ability to transform teaching practice and student learning.

DIGITAL TEACHING PLATFORMS IN ACTION

The DTP supports teachers and students in classrooms equipped with one-to-one computing. In this environment, each student has a laptop, or some equivalent computational device, with a wireless connection to the network. The teacher also has a networked workstation connected to an interactive display, or even a projector. Under the teacher's direction, the interactions between teacher and student and among students are facilitated by the cluster of networked computers.

The DTP delivers the content of each lesson. It contains a comprehensive curriculum of guided learning sequences that include applet activities, multimedia presentations, practice exercises, and games. The vignettes below illustrate the use of this platform with mathematics lessons in a 5th-grade classroom. Before class the teacher uses planning tools to prepare; during class he or she uses multimedia to introduce a topic, an applet to explore a mathematics concept, and practice exercises. After class, the teacher can review each student's progress and trends in the class performance, and begin the process for planning tomorrow's lessons.

Vignette 1

Mr. Jones teaches 5th grade and is preparing for a math lesson on finding common denominators. This is a new fractions concept for the class, so he plans to use the Fraction Bar application to have students explore fractions of equal value (Figure 1.1). The integrated curriculum material also includes an animation to introduce the concept and several related practice activities.

Jones opens the lesson planning tool and selects the learning sequence on common denominators. From this collection of activities, he selects an animation and several exercises and adds them to the lesson plan.

Students use the Fraction Bar to create fractions with different numerators and denominators. First, they select a denominator, and the application creates a horizontal bar with the corresponding number of boxes. Then they click any box in the bar to fill it with color; the numerator increases to show the corresponding fraction. Students can also click on a filled box to remove the color and decrease the numerator. By creating two parallel bars with the applet, students can test two fractions for equivalence by comparing the lengths of their filled boxes.

Jones previews the application and then adds it to his lesson, along with some questions to guide student discussion. He saves his revised learning sequence and assigns the activities to the class.

The next morning in math class, Jones begins the lesson with the animation that shows the "Magic Machine" transforming one fraction into an equivalent fraction—the fraction 1/2 becomes 3/6. Next Jones explains how to use the fractions bar applet and tells the students to begin their first activity. Students open their laptops. On their student desktop, they see the activity, several practice exercises, and some guiding questions for class discussion.

The students are familiar with the interface, and they immediately open the activity and begin work. They use the Fraction Bar to create fractions that have different denominators, but are the same length. When they find examples, they save them to the Gallery. Later, Jones displays the Gallery on the interactive whiteboard and the class discusses the examples.

As the first vignette shows, teachers use the DTP to plan their lessons and to customize learning sequences. The DTP also lets them assign assessments to students and create reports of student progress. Because each student uses a laptop or equivalent device during class, the teacher can monitor individual progress and communicate unobtrusively with each student.

The students' workspace is simple and consistent. Students see only the activities that they are assigned, so they are not distracted by materials meant

Figure 1.1. The Fraction Bar screen lets students explore fractions with different denominators.

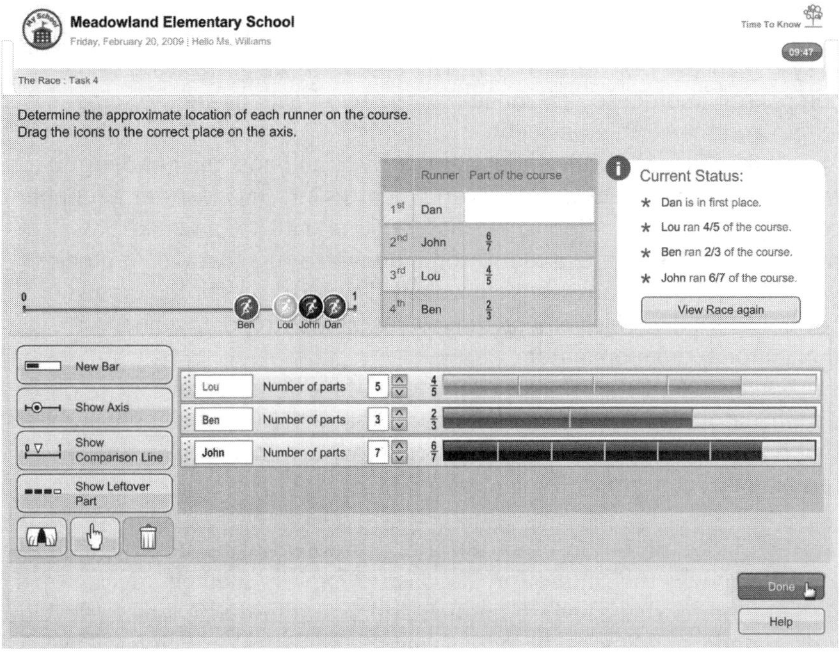

for others or by activities that will be used later. They quickly learn to navigate the interface to find and complete their assignments.

Vignette 2

In Mr. Jones's math class, students work in pairs using an application to explore equivalent fractions. The "Magic Machine" lesson on equivalent fractions will challenge students to find a rule for determining which fractions are equivalent. Rather than simply stating the rule and then providing lots of practice exercises with it, the lesson begins by providing students with tools to explore equivalent fractions, and then opens up to explore the rule.

One student builds fractions with the fraction bar applet. The student creates the fractions by filling in the blocks for the numerator with a pattern of alternating colors. To depict the fraction 4/8, the student creates a bar with 8 boxes and then fills in the first box on the left, the third box from the left, the fifth box, and the seventh box. This creates a pleasant patchwork design. Next the student creates the fraction 3/6 in a similar way. But the two fractions bars, filled in this way, are difficult to compare for equivalence by comparing lengths.

After a few minutes of puzzling over this, the student seems to understand the problem—it is too difficult to compare the lengths of the fractions. The student clears the color from the boxes and fills them in systematically from left to right. This creates a straightforward visual comparison in order to determine that the two fractions are the same length and therefore equivalent.

As the students work through this activity and post their findings to the Gallery, Jones fields questions and mentors individuals. After a number of examples are submitted to the Gallery, Jones initiates a whole-class discussion. Students are asked to come up with a rule that would predict when different fractions were equivalent. This sparks a spirited discussion. Several alternative rules emerge, involving multiplying or dividing numerator and denominator.

Some students notice that nearly all of the examples used denominators of 2 and 3, and they guess that these were the only numbers that work. Others suggest that they test other denominators before reaching this conclusion.

This guided exploration of an intriguing problem using the fractions bar applet provides the setting for the class to explore mathematical properties, to discuss what they are finding, and from those activities to develop a deep understanding of the underlying mathematical principles. The boy who creates the visual pattern illustrates how in the constructivist approach students do not always follow a direct line from problem to solution.

Because the teacher is present, the content of the DTP can include open-response activities. In the second vignette, we see how the Time To Know version of a DTP has capitalized on this quality by building a strong constructivist pedagogy into the content it presents.

In DTPs students can work with open-ended tools to explore the principles and concepts of mathematics and language arts. Led by the teacher through this exploration, experimentation, and discussion, students can construct a deeper understanding of these concepts and learn to extend them to new situations. The applications and applets, such as the fractions bar used in the vignette, provide the opportunity for constructivist learning. Much like the hands-on manipulative materials of a traditional mathematics class, these applets promote exploration and discovery.

Vignette 3

Jones then instructs students to begin work on their individual assignments. These are selected exercises and gamelike activities that give the students a chance to practice with the concept of equivalent fractions. When he planned for this class, Jones assigned specific activities to individual students, based on their interests and capabilities. He knew, for example, that several students already had a good grasp of fractions concepts and were ready for some challenging problems; others needed to take smaller steps and work on prerequisite skills before moving forward. With this in mind, Jones assigned students different activities; the DTP system can also adjust assignments based on past performance.

At this point the students open their laptops, select the assigned activity, and begin work. Each student sees only the activities that have been assigned to him or her. The students work independently, side by side, and usually do not realize that they have different tasks to complete.

As students work through these exercises, Jones monitors their progress by walking around the room. He spends a few minutes helping one particular student and then goes to his workstation at the front of the room, where he reviews a status report of student progress. He notices that the two students who are working collaboratively on a challenging assignment appear stuck, so at his computer he assigns the pair a different activity and then visits them to see why they are having difficulty.

As he reviews the various students' screens on the teacher computer display, he realizes that many of the students are stuck on this problem. He puts the work from one of the pairs of students showing their progress on the interactive display device, and presses the "Eyes Front" button on his

display, sending a message to each laptop. Students stop work and close
their computers as Jones runs a short whole-class discussion about the
particular problem.

That evening, Jones reviews the student reports on the activity and
begins his preparations for the next day. He will continue the fractions
work, with a matching game on equivalent fractions. Students will also
build fractions by cutting up strips of paper and compare these concrete
constructions with their work on the computer.

This vignette shows how the DTP keeps the teacher in charge of the lesson,
while providing the tools and resources that he needs to ensure that the class
runs smoothly. These resources range from multimedia demonstrations that
involve the entire class to small-group projects and individual assignments.
The platform ensures that students understand their assignments, and can
move quickly from one activity to the next without losing time or momentum.

The DTP also helps the teacher individualize assignments to students.
Individualization–matching students to learning activities based on interest
and capability–is a key element of personalized learning. In traditional settings, individualization can be logistically complicated and can disrupt the
flow of instruction, but with DTPs individualization is straightforward and
can be handled before class begins.

DIGITAL TEACHING PLATFORM IN CONTEXT

In this section we turn our attention to Comprehensive Curriculum and
Assessment Systems– elaborate computer products that some schools use to
support teaching and learning. These systems provide teachers with administrative tools to make assignments and review student results. The systems
include mechanisms that enable students to study lessons, complete assignments, and take tests.

This class of products does not include the more limited, special-purpose
applications in schools, such as science simulations, grade book applications,
assessment products, video streaming services, and so on. We focus on products that address the entire teaching and learning enterprise.

We identified three different types of comprehensive products. They are
described here and analyzed in the section that follows. We also include the
traditional textbook and its digital equivalent, the e-textbook, in this analysis.

Course Platform Learning Management Systems

Course Platform Learning Management Systems (LMSs) provide software for creating and refining course content, for designing and administering

assessment, and for communication and collaboration. Course Platform systems have tools for creating and managing teacher accounts and student accounts, for importing content, and for managing results. They provide detailed reports that can be used to create new assignments.

These systems also provide some tools for students, allowing them to see their work or test what they have been assigned, as well as providing them a mechanism for returning the completed work to the teacher. The teacher must then correct the work and enter those results into the system. Tests are created from closed-response questions and are corrected by the system. Using those data, the system then creates complex reports on student accomplishments.

These systems do not provide the content of the curriculum: the activities, practice pages, reading assignments, assessment questions, and so on. That content is created or entered by the district or by the teacher. Districts can also purchase content from third-party vendors or from other districts. Examples of products in this category include Blackboard, Desire2Learn, Moodle/Moodlerooms, Sakai, Project, School Town, Pearson/Tapestry, Edmin, Edline, and SchoolNet.

These systems are most appealing to schools that have a lot of quality content and are looking for a system that will allow them to organize that content into online courses and to deliver those courses efficiently. For example, the Course Platform systems are often used to support virtual high schools and other online courses.

These systems make only moderate demands on the technology: Teachers must have access to a computer, but it need not be in the classroom. Students too must have computer access, but they don't have to use the computer during class. Typically, these systems require fairly complicated installation procedures, including integration with student information systems (SIS) and human resource (HR) systems.

Course Delivery Learning Management Systems

Course Delivery Learning Management Systems provide both the content of the course and the platform for instruction. Like the Course Platforms, these systems have both teacher and student accounts. The system assigns work to students, creates and assigns tests, and reviews the results.

These systems provide all the content needed for the course: instructional content, exercise assignments, and test questions. They often provide elaborate multimedia elements as well. These systems do not allow the district or the teachers to add their own content.

The Course Delivery LMS, like the Course Platform LMS, is designed to operate without a teacher present. Examples of products in this category include CompassLearning/Odyssey, Plato Learning, Riverdeep Destination Series,

Ignite! Learning, K–12, American Education Corporation's A+, McGraw Hill's SRA Real Math, Pearson NovaNet, and Pearson SuccessMaker.

These systems are designed for use outside of class, and they do not require additional management by the teacher. For that reason, Course Delivery LMSs are ideal in computer labs or in after-school environments; they are rarely used in classrooms. The implementers of these systems are programs geared to meet the remedial needs of specific students, to supplement test-preparation curriculum, or to provide an efficient method for using computer labs. They are often used for credit recovery programs for students who have already failed a course or in pull-out activities in the back of a classroom for students who are either advanced or require remedial work. A school with a computer lab can operate a Course Delivery LMS quite effectively.

Digital Teaching Platforms

Digital Teaching Platforms provide comprehensive courseware with tools for teachers and students like the Course Delivery systems. The difference between the two is that the DTP is designed for classroom use and requires one-to-one hardware and a wireless environment. The curriculum is teacher-centered, not teacher-proof.

Time To Know is the only commercial example of a comprehensive Digital Teaching Platform. Three other products have some of the features of DTP and represent a transition in this direction: Renaissance Learning, Discovery Science, and Carnegie Algebra Tutor. Chapters 3 and 4 in this book discuss research-based DTPs that typically focus on a single curriculum area.

DTPs are used in classrooms. The audience for these products is composed of districts that want teachers to use the computer as a regular part of their classroom instruction. A school must have one-to-one computing in every class that uses a Digital Teaching Platform. They can share laptops between classes (often called the *computers on wheels* approach), but this is not optimal.

Print and Digital Textbooks

A textbook is an analog version of the comprehensive system for learning that provides all of the content needed to support instruction in a given subject. The textbook also provides many tools for the teacher, including pedagogical guidelines, grading mechanisms, practice exercises, lesson sequencing, and so on. Indeed, the teacher's edition of the textbook is substantially larger than the student edition.

A digital textbook is generally an exact duplicate of the print book in a PDF or other machine-readable form. Textbooks are designed to be used in classrooms by teachers and students. The exact use of digital texts is less clear. Nearly every school uses textbooks. Print texts make no technological demands, while digital texts can be integrated with other technological services (e.g., websites, online dictionaries, digital whiteboards, and assessment programs).

Eight Features of a 21st-Century Classroom

In Table 1.1 we analyze and compare features of the different comprehensive systems of curriculum and assessment. To structure this analysis, we examine eight aspects of the 21st-century classroom.

1. *Interactive Digital Environment*: Does the product provide some kind of digital tools for the school or teacher? Does it enable digital input from the teacher? Does it include student accounts and facilitate student input?
2. *Teacher Administrative Tools*: Does the product provide specific tools for teachers to use in their teaching, such as lesson assignment and management, assessment assignment, automated test reports, and grading tools?
3. *Student Tools*: Does the product provide individualized instruction to students? Does it include tools for receiving assignments and turning them in? Does it include an assessment system?
4. *Course Authoring Tools*: Does the system provide tools for entering original content? Does it structure the entry of content with templates for lessons and for assessments? Does the system include tools for importing third-party content?
5. *Curriculum Content*: Does the system provide the instructional content of the curriculum and assessment? Does that content include multimedia elements and interactive applets? Does the system enable individualized instruction? Is it aligned to state standards?
6. *Assessment Content*: Does the system provide the assessment content of the curriculum, including test questions? Does it provide automated reports based on those questions? Is the assessment individualized? Are the results of the assessment linked back to the curriculum?
7. *Classroom Support*: Must the teacher be present, managing the classroom? Does the system provide tools for real-time classroom management? Can the teacher use the system during class to monitor assignments and assessments? Does the system provide tools for integrating interactive display technology?
8. *Pedagogical Support*: Does the system support open-response problems? Does it enable creative problem-solving, project work, brainstorming, and other opportunities for unique student responses? Does it facilitate both large- and small-group work? Does it provide tools for collaboration and solution sharing?

Table 1.1. Comparisons Between Different Comprehensive Learning Systems

21st-Century School Environment	Course Platform LMS	Course Delivery LMS	Digital Teaching Platform	Textbook	e-book
Interactive Digital Environment				No	No
Computer-based delivery	☑	☑	☑		☑
Teacher accounts	☑	☑	☑		
Student accounts	☑	☑	☑		
Digital student interaction	☑	☑	☑		
Used in distance-learning situations	☑	☑			
Teacher Administration Tools					
Lesson assignment/management	☑	☑	☑	☑	☑
Assessment assignment/management	☑	☑	☑	☑	☑
Automated progress reports	☑	☑	☑		
Grading tools	☑	☑	☑	☑	☑
Student Administration Tools					
Individualized instruction	☑	☑	☑		
Assignment drop box	☑	☑	☑	☑	☑
Assessment delivery system	☑	☑	☑	☑	☑
Course Authoring Tools		No		No	No
Content entry systems	☑		☑		
Lesson templates	☑		☑		
Assessment templates	☑		☑		
Mechanisms for importing content	☑		☑		

	No		Some
Curriculum Content Features			
Instructional content provided		☑	☑
Assignment content provided		☑	☑
Includes integrated multimedia content	☑	☑	
Includes interactive applets	☑	☑	
Enables individualized instruction	☑	☑	
Alignment to standards	☑	☑	☑
Assessment Content Features	No		
Includes test questions	☑	☑	☑
Assessment report templates	☑	☑	☑
Individualized assessment	☑	☑	
Results linked to curriculum	☑	☑	
Classroom Support Tools	No		
Teacher manages learning in classroom		☑	☑
Tools for real-time classroom management	☑		
In-class assignment monitoring	☑		
In-class assessment monitoring	☑		
Interactive display integration	☑		
Pedagogical Support Tools	No		
Curriculum allows open response		☑	☑
Enables problem solving, creativity, etc	☑	☑	☑
Facilitates large- & small-group work	☑	☑	☑
Tools for collaboration and sharing	☑	☑	☑

Comparison by Features

Table 1.1 summarizes our comparison of the systems based on the eight features of the 21st-century classroom. All three types of comprehensive systems include an interactive digital environment and administrative tools for teachers and students. They are very different with respect to the source of content: The Course Platform LMSs do not include content, but do provide tools for authoring content, for importing it from other sources, and for customizing that content.

The Course Delivery LMSs and the DTPs provide all content. The content includes both curriculum and assessment. These systems also provide tools for individualizing instruction and for delivering interactive applets. Course Delivery LMSs do not allow teachers to enter their own content or to customize it. DTPs provide tools for manipulating lesson content and importing new types of content.

The Digital Teaching Platform differs from the Course Delivery LMS in terms of classroom operation and pedagogical support. Through the monitoring of assignments and assessment, DTP systems offer tools for management of the classroom by the teacher and real-time evaluation of students.

Because the teacher is present during learning, the DTP systems can include open-response problems. This allows the curriculum to move beyond direct instruction and multiple-choice assessment to curriculum that involves creativity, brainstorming, project work, and group problem solving. DTP systems also provide tools for small-group work, collaboration, and the sharing of student work.

It is important to explain why we included the print and e-textbooks in our comparison. The textbook is a highly evolved product that has responded to teacher and administrator demands for over a century. While there are obvious shortcomings beyond price and weight, it provides a basis for considering critical features of a teacher-oriented comprehensive teaching and learning environment. The e-textbook, while having the potential to reduce price and certainly to reduce weight, is at best a compromise. By replicating the textbook, it fails to take advantage of the kind of interactivity that marks the evolution of the DTP.

The other comprehensive systems fall short even in comparison with the textbook, because from an information-processing point of view they merely automate or magnify individual capabilities, rather than compose a system of capabilities. The essence of product design is function, not features. Both the textbook and the DTP have the former as well as the latter.

The most important pattern in the table is that the LMS systems are strong in the categories at the top of the table—in interactivity and student and teacher administration. And the textbook is strong in the categories at the bottom of the chart—in classroom and teacher support tools. The DTP crosses both of these boundaries due to the design that supports the teacher.

DTPs provide the closed assess-teach feedback loop that helps with practice and personalization (see Figure 1.1), but they also include a second feedback loop that flows through the teacher in the typical interactions in a normal classroom. The teacher evaluates student responses and makes prescriptive decisions about each student based on that evaluation (see Figure 1.2).

The DTP is an integrated solution that combines features of diverse products. Figure 1.2 inserts the DTP within the broader context of the school. We can begin to see how some of these subsystems are contained in the design of the DTP. These subsystems include:

- *Instructional Process Systems.* These handle administrative functions, but not much else (cf. SchoolNet, Riverdeep Learning Village, Edmin Inform, Pearson eCollege and eSchool).
- *Course/Content Authoring/Creation.* These tools are part of some LMS platform systems, but not all.
- *Content Management Systems.* CMSs are not organized into courses (cf. Discovery Streaming).
- *Web Content Aggregators.* These mainly target the library /media specialist, are not organized into curriculum parts or courses, and do not have any administrative functions (cf. Hot Chalk).
- *Portals.* These are not organized into modules or courses (cf. School Fusion, School Wires, Edline).
- *Student Support Systems.* These are intended for use by students with teacher or parent assistance or intervention (cf. Study Wiz, K–12).

Figure 1.2. The DTP accommodates personalization through the inner loop and open-ended explorations through the teacher. This system is embedded within the structure of the school.

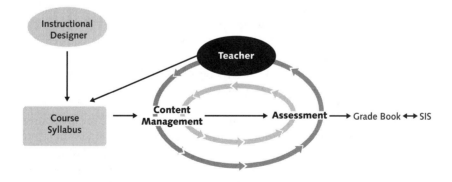

DESIGNING THE DTP

This section examines the research behind the use of DTP systems in classrooms, looking at three research categories: technology, classroom practice, and pedagogy.

Research: Technology

The hardware used in the Digital Teaching Platform–laptop computers or equivalent devices and a wireless network–is less than 10 years old, and research findings that document this infrastructure's impact on teaching and learning are sparse. Nevertheless, the one-to-one computing environment has spawned a number of studies; although the results of these investigations are encouraging, the findings are limited and one must draw inferences with care (see Chapter 2, this volume).

Much of the research on one-to-one computing takes an undifferentiated view of computers in classrooms. These studies often compare technology-intensive classrooms to similar classrooms that are not using the technology. The comparisons include little analysis of how the computers are actually used or the part played by the teacher or the instructional software. In fact, most one-to-one classrooms use computers for web research or for typical Microsoft Office-type tools, such as word processing, spreadsheets, and presentations (see Chapter 2, this volume).

Current research is beginning to focus on various contributing factors, moving beyond technology usage to examine precisely how the infrastructure facilitates teaching and learning. These studies have a common finding: How the teacher uses the technology contributes significantly to the effectiveness of that technology.

Classrooms with Technology versus Those Without. A number of studies illustrate the findings and limitations of high-level comparisons. A research team from Boston College evaluated a wireless initiative in western Massachusetts in which students were equipped with wireless laptop computers. The study examined the student scores on the Massachusetts statewide examination (the MCAS) and found a significant improvement in the technology classrooms across a 2-year span (Bebell and Kay, 2008).

A study of California middle school students found that laptop students significantly outscored students in conventional classrooms in the areas of mathematics and language arts (Gulek & Demirtas, 2005). In Germany, a study found that laptop students made greater gains than students in a comparison group on technology literacy (productivity tools; skill in using the Internet; and knowledge of hardware, software, and operating systems), especially for girls (Schaumburg, 2001).

Two recent studies of technology with large numbers of students failed to demonstrate that technology in the classrooms was consistently effective. A 4-year evaluation of technology immersion in Texas showed that in several instances the treatment groups outperformed the control classrooms, but that in other cases the two groups were the same. This study also found that only 25% of the *immersion* classrooms used technology at a high level, although the level of use and the proficiency of the teachers increased over the 4 years of the study (Shapely, Sheehan, Maloney, & Caranikas-Walker, 2009). Also, a study by the Institute of Education Sciences (IES) of the Department of Education found no significant gains in the treatment group of a controlled study (Dynarski, Agodini, Heaviside, Novak, Carey, Campuzano, et al., 2007).

Variables in Technology Implementation Impact Its Effectiveness. As researchers move beyond simple comparisons of classrooms with computers versus classrooms without computers, they are finding important underlying variables. In the research on one-to-one computing, studies consistently point to the importance of the nature of the implementation: Was the technology used effectively? Were the teachers proficient with it? How rigorous was the courseware?

A recent review of the research on one-to-one computing (Lemke & Fadel, 2006) found several studies that identified an increasing student engagement in learning. These studies showed that in technology-intensive classrooms with effective implementation, instructional practices shifted to more collaborative, small-group work; used curricula that were more student centered and problem based; and produced more higher-order thinking skills. These gains were predicated on fidelity of the implementation to the instructional program as designed. Teachers who used the technology effectively were more likely to produce gains than teachers who were unprepared for the technology. School leadership and school culture were strong correlates of that fidelity.

Lemke and Fadel (2006) concluded that new studies must pay careful attention to these factors, examining specifically the roles of leadership, professional development, school culture, and curricular redesign. At the same time, the review found few rigorous research studies on the one-to-one model and advised caution in making inferences from this limited scholarly literature.

A more recent study that focused on the one-to-one use of laptops in high school (Zucker & Hug, 2007) found that technology as a sole change factor is not enough to produce gains in student learning and teacher effectiveness. The hardware must be accompanied by changes in teaching, testing, and professional development. Indeed, the complexity of the technology was a challenge to successful implementation. In this study, teachers had to learn to manage their classes in different ways; they had to keep the hardware functioning; and they had to find adequate software and learn to use it. The teachers who surmounted these challenges produced the greatest results.

The importance of multiple factors in implementation is documented by technology coordinators. In a survey, coordinators of one-to-one computing programs rated their areas of interest. Although teacher professional development was at the top of the list, 64% reported a need for content resources (Wilson, 2008). A preliminary study of the Maine Laptop Initiative, a statewide implementation of one-to-one computing in middle school, found that teachers who were proficient with technology used it more effectively. They were more likely to report that the laptops had a positive impact on students, to collaborate with colleagues and students, and to conduct online assessments (Sargent, 2003).

These findings are highly relevant to the analysis of the DTP. The hardware and course content, by themselves, will always depend on the teacher's skills with these tools. In recognizing the importance of the teacher, Time To Know includes an extensive program of professional development that addresses the pedagogy of the platform as well as the technology (cf. Rockman and Scott, Chapter 11 of this volume). Looking ahead, investigations of one-to-one computing are increasing. The impact of this technology on teaching and learning has been anticipated by researchers around the world (see Chan, Roschelle, Hsi, Kinshuk, Sharples, Brown, et al., 2006, for an analysis of the related research opportunities).

Research: Classrooms

Using a DTP in the classroom opens up new opportunities for teaching and learning, but opportunities for more sophisticated pedagogy also pose challenges for the teacher (Zucker & Hug, 2007). This section considers the challenges inherent in the task of managing the classroom equipped with this technology.

Jon Saphier and Robert Gower, in their seminal work *The Skillful Teacher* (1997), identify six challenges that must be faced in effective classroom management: attention, momentum, time, space, routines, and discipline. Technology offers many opportunities to orchestrate the choreography of classroom management, and the discussion below shows how the features of the Time To Know DTP have been designed to aid the teacher in each of these areas.

Attention. Students learn only when they attend to their learning. Teachers must get students on task during class time by engaging them in legitimate curriculum activities. In fact, researchers have documented that time on task is positively correlated with achievement (Bennett, 1978). Time To Know engages students through its visual demonstrations and animations. The interactive applets challenge them to explore problems and patterns. The LiveText feature scaffolds their reading skills and motivates them to keep reading. At the same time, real-time progress reports ensure that students are working on activities that are productive. All tasks and materials in the Time To Know DTP are designed to be relevant and engaging.

Momentum. The teacher must coordinate the flow of events during class and provide smooth, rapid transitions between activities (Kounin, 1970). Breaks in momentum are a distraction and interfere with students' concentration. Time To Know helps maintain class momentum by giving the teacher tools for directing students through the transitions from group discussion to individual practice. The Eyes to the Board tool signals students at their laptops to stop their independent work and to participate in a large-group experience. The activities within each learning sequence are also designed to flow in a meaningful way.

Space and Time. Teachers must organize the physical space of the classroom in order to maintain momentum and routine. They must manage events, regulate schedules, and allocate time appropriately. Teachers must use that time efficiently, and they must set a pace for all activities that meets the needs of individuals as well as the whole class (Stallings, 1980). In analyzing the use of computers in classrooms, Roschelle and Pea (2002) depict the ability of one-to-one computers to augment physical space with important information exchanges among students and teachers.

Time To Know and students' wireless computers provide a mechanism for organizing the physical space. Students work individually or in groups. They move to and from the whiteboard in the front of the room. They can easily relocate their computers for each of these activities while still being monitored by the teacher's workstation. Also, the T2K planning tools help teachers use class time most efficiently.

Routines. Classes are managed most efficiently by building procedural routines and using them effectively. Students must know what these routines are and how to engage in them. Time To Know helps develop these routines by deploying a uniform user interface for all activities and applets. When students open their laptops, they quickly begin to navigate their assignments, even though the activities in those assignments may be completely new to them. These routines also simplify the many transitions during class.

Discipline. From time to time, all teachers must respond to resistant students. Rules must be clear and specific. Positive expectations must be repeated. Students must have a sense of influence on the life of the classroom

(Gordon, 1974). Students often become frustrated when they are working on assignments that are too hard, and they are bored when their assignments are too easy. By customizing all assignments to students individually, and by adjusting these assignments during class, the teacher keeps students working at their optimal level, reducing the number of discipline issues.

The classroom is a complex environment that requires thoughtful preparation in planning followed by a skillful choreography in execution. The six attributes here delineate that choreography, illustrating how the T2K platform supports these tasks and, when used effectively, make the teacher more productive. When all this comes together, students operate more independently, making the transitions from one type of activity to the next without disrupting their learning.

Research: Individualization, Practice, and Assessment

Extensive educational research documents the importance of guided practice in learning skills and concepts. In 2008, a national panel in mathematics education concluded that "curriculum must provide sufficient practice and in fact few U.S. curricula do so. Pedagogy should develop proficiency in students. Proficiency means that students understand the key concepts, achieve automaticity, develop flexible, accurate, automatic execution of standard algorithms, and use these competencies to solve problems" (National Mathematics Advisory Panel, 2008).

Research on reading also finds that practice develops skills, especially when coupled with timely feedback (National Institute of Child Health and Human Development, 2000). Studies find that frequent feedback to students about their learning yields substantial learning gains (Black & Wiliam, 1998).

The role of practice in developing expertise has been studied extensively. Research shows that *deliberate* practice—practice that is thoughtful and well supported with feedback from a teacher—is essential to developing expertise in many disciplines, including music, sports, mathematics, chess, and surgery (Ericsson, Charness, & Feltovich, 2006).

Practice is effective only when it is accompanied by timely feedback. Research in mathematics education finds a value in using technology to administer formative assessments when the assessment results are then used to individualize assignments (National Mathematics Advisory Panel, 2008). Similarly, in reading there is an important role for practice, coupled with diagnostic assessment. These assessments can guide instruction on a moment-to-moment basis and can respond to individual needs (National Institute for Literacy, 2007).

Contemporary research also finds a strong connection between assessment and student production. Students must learn to evaluate their own work during the production process; this evaluation must happen during each productive act, including moments of deliberate practice. Students must have tactics they use to modify their work as they produce it. These skills or tactics can be developed with direct authentic evaluative experience, and the instructional system must supply these (Sadler, 1989).

Accurate, timely assessment is also related to effective use of individualized practice. Stiggins (2004) postulates that maximum learning comes from active engagement between the teacher and student; this engagement allows students to decide if they are likely to succeed and if meeting the standards is worth the effort. In other words, students examine these assessment factors on a personal level.

Stiggins concludes that many current assessment practices, especially high-stakes tests, do not provide this kind of information to students. Instructional decisions best occur in a fluid day-to-day instructional environment, not once a year in standardized tests. Using online assessment tools, teachers and students can assess individual learning and instructional progress quickly and efficiently. This approach to assessment has additional analytical power for the teacher because the results are both individualized by the student and combined into a class analysis. Aggregating data in this way can be critical to planning for the group (Roschelle & Pea, 2002).

Finally, the role of individualization through technology leads to a view of "personalized learning." As Howard Gardner (2009) describes it:

> Well-programmed computers offer many ways to master materials. Students or their teachers will choose the optimal ways of presenting the materials. Appropriate tools for assessment will be implemented. And best of all, computers are infinitely patient and flexible. If a promising approach does not work the first time, it can be repeated, and if it continues to fail, other options will be readily available. (p. 86)

This research demonstrates clearly the importance of customizing instruction and practice with tools like those in the T2K platform. Teachers make assignments to individual students as part of the planning process, and they can adapt these assignments during class based on student work and assessment. This keeps the practice and assessment tasks closely linked, and helps the teacher keep all students working at an optimal level at all times.

The practice elements can also be combined with other types of activities. Some students can work on a practice assignment while others are using open-ended applets or working with game activities, viewing media, or reading text. While all these activities are under way, the teacher can spend time mentoring struggling students individually. The customization made possible by the DTP includes both types of activities as well as the developmental level of those activities.

Research: Pedagogy

A DTP implements a specific pedagogical approach. The Time To Know system and DTPs, as described in this book, are designed around principles of *social constructivist* learning.

In the constructivist view, meaning is developed by the individual; it is not something that exists in the world apart from the individual. Learners construct new knowledge and understandings based on what they already know and believe. Student learning is shaped by developmental level and experience. Sociocultural background knowledge is embedded in a setting and mastered through authentic, realistic tasks. Learners build a personal knowledge of reality and create novel and situation-specific understandings. Instruction must provide rich, loosely structured experiences that encourage meaning-making without imposing a fixed set of knowledge and skills. This guidance can come in the form of coaching, mentoring, or apprenticing (Dede, 2008). Curriculum built on constructivist principles must develop conceptual understandings together with fluency and problem-solving skills in a manner that makes these attributes mutually supportive (National Mathematics Advisory Panel, 2008).

In the constructivist approach, instruction is a process that supports knowledge construction rather than communicating that knowledge. The teacher serves as a guide, rather than as the expert who transfers knowledge to students. Learning activities are authentic and leverage the learners' puzzlement and curiosity that arise when their faulty or incomplete knowledge fails to predict what they observe. Teachers encourage students to reflect on these experiences, to seek alternative viewpoints, and to test a variety of ideas. Student motivation to achieve these goals is determined by factors such as challenge, curiosity, choice, fantasy, and social recognition (Malone & Lepper, 1987; Pintrich & Schunk, 2002).

The National Research Council lists the essential goals of learning in a constructivist approach: building a deep foundation of factual knowledge and procedural skills; developing conceptual frameworks; organizing domain knowledge as experts do; and improving the thinking processes (National Research Council, 2005).

Student motivation to achieve these goals is determined by a variety of intrinsic and extrinsic factors, such as satisfaction from achievement, contributing to others, and challenge and curiosity (Pintrich & Schunk, 2002).

Researchers whose theories were important in the development of this school of thought include Anderson (1993), Bruner (1960, 1968), Piaget (1967, 1974), Mayer (1977), Norman (1980), Newell and Simon (1972), Palincsar and Brown (1984), and Vygotsky (1986). A number of design strategies based on these theories often aimed to help students understand disciplinary knowledge (Case, 1992; Hunt & Minstrell, 1994; Lee & Ashby, 2001). The theory has been especially influential in mathematics education (Glasersfeld, 1995a & 1995b).

Recent writers have analyzed constructivism in specific contexts. Dede reviews studies that apply this perspective to information and communications technologies and finds that these studies, covering a broad range of topics, tend to return positive results (Dede, 2008). Others have articulated techniques for implementing the constructivist approach in day-to-day classroom practice (Brooks & Brooks, 1999; Fostnot, 2005; Gagnon, Collay, & Schmuck, 2005). With respect to classroom practice, Perkins cautions practitioners to approach constructivism with a pragmatic bent, counseling them to concentrate on what works (Perkins, 1999).

Time To Know as a Social Constructivist Platform

Time To Know is designed on constructivist principles. It engages students by having them do meaningful tasks in mathematics and reading/language arts. It provides open-ended applets that students use to explore specific problems or concepts. In mathematics, these applets provide an environment for exploring specific concepts; vignettes 1 and 2 illustrate this with the applet fraction bar. In reading language arts, a function called LiveText gives students tools to interact with reading material and provides guided support for developing reading skills and the comprehension of text.

The Gallery feature provides a venue in which students post their work and review the work of their peers. The Gallery also serves as a mechanism the teacher can use to report and analyze student work and to let students see it being shared with others. Both implementations of the Gallery can guide class discussion. Long-term assignments stimulate inquiry learning based on student projects. These elements are all important in the constructivist view. Roschelle also points out that technology makes it easier for teachers to target prior understanding, engage students in discussion, and provide frequent feedback. He reminds readers that "teacher implementation of these practices is the main cause of improved student performance," again raising the issue of program effectiveness (Roschelle, Penuel, & Abrahamson, 2004).

TECHNOLOGY AS AN AGENT OF CHANGE IN THE CLASSROOM

In 1993, Larry Cuban wrote an article in the *Teachers College Record* with the title "Computers Meet the Classroom: Classroom Wins." In the article, Cuban analyzed the place of technology in education and suggested reasons for the slow adoption of technology at that time. He claimed that the reason was not funding or training or the technology, but rather a misunderstanding of the role of schools in society.

Cuban's essay remains surprisingly appropriate to this analysis of the use of technology in today's classrooms. Cuban posited three scenarios for the future of technological innovation in schools. In the first scenario, the *technophile* predicts that technology will make schools more efficient and therefore more productive, as computers liberate students and teachers from drudgery and inflexible approaches. These instructional delivery systems enhanced with technology will take a central role in classroom practice, transforming it dramatically, and the systems may even grow so intelligent that they can replace the teacher as deliverer of information. Although there were many who supported the technophile view in 1993, there are few supporters today and little interest in artificial intelligence in the classroom.

The second scenario, the *preservationist* view, supports prevailing cultural beliefs about teaching, learning, and the relationships among teachers and students. For the preservationist, technologies should not substantially alter existing ways of organizing schools for instruction. The educational system is designed to pass on today's values and knowledge to the next generation, and in the preservationist view technology is designed to support that role. This is exemplified in technology literacy courses and computer science curricula that add technology to the body of knowledge that must be transmitted. Providing software as a part of a textbook adoption or using technology as a tool for test preparation are other illustrations of the preservationist approach. In this view, technology is important but peripheral to the business of teaching students.

A critical element of the preservationist approach is that it maintains a strong role for the teacher as the transmitter of information. Indeed, the use of technology must be adapted by teachers to the "durable grammar of the classroom and school" (Cuban, 1993, p.195). As Saul Rockman put it, "What a teacher *does* with it is more important than what the *it* is" (Rockman, 1991, p. 25, italics in original). The preservationist approach is cautious toward major changes and respects traditional aims for schooling, reinforcing what schools have done for over a century (Cohen, 1990).

The *cautious optimists* provide the third scenario. They predict a slow growth of hybrid schools and classrooms in which computers produce steady but gradual changes in teaching and schooling. In this view, "schools can become small learning communities where students and adults teach one another through a deliberate and slow application of technology to schooling" (Cuban, 1993, p. 196). This scenario projects a gradual evolution to a fundamentally changed perspective. Technology can provide the scaffolding for students and teachers to teach one another. Classrooms develop from teacher-directed environments to workplaces where peers help one another and teachers serve as mentors.

In looking to the future in 1993, Cuban predicted that the preservationist approach would best describe classroom use of technology in the short run, but that in the longer term the cautious optimist approach would gain ground, especially in elementary schools. Cuban's analysis of technology and his predictions remain compelling in today's world. Certainly, the preservationist approach is the best description of how technology is used today. Technology still cannot provide many of the futurist visions of the technophile and not enough time has passed for the optimist approach to gain much of a foothold, although futurists like Christensen see a technological transformation of schools just around the corner (Christensen et al., 2008).

THE FUTURE OF DIGITAL TEACHING PLATFORMS

Since Cuban's analysis, the technology platform has advanced in significant ways for education. Today, computers are powerful multimedia machines that have wireless high-speed connections to a global network populated with an immense array of assets. Nevertheless, the use of technology in schools has not changed substantially—it remains a peripheral element to educational practice.

Cuban's analysis can be applied to this review of the Digital Teaching Platform as exemplified by the Time To Know product. That analysis reveals an intriguing combination of preservationist and optimist capabilities. With its focus on teacher-led classrooms, tools for managing classroom operation, and attention to practice and assessment, the DTP is strongly preservationist. These tools and curriculum address the essential features of traditional schooling, such as focusing on learning standards, measuring learning with high-stakes tests, and creating classroom groups of students based on age.

With its student-centered applets, attention to student collaboration, constructivist pedagogy, and authentic student work, the DTP is also cautiously optimistic, with a neo-progressive orientation. It supports students exploring phenomena, constructing understanding, and guiding their own learning. It aids the teacher as a mentor and coach.

This finding, that the DTP is both preservationist and optimistic, is amplified by the examination of four significant innovations that DTP brings to the classroom. Two of these innovations are clearly preservationist in their benefits: the role of individualization and the use of rapid diagnostics. Both show how the DTP is designed to prepare students efficiently for high-stakes tests on the accepted standards. Two other innovations, constructivist pedagogy and cooperative groups, move in the direction of cautious optimism by nudging teachers toward mentoring and students toward exploration, creativity, and peer collaboration.

Individualization and Independence

Perhaps the most powerful efficiency of a Digital Teaching Platform like Time To Know is its ability to individualize student learning quickly during the course of regular classroom events. This allows students to work more effectively with greater investment in their learning. Research indicates that guided practice must be regularly tailored to the needs, interests, and capabilities of each student and that generic practice assigned to a group is highly inefficient. The DTP makes this individualization possible to a new level.

Individualization also gives students a sense of independence—from both the teacher and from the necessity of following along with other students—and that encourages them to make greater effort. This level of individualization is less practical when using traditional classroom materials.

Individualizing education by providing customized learning for each student is a powerful lever for transforming schools. The T2K platform approaches the problem by providing the teacher with tools for individualization. Technophile Clay Christensen agrees with the critical role of individualization but finds the solution in the technology rather than in the teacher's expertise (Christensen et al., 2008).

While we are intrigued by Christianson's prediction that 50% of high school courses will be online by 2020, we feel that he missed the input of the disruptive technology of Digital Teaching Platforms. The predictions ignore the role of the teacher. Instead we might predict that 50% or more of the curriculum will be online, as we move from print to digital, but that there is still a crucial role for the teacher (our preservationist legacy).

Diagnostics with Rapid Response

Assessment is effective as a teaching tool only when it is fitted exactly to the curriculum, it is delivered in a timely fashion, and the results are used immediately to guide the deployment of new lessons. Time To Know makes all of these requirements feasible. Teachers develop assessments that match what they are teaching. They administer these assessments to students, individuals, groups, or the whole class, at exactly the right time. And they review the results immediately after the students have completed the assessment.

Assessment fits closely with the individualizing capability, adding the critical diagnostic element. This approach to teaching and assessing keeps students on track, motivated, and alert to their progress. These two innovations in classroom practice, individualization and diagnostics, work together to provide efficiency in teaching and learning.

Constructivist Teaching with Rigorous Practice

The constructivist approach in the T2K pedagogy brings a strong element of neo-progressive thinking. This approach places a premium on creativity, deep understanding, and life-long learning. To implement a constructivist approach, however, teachers must pose many open-ended problems; spend less time lecturing; and invest more time in coaching, observing, and questioning.

This pedagogy does not dismiss the need for facility in reading and mathematics, and therefore the role of rigorous practice plays a key role. T2K combines this practice with open-ended problem solving supported with tools, applets, and group discussion.

Blend of Individual Work and Cooperative Groups

The combination of constructivist pedagogy and rigorous practice requires restructuring the classroom. Students work individually and as a whole class. But they also join in cooperative groups for many problem solving activities and discussions.

The challenge to the teacher is the choreography required to manage these various groups. The DTP provides tools for dealing with these needs. As a result, it nurtures community, sharing, and cooperation.

The Human Element of the Digital Teaching Platform

There is indeed the potential for a disruptive change in classrooms that have adopted one-to-one networked technology, digital curricula, and interactive whiteboards (cf. Christianson, 2003). The Digital Teaching Platform is a design that facilitates this change by leveraging technology to reinsert the human element. The key to this change is providing digital support for the teacher and students: support for the teacher for class preparation, for classroom management, for personalization, and for assessment; support for the student for open-ended exploration, for personalization, for 21st-century skills, and for collaboration.

REFERENCES

Anderson, J. (1993). *Rules of the mind.* Mahwah, NJ: Erlbaum.

Bebell, D., & Kaye, J. (2008). *Berkshire Wireless Learning Initiative year 3 evaluation results.* Boston: Boston College.

Bennett, N. (1978). Recent research on teaching: A dream, a belief, a model. *Journal of Education, 160,* 5–37.

Black, P., & Wiliam, D. (1998). Assessment and classroom learning. *Assessment in Education, 5*, 7–74.

Brooks, M., & Brooks, G. (1999). The courage to be constructivist. *Education Leadership, 54*, 18–24.

Bruner, J. (1960). *The process of education.* Cambridge, MA: Harvard University Press.

Bruner, J. (1968). *Toward a theory of instruction.* New York: Norton.

Case, R. (1992). *The mind's staircase: Exploring the conceptual underpinnings of children's thought and knowledge.* Mahwah, NJ: Lawrence Erlbaum Associates.

Chan, T., Roschelle, J., Hsi, S., Kinshuk, M., Sharples, T., Brown, J., . . . Hoppe, U. (2006). One-to-one technology-enhanced learning: An opportunity for global research collaboration. *Research and Practice in Technology Enhanced Learning, 1*, 3–29.

Christianson, C. (2003). *The innovator's dilemma: The revolutionary book that will change the way you do business.* New York: Harper.

Christensen, C., Horn, M., & Johnson, C. (2008). *Disrupting class: How disruptive innovation will change the way the world learns.* New York: McGraw-Hill.

Cohen, D. (1990). A revolution in one classroom. *Educational Evaluation and Policy Analysis, 12*(3), 327–345.

Cuban, L. (1993). Computers meet classroom: Classroom wins. *Teachers College Record, 95*, 185–210.

Dede, C. (2008). Theoretical perspectives influencing the use of information technology in teaching and learning. In J. Voogt & G. Knezek (Eds.), *International handbook of information technology in primary and secondary education* (pp. 43–62). New York: Springer.

Dynarski, M., Agodini, R., Heaviside, S., Novak, T., Carey, N., Campuzano, L., . . . Sussex, W. (2007). *Effectiveness of reading and mathematics software products: Findings from the first student cohort* (Publication NCEE 2007-4005). Washington, DC: U.S. Department of Education, Institute of Education Sciences.

Ericsson, K., Charness, N., & Feltovich, P. (2006). *The Cambridge handbook of expertise and expert performance.* Cambridge: Cambridge University Press.

Fostnot, C. (2005). *Constructivism: Theory, perspectives, and practice.* New York: Teachers College Press.

Gagnon, G., Collay, R., & Schmuck, R. (2005). *Constructivist learning design: Key questions for teaching to standards.* Thousand Oaks, CA: Corwin Press.

Gardner, H. (2009, April 15). The next big thing: Personalized education. *Foreign Policy.* Retrieved from http://www.foreignpolicy.com/articles/2009/04/15/the_next_big_thing_personalized_education., p. 86.

Glasersfeld, E von. (1995a). A constructivist approach to teaching. In L. Steffe & J. Gale (Eds.), *Constructivism in education* (pp. 3–15). Hillsdale, NJ: Lawrence Erlbaum.

Glasersfeld, E von. (1995b). Sensory experience, abstraction, and teaching. In L. Steffe & J. Gale (Eds.), *Constructivism in education* (pp. 369–383). Hillsdale, NJ: Lawrence Erlbaum.

Gordon, T. (1974). *Teacher effectiveness training.* New York: Peter Wyden.

Gulek, J., & Demirtas, H. (2005). Learning with technology: The impact of laptop use on student achievement. *Journal of Technology, Learning, and Assessment, 3.* Retrieved from http://www.jtla.org.

Hunt, E., & Minstrell, J. (1994). A cognitive approach to the teaching of physics. In K. McGilly (Ed.), *Classroom lessons: Integrating cognitive theory and classroom practice* (pp. 51–74). Cambridge, MA: MIT Press.

Kounin, J. (1970). *Discipline and classroom management.* New York: Holt Rinehart and Winston.

Lee, P., & Ashby, R. (2001). Empathy, perspective taking and rational understanding. In O. Davis Jr., S. Foster, & E. Yaeger (Eds.), *Historical empathy and perspective taking in the social studies* (pp. 21–50). Boulder, CO: Rowman and Littlefield.

Lemke, C., & Fadel, C. (2006). *Technology in schools: What the research says.* Culver City, CA: Metiri Group for Cisco Systems.

Malone, T., & Lepper, M. (1987). Making learning fun: A taxonomy of intrinsic motivations for learning. In R. Snow & M. Farr (Eds.), *Aptitude, learning and instruction, volume 3: Conative and affective process analyses.* Hillsdale, NJ: Lawrence Erlbaum.

Mayer, R. (1977). The sequencing of instruction and the concept of assimilation-to-schema. *Instructional Science, 6,* 369–388.

National Institute for Literacy. (2007). *What content-area teachers should know about adolescent literacy.* Washington DC: National Institute of Child Health and Human Development. (ERIC Document Reproduction Service No. ED500289)

National Institute of Child Health and Human Development. (2000). *Report of the National Reading Panel. Teaching children to read: An evidence-based assessment of the scientific research literature on reading and its implications for reading instruction* (NIH Publication No. 00-4769). Washington, DC: U.S. Government Printing Office.

National Mathematics Advisory Panel. (2008). *Foundations for success: The final report of the National Mathematics Advisory Panel.* Washington DC: U.S. Department of Education.

National Research Council (Donovan, M., & Bransford, J., Eds.) (2005). *How students learn: History, mathematics, and science in the classroom. Committee on How People Learn, a targeted report for teachers.* Washington, DC: The National Academies Press.

Newell, A., & Simon, H. (1972). *Human problem solving.* Englewood Cliffs, NJ: Prentice Hall.

Norman, D. A. (1980). Twelve issues for cognitive science. *Cognitive Science, 4,* 1–32.

Palincsar, A., & Brown, A. (1984). Reciprocal teaching of comprehension monitoring activities. *Cognition and Instruction, 1,* 117–175.

Perkins, D. (1999). The many faces of constructivism. *Education Leadership, 57,* 6–11.

Piaget, J. (1967). *The child's conception of the world.* Totowa, NJ: Littlefield, Adams.

Piaget, J. (1974). *To understand is to invent: The future of education.* New York: Grossman.

Pintrich, P., & Schunk, D. (2002). *Motivation in education: Theory, research, and applications* (2nd ed.). Upper Saddle River, NJ: Merrill-Prentice Hall.

Rockman, S. (1991). Telecommunications and restructuring: Supporting change or creating it. In A. Sheekey (Ed.), *Educational policy and telecommunications technologies* (pp. 24–35). Washington, DC: U.S. Department of Education.

Roschelle, J., & Pea, R. (2002). A walk on the WILD side: How wireless handhelds may change computer-supported collaborative learning. *International Journal of Cognition and Technology, 1,* 145–168.

Roschelle, J., Penuel, W. R., & Abrahamson, L. A. (2004). The networked classroom. *Educational Leadership, 61*, 50–54.

Sadler, D. (1989). Formative assessment and the design of instructional systems. *Instructional Science, 18*, 119–144.

Saphier, J., & Gower, R. (1997). *The skillful teacher: Building your teaching skills.* Acton, MA: Research For Better Teaching.

Sargent, K. (2003). *The Maine Learning Initiative: What is the impact on teacher beliefs and instructional practice?* Portland, ME: University of Southern Maine, Center for Educational Policy, Applied Research and Evaluation.

Schaumburg, H. (2001, June). Fostering girls' computer literacy through laptop learning: Can mobile computers help to level out the gender difference? Paper presented at the National Educational Computing Conference, Chicago, IL.

Shapely, K., Sheehan, D., Maloney, C., & Caranikas-Walker, F. (2009). *Evaluation of the Texas immersion pilot.* Austin, TX: Texas Center for Educational Research.

Stallings, J. (1980). Allocated academic learning time revisited, or beyond time on task. *Educational Researcher, 9*, 11–18.

Stiggins, R. (2004). New assessment beliefs for a new school mission. *Phi Delta Kappan, 86*, 22–27.

Vygotsky, L. S. (1986). *Thought and language.* Cambridge, MA: MIT Press.

Wilson, L. (2008, March). *One-to-one programs: A report to national directors of CoSN.* Presentation at the 2008 Meeting of the Consortium for School Networking (CoSN).

Zucker, A., & Hug, S. (2007). *A study of the one-to-one laptop program of the Denver School of Science and Technology.* Denver, CO: Denver School of Science and Technology. Retrieved from http://www.scienceandtech.org/documents/Technology/DSST_Laptop_Study_Report.pdf

CHAPTER 2

One-to-One Computing
The Evolving Infrastructure for Digital Teaching Platforms

Thomas Greaves

This chapter examines the continuing trend toward one-to-one computing in schools and the emerging role of Digital Teaching Platforms in supporting that trend and promoting *disruptive* change.

This chapter looks at the role of technology in schools historically, the one-to-one research findings from Project RED, potential problems and challenges in the implementation of one-to-one initiatives, key implementation factors for success, and the potential impact of one-to-one computing if implemented correctly.

EARLY ROLE OF TECHNOLOGY IN SCHOOLS

For over 40 years, educators have been interested in the potential of computer technology to improve education. Some even hoped that technology might hold the key to a transformation of our school systems. This interest and these hopes were driven by the advantages of computer technology over other technologies like television—advantages such as sophisticated diagnostic assessment and communications capabilities, and a personalized, interactive learning experience.

In the 1960s and 1970s, computer technology in educational institutions, primarily in universities, relied on large, expensive installations based on a central processing computer and extensive telecommunications equipment. At that time, the cost of student computing was about 10 dollars per student hour, compared with less than 10 cents today (Greaves, Hayes, Wilson, Gielniak, & Peterson, 2010).

The concept of the Learning Management System (LMS), began in these early days with the Programmed Logic for Automated Teaching Operations (PLATO) system. This was in many ways ahead of its time, serving as a course repository and controlling the delivery of content, online testing, and communications. It even harnessed the power of a connected learning community through an early version of chat and discussion boards.

The advent of the microcomputer promised to solve the cost issues for schools, and in the late 1970s and early 1980s schools began to acquire one computer to be shared among several classrooms. The computer was generally placed in the library or moved around the school on a cart, almost always under the direction of one teacher who had funded the purchase via bake sales and other efforts, and who was responsible for maintenance and repairs. Early tool software applications included Logo, Basic, and Bank Street Writer, followed by early educational games such as *Gertrude's Secrets, Agent USA,* and *Where in the World Is Carmen Sandiego?*

The next major development was one lab with roughly the number of an average class size, say 30, of standalone computers per school. Students would typically spend one class period a week in the lab, where the teacher booted up 30 copies of programs such as *Oregon Trail.* The logistics of dealing with stacks of floppy disks seriously impacted the time available for instruction; and, again, the emphasis was on tool software and supplementary educational games. Students were often sent to the lab for recreational activity, and little thought was given to improving achievement through the use of technology.

In 1988, national attention began to focus on the student-computer ratio after the publication of *Power On!* from the U.S. Department of Education (U.S. Congress, 1988), which stated that the national ratio of students to computers was 100 to 1 in 1981, the first year these data were tracked. By 1988, the ratio was 30 to 1, and the ratio dropped every few years, eventually reaching today's level of 3 to 1 (Gray, Thomas, & Lewis, 2010). However, until very recently the focus was primarily on input, or increasing the number of computers in schools, rather than output, or improving learning outcomes.

In the late 1980s, with the advent of low-cost, high-speed networks, the preferred method of implementation of computers in classrooms shifted first toward networked labs and then toward a few computers in the back of the classroom. The first networks were not capable of connecting classrooms, but this changed when IBM introduced the Token Ring network in 1985. Schools then began to move the computers physically closer to instruction, into classrooms, although networked labs continued to play an important role. Integrated Learning Systems (ILSs) such as Jostens, CCC, and WICAT, which relied on networked labs, were common throughout all grades, primarily focusing on a drill-and-practice approach to basic skills in a remedial setting. High schools often established a networked lab dedicated to one application such as word processing, desktop publishing, spreadsheets, or databases.

Clearly, in order for students to gain the benefits of personalized, interactive learning, each student would need access to a computer. In the late 1980s and early 1990s, small, experimental programs, like the Apple Classroom of Tomorrow and the Indiana Buddy Project, provided a desktop computer for each student at home and at school, with data carried back and forth on floppy disks.

In the early to mid-1990s, as the functionality of laptop computers improved, more schools began to experiment with the one-to-one computing concept. In 1990, the Methodist Ladies College in Melbourne, Australia, became the first school in the world to provide laptops for all students in grades 5–12 ("History of MLC," n.d.), and in 1995, Microsoft brought the Anytime Anywhere Learning concept to 26 private schools and 16 public school districts in the United States (Rockman et al (REA), 1997). In 1999, Governor Barnes of Georgia initiated a comprehensive one-to-one pilot in ten schools; and in 2000, the governor of Maine, Angus King, used budget surpluses from 1999 and 2000 to create the Maine Learning Technology Endowment, which equipped every middle school with student and teacher laptops in the fall of 2002.

Driven by the Internet, Learning Management Systems evolved from closed systems that managed the delivery of proprietary content to more open systems that supported content from a variety of sources. The Learning Management Systems of today have sophisticated subsystems that deliver online courses, manage online learning object repositories, and provide searchable content. However, unlike Digital Teaching Platforms, they are designed to function independently of the classroom or teacher.

At the same time, the hardware and software infrastructure and the reliability of laptops have improved dramatically. The speed of wireless local area networks has improved, along with robust, self-tuning features. Schools and vendors have increased their technical capacity to handle the installation of large implementations.

In 2006, a major shift in devices and deployment strategies began. According to the 2006 *America's Digital Schools* survey of the 2,500 largest districts, schools forecast that mobile devices and laptops would grow from 17% of the installed base to 50% by 2011 (Greaves & Hayes, 2006). This led to a reduction in computer labs and computers in the back of the classroom and a rapid growth of one-to-one programs and carts on wheels with 30 or more laptops.

By 2011, over 2,000 schools in the United States had a one-to-one laptop program in a full grade or in the whole school, with more than half a million students involved. Compared with early laptops, battery life was up 500%, weight had dropped by 80%, screen resolution had improved by 400%, and the total cost of ownership had gone down 70%. Student computing devices had evolved to include tablets, slates, and smartphones. While student computing devices will continue to evolve rapidly, today's models are unquestionably able to support teaching and learning effectively (Dede & Bjerede, 2011).

A wide variety of technology implementations still exists in schools, with labs and small groups of classroom computers continuing to play a role. In addition, classroom hardware continues to evolve as more schools add interactive whiteboards, student response systems, cameras, and other technologies that lead to technology-intensive instructional environments.

In 2010 Digital Teaching Platforms (DTPs) emerged that were built on the LMS knowledge base, and had revolutionary advances in teacher control of the one-to-one classroom and integrated core curriculum. The DTP classroom exploited the unique capabilities of one-to-one computing for the first time, and required that every student and teacher have a computing device.

CURRENT STATUS: FINDINGS FROM PROJECT RED

By any measure, the results of 15 years of laptop computing in schools are mixed. Many schools are doing well, and a few are doing extremely well. Maine has sustained its program and expanded it to the high schools. The Michigan Freedom to Learn program has funded one-to-one computing for over 23,000 students in 100 school districts in the state. One-to-one computing is an international movement, with schools in Australia, the United Kingdom, Singapore, and Uruguay leading the way.

On the other hand, the 2008 research study by *America's Digital Schools* revealed that only 33% of U.S. school districts with one-to-one programs believed that their program was key to substantial improvement in student achievement (Greaves & Hayes, 2008).

The 2010 Project RED survey of 1,000 schools sought to explain some of the reasons why many one-to-one implementations fall short of expectations, and to identify the factors that make some implementations perform dramatically better than others. The study showed that one-to-one technology alone can only go so far in improving student performance, that the key implementation factors involved in producing high-performing one-to-one schools are poorly understood, and that there is no clear consensus among educators on the best implementation practices (Greaves, Hayes, Wilson, Gielniak, & Peterson, 2010).

Key Implementation Factors

To determine which one-to-one implementation factors are linked most strongly to educational success, the Project RED survey used 11 widely accepted success measures, including high-stakes test scores; teacher attendance; AP course enrollment; and graduation, dropout, and disciplinary action rates (Greaves et al., 2010).

Nine key implementation factors were identified:

1. Integrating technology classes into every intervention class period
2. Implementing change-management leadership by school principals
3. Practicing daily online collaboration by students
4. Integrating technology into the core curriculum at least weekly
5. Performing online formative assessments at least weekly
6. Having a low student-computer ratio
7. Taking frequent virtual field trips
8. Using search engines by students daily
9. Training principals in teacher buy-in, best practices, and technology-transformed learning

Several of these factors—the integration of technology into intervention classes and the core curriculum, daily online collaboration among students, and online formative assessments—are integral to the emerging category of comprehensive DTPs.

An effective one-to-one implementation in schools is complex, and inattention to just one factor can impact success. For example, a school that implements most of the key factors without an integrated approach to core curriculum or appropriate change-management leadership is unlikely to reap the potential benefits (see Figure 2.1).

These one-to-one key implementation factors are not widely practiced, and it appears that most schools may not be aware of them. The Project RED study found that only 1% of schools surveyed had implemented all nine factors and that most schools had implemented three or less (see Figure 2.2). In addition, a large body of experience points to other important practices that are not widely implemented, such as a phased rollout of student laptops, rollout of teacher laptops before student laptops, and a sustained program of professional learning.

Awareness of First- and Second-Order Change Principles

Another critical factor in the disappointing performance of one-to-one implementations to date is the pervasiveness of first-order versus second-order change mechanisms in schools. According to Larry Cuban:

> First-order changes assume that the existing organizational goals and structures are basically adequate and what needs to be done is to correct deficiencies in policies and practice. . . . Second-order changes aim at altering the fundamental ways of achieving organizational goals because of major dissatisfaction with current arrangements. (1988, p. 229)

Figure 2.1. One-to-one computing works when properly implemented.

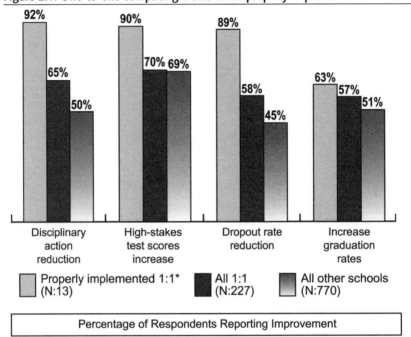

Properly implemented 1:1*
(N:13)

All 1:1
(N:227)

All other schools
(N:770)

Percentage of Respondents Reporting Improvement

*Properly Implemented 1:1: Those schools practicing the top four key implementation factors (intervention classes every period, principal leads change management, online collaboration daily, core curriculum weekly).

Schools are working with first-order change when they do old things in new ways—for example, when students word-process rather than type an essay. First-order changes can lead to improvements, but they are not transformative. However, schools generally pin their hopes for reform on these types of changes.

When schools do new things in new ways, they are working with second-order change—for example, when they move from teacher-centered to student-centered learning. Although second-order change can appear challenging, some types of second-order change have the transformative power that educators have been seeking since the microcomputer revolution began. These involve facilitating inquiry-based learning and the deep use of primary source material. This has the potential to increase student performance levels substantially, address all student populations, scale to the largest educational entities, and be sustained during changing economic times (National Research Council, 2005).

Educators have sometimes questioned whether students need to use technology every day in order to improve performance, and it is true that if

Figure 2.2. Few schools deploy many key implementation factors.

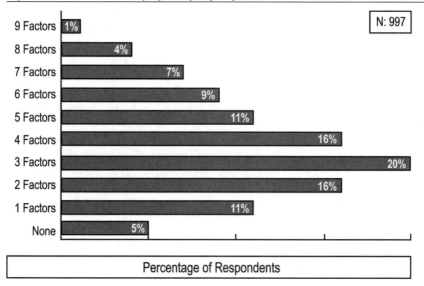

Only 1% of schools have implemented all nine KIFs, and most schools have implemented three or less. Given the nature of the nine items, it is clear that money is not the issue.

technology is no more than an add-on to an established way of doing things, daily use may have little impact. However, with second-order change, in schools with technology interwoven throughout the teaching and learning process by means of a DTP, daily use follows naturally and is more likely to impact achievement levels.

Hitherto, educators may have been justified in looking to the evolving state of laptop technology for the reason behind the lackluster performance of one-to-one schools, but no longer. The laptop technology, infrastructure, and DTPs are there, but the key implementation factors and second-order change mechanisms are still not widely understood.

Impact of One-to-One Technology and Implementation Factors

The Project RED study showed that the student-computer ratio is important to student achievement levels and highlighted the importance of proper implementation, which outweighed student-computer ratio in terms of its impact on student test scores. For example, a school with a four-to-one student-computer ratio that implemented many of the key factors had higher test scores than a one-to-one school that implemented none. Clearly the key factors played a major role in student success. However, one-to-one schools did not behave like other schools, and two-to-one schools behaved more like three-to-one schools than one-to-one schools. Something appeared to be different in the one-to-one teaching and learning environment, most likely students' ubiquitous access to personal technology (Greaves et al., 2010).

The research also found that although the implementation factors outweighed the student-computer ratio in terms of impact on student performance, one-to-one computing environments have many benefits that are conducive to improved student performance (see Figure 2.3). Personalized instruction flourishes. More principals model and provide professional development for teachers—one of the key implementation factors identified by the study. Principals and other leaders have much higher expectations that technology tools will be used for collaboration, research, and instruction. One-to-one schools also have higher rates of professional collaboration and

Figure 2.3. Ubiquitous technology has direct impact on performance measures.

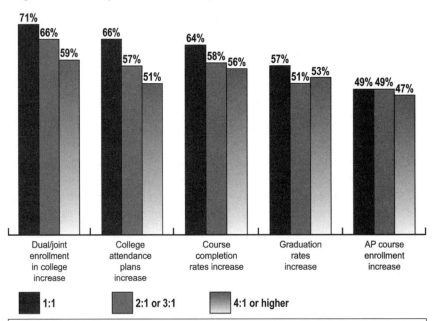

Improvements Due to Technology Deployment: High Schools by Student-Computer Ratio

parental involvement, and they report greater increases in dual/joint enroll-ment in college and rate of course completion.

The research strongly suggests that these schools are well positioned to increase student achievement as they become more aware of the key imple-mentation factors.

Reports from the Field: Challenges to Implementation

But what about the less successful one-to-one initiatives? Some schools surveyed by Project RED may have adopted one-to-one computing based on top-down directives without securing teacher buy-in. They may have lacked adequate levels of professional development, or purchased the hardware without adequate courseware, or used the laptops only for word processing and limited web browsing. It is probably safe to say that many schools focused primarily on the hardware and overlooked the importance of other factors.

Most schools do not start the implementation process with a thorough project plan, which can include 500 to 1,000 tasks or more. Most project plans, if they exist at all, specify only 50 to 100 tasks. In addition, there is little or no understanding of interlocking dependencies. For example, if several departments in a school each implement solutions that require a sig-nificant amount of Internet bandwidth, they generally find that when school starts, there is insufficient bandwidth for all students and all applications, so students may be asked to bring a book to read while the Internet pages load. Similar schoolwide delays may cause the entire laptop program to be seen as a failure, when in fact the problem is the infrastructure supporting the lap-tops. There are hundreds of similar interlocking dependencies in one-to-one implementations.

Unfortunately, change-management training is still largely absent. In one middle school where no change-management training was offered, stu-dents in a current events class received an assignment on a half-page of paper and were instructed to go to a single web site and write a two-page report on lined paper. The use of technology was extremely limited, and personalized learning was completely absent. However, in another middle school where administrators had received change-management training, students chose their own current events topic and researched it using news sources from at least three different countries. They each wrote a five-page report, asked a fellow student to peer-review it, and submitted it electroni-cally to the teacher. Technology was used to transform and personalize the learning experience.

One program of note in these reports was run in the Mooresville Graded School District in Mooresville, North Carolina (Learning Matters, 2011). This district supported its one-to-one implementation with a phased rollout of student laptops, teacher laptops before student laptops, and ongoing summer institutes for professional learning. In 2009–2010, Mooresville was one of only six districts in the state that made all of its Annual Yearly Progress (AYP) targets and also had the highest number of targets met (see Table 2.1). All schools in the district were recognized as Schools of Distinction, and one elementary school was recognized as an Honor School of Excellence. And Mooresville ranks 101st out of 115 districts in the state in per-pupil expenditures.

In another successful one-to-one implementation, at Canadian High School in Canadian, Texas, the number of available classes was limited because of the school's small size (212 students). So the school board allowed the school to pay for students to take any online course if the course was not offered locally (Beilue, 2010).

Financial Considerations

Schools currently operate in a regulated environment based on the teacher-centered, print-driven classroom. To facilitate second-order change, policies will need to change in many areas, including seat time, textbook adoption requirements, and textbook funding streams.

Most current school financial systems do not support the development of one-to-one transformed schools because insufficient incentives are available. For example, if a student fails a class, the state gives the district an identical per-student allotment to try again the same way. However, technology-based intervention methods could be used from the beginning to increase the chances of success. And although one-to-one schools offer substantial cost-saving efficiencies, states do not fund the initial investment.

Table 2.1. Mooresville Graded School District Before/After Digital Conversion

Category	2006–2007	2009–2010
End of Course/End of Grade Pass Rate	70%	86%
Graduation Rate	77%	86%
Students Going to College	74%	86%
Short-Term Suspensions	549	310
Dropouts	5.3%	2.3%
Attendance	94%	96%
Free/Reduced Lunch	31%	39%

Source: Sump-McLean, T., 2010

The initial costs of one-to-one computing may appear daunting in today's challenging economic climate. However, the Project RED survey also looked at the potential cost savings of one-to-one technology and found that schools with properly implemented programs were able to achieve substantial savings in many areas, from reduced copying and paperwork costs to savings at the state and local level to lower dropout rates (see Figure 2.4). The survey also pointed to some of the broader savings at a national level, for example, a reduction in the huge economic costs of dropouts.

The cost differential between a typical three-to-one school and a fully implemented one-to-one school, including support, professional development, curriculum software, and a DTP, is approximately $295 per student per year. Potential net savings are estimated to be at least $164 per student per year (Greaves et al., 2010).

Some of these savings are realized immediately, and others over a few years. The savings should improve as the systems improve, provided that schools adopt second-order change mechanisms and fully exploit the availability of DTPs and other technologies. And costs are projected to continue to drop over time, consistent with the historical pattern of the industry.

Figure 2.4. Disciplinary actions decreased due to technology and principal leadership.

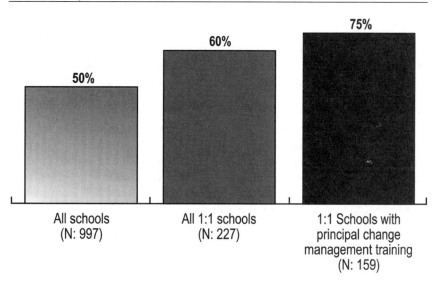

LOOKING TO THE FUTURE

Over the next few years, the changes already under way should continue and gather momentum. Over the long term, as second-order change mechanisms take hold, change will become more disruptive and transformative.

Near-Term Outlook

We can expect that more schools will become aware of the key implementation factors and adopt Digital Teaching Platforms and next-generation Learning Management Systems with enterprise solutions.

We can expect to see improvements in the change-management skills of school leaders, an area that is beginning to receive more attention. The transition from print to digital instructional materials should continue. Many schools will begin to use student-owned rather than school-owned devices, leading to cost savings.

The continued transition to mobile computing will coincide with the shift in the role of servers from data centers to a cloud environment. District policy decisions around cost, data security, and functionality will be based on cloud computing. As Internet bandwidth increases, online assessment solutions will become increasingly practical. We can also expect to see new applications and tool software that fully exploit a one-to-one environment. It is highly likely that new classes of engaging and educational apps will appear.

With students always connected, assessment software will be joined by the next generation of diagnostic software, capable of identifying the causes of student difficulties at a much more granular level (see Chapters 5 and 8). Today's assessment solutions too often function like autopsies, diagnosing the problem when it is already too late, but in a few years teachers should be able to address the underlying causes while intervention is still possible.

As the nation's cellular data infrastructure moves from 3G to 4G, and on to 5G, more and more students will be connected all the time. The Federal Communications Commission (FCC) is already funding several pilots of this approach with E-rate infrastructure funds. This transition will create new applications that exploit always-on, ubiquitous computing. These changes should lead to improved student performance across implementations.

At the same time, research will continue, with greater consistency in the measured variables and a continued focus on understanding the cost savings of properly implemented solutions.

Long-Term Outlook

Looking toward the future of DTPs, I predict a number of likely outcomes in the next 5 to 7 years: All students, faculty, and staff will enjoy 24-hour connectivity (4G, 5G) inside and outside of school; the transition from print to digital materials will be complete in many curriculum areas; learning will be fully personalized; the transition to student-owned devices will be complete, with students bringing their devices to school just as they bring their calculators today; and legislation and policies will change to facilitate second-order change.

As implementations improve and as second- and third-generation DTPs and LMSs come online, second-order change should become common, with students learning at increased rates.

The move to second-order change will require enormous changes in the curriculum, and what works for high schools may not work for the elementary grades because of differences in social and intellectual development. The lower grades may need to keep the same course of study but delve deeper. For example, the 3rd-grade class in the United Kingdom that recently conducted original research and published an article on bees in a peer-reviewed journal may be a forerunner of things to come (Scientific Journal Club, 2011). High school students may begin to graduate with an advanced degree or college credits. This development is already under way at the Whale Branch Early College High School in Beaufort County, South Carolina, where students are expected to graduate with an Associate Degree from the community college on the same campus.

High-stakes tests will need to change to accommodate second-order change schools, since the current instruments cannot adequately measure students who are learning at higher rates than today. School and classroom organization will also need to change to accommodate more advanced learning rates.

Financial planning in schools will need to capitalize on the positive financial impact of properly implemented technology and the downward trend in total cost of ownership. The funding picture will need to change based on an increased understanding of the powerful business case for one-to-one computing.

As second-order changes take hold, we should reach the tipping point in the effort to transform schools via the use of technology.

THE FUTURE OF DIGITAL TEACHING PLATFORMS

Only a handful of software applications fully exploit the potential of one-to-one implementations. Adapting existing software to one-to-one computing yields many benefits, but these are of a first-order change variety.

The secret to second-order change is to move from a teacher-centered to a fully personalized, student-centered classroom, which requires a move from print to digital format and a computing device for every student. The device and its digital content must be available wherever textbooks are currently available. This implies WiFi inside the school, and 3G, or preferably 4G, outside the school. Most software runs well in a wired or wireless LAN environment, but some software may have difficulties in less robust, higher-latency, 3G or 4G environments.

The new category of DTP goes well beyond traditional software applications and requires a one-to-one ratio to be fully useful. DTPs provide much of the software component of personalized learning to complement the one-to-one hardware environment.

DTPs support the student-centered classroom by facilitating the transition of the teacher from the sage on the stage to the guide on the side, and the conversion of core curriculum delivery from a paper-based to a digital format. They relieve teachers of many mundane tasks and free up time for effective teaching. They allow teachers to combine commercially developed materials, open-source materials, and teacher-developed materials into cohesive lessons that match the requirements of each student. They allow students to collaborate, comment, and respond to mini-polls, leading to increased engagement in the learning process.

DTPs are still a new development. Over time, their functionality and effectiveness will increase still further and help facilitate second-order change in one-to-one computing schools.

DTPs will help move one-to-one implementations to the next level, as educators become aware of the impact of a teacher-managed digital environment, integrated core curriculum, and advances over the lab-based curriculum software of LMSs.

The personalization engines built into DTPs will become vastly more powerful than they are today. Since students in a DTP classroom use guided discovery to learn concepts at a deep level, rather than by relying on drill and practice, we can expect to see understanding and achievement levels improve.

The benefits of educational technology have been a long time coming. Have we now reached the point where, after 40 years, a few schools are beginning to implement one-to-one computing practices that can revolutionize schools? The answer appears to be a cautious "yes." The capability and knowledge now exist to move schools toward a new paradigm—a goal that can be accomplished over time by redesigning schools to a new level of technology and curriculum integration supported by DTPs, and by improving implementation practices, teaching, policies, professional learning, and leadership skills.

REFERENCES

Beilue, J. N. (2010, May 26). Harvard by way of Mexico, Canadian. *Amarillo Globe News*. Retrieved from http://amarillo.com/stories/052610/new_news5.shtml.

Cuban, L. (1988). *The managerial imperative and the practice of leadership in schools*. New York: SUNY Press.

Dede, C., & Bjerede, M. (2011). *Mobile learning for the 21st century: Insights from the 2010 Wireless EdTech Conference*. Retrieved from the Wireless EdTech Conference website: http://wirelessedtech.com/wp-content/uploads/2011/03/ed_tech_pages.pdf

Gray, L., Thomas, N., & Lewis, L. (2010). *Educational technology in U.S. public schools: Fall 2008* (NCES 2010–034). U.S. Department of Education, National Center for Education Statistics. Washington, DC: U.S. Government Printing Office.

Greaves, T., & Hayes, J. (2006). *America's digital schools: Mobilizing the curriculum*. Shelton, CT: MDR.

Greaves, T., & Hayes, J. (2008). *America's digital schools: The six trends to watch*. Shelton, CT: MDR.

Greaves, T., Hayes, J., Wilson, L., Gielniak, M., & Peterson, R. (2010). *The technology factor: Nine keys to student achievement and cost-effectiveness*. Shelton, CT: MDR.

Learning Matters. (2011, April 8). The Mooresville tech revolution. Retrieved from http://learningmatters.tv/ blog/on-pbs-newshour/the-mooresville-tech-revolution/5526/.

History of MLC. (n.d.). Retrieved from Methodist Ladies College website: http://www.mlc.vic.edu.au/about/ history_of_mlc_60.htm

National Research Council (Donovan, M., & Bransford, J., Eds.). (2005). *How students learn: History, mathematics, and science in the classroom. Committee on How People Learn, a targeted report for teachers*. Washington, DC: The National Academies Press.

Rockman et al (REA). (1997, June). *Report of a laptop program pilot: A project for Anytime Anywhere Learning by Microsoft Corporation*. San Francisco, CA: Author.

Scientific Journal Club. (2011). Bees think, and they also have color preferences! Retrieved from http://scientificjournalclub.blogspot.com/2011/04/bees-think-and-they-also-have-color.html

Sump-McLean, T. A. (compiler). (2010). *Mooresville Graded School District: Continuing to look forward* (Chart). Mooresville, NC: Author.

U.S. Congress, Office of Technology Assessment. (1988). *Power on! New tools for teaching and learning*. (OTA-Set-379). Washington, DC: U.S. Government Printing Office.

CONTENT AND PEDAGOGY

Part II examines DTP pedagogical-content design in science, reading, and mathematics. While focusing on these specific curricula, the authors also provide generalizations of their research to all curriculum areas.

Chapter 3 describes the advantages of the Web-based Inquiry Science Environment (WISE) as a DTP. WISE is a learning environment that supports development of instruction and assessments grounded in cognitive-science research. WISE supports designs that emphasize inquiry instruction, and its assessments measure knowledge integration in a psychometrically rigorous manner, tapping the relationships students establish between concepts. Benchmark assessments were used in a cohort comparison study to compare typical and WISE instruction for two key science concepts in six courses, with results indicating that instruction with WISE units can be highly effective in retaining and even enhancing understanding.

Chapter 4 provides an overview of technologies that support individualized reading instruction. Teachers can incorporate these technologies in classrooms to aid both small-group learning and one-on-one tutoring of individual students. It also emphasizes technologies that help students comprehend text beyond the word and into the realm of sentence and discourse meaning. The chapter is divided into four sections: identifying levels of language and discourse that need to be considered in a comprehensive model of reading intervention; presenting some automated metrics for scaling texts on text complexity at multiple levels of language and meaning; giving some examples of technology that can diagnose reading deficits and train students to rectify such deficits; and exploring the reading process in more advanced digital environments that consider student motivation and incorporate multiple media, tasks, and pedagogical objectives. Teachers and other professionals can use these new technologies effectively in a Digital Teaching Platform.

Chapter 5 describes an intelligent tutoring system for middle school mathematics (pre-algebra and algebra) that is designed to extend already proven effective teaching practices. The authors show how the technology is well situated to create new normative pedagogical practices, as it is rooted in six anchors of pedagogical change enabled by technology. The relative advantage for teachers using DTP technology is garnered through ease-of-use, efficiency, and the ability to observe improvements in student engagement. The chapter reviews the tutoring system ASSISTments (a web-based assessment system that provides tutoring based on student responses), provides three compelling examples of the system in action, and concludes with a discussion on what these illustrations tell us about teaching and learning with intelligent tutoring systems.

Chapter 6 introduces a Digital Teaching Platform that addresses the practice of teaching mathematics in engaging and motivating ways with a focus on potential added benefits of these networked technologies in new classroom environments. Elements of a networked classroom, with implications for curriculum and pedagogy, highlight their discussion of classroom connectivity technology. To support how such resources can transform student learning and motivation, the chapter outlines what is necessary to effectively integrate such environments, translating some 10 years of research and development into core implementation principles. The conclusion makes recommendations for future use in terms of technology design, learning, and teaching.

CHAPTER 3

Insights for Teaching and Learning Science

Marcia C. Linn

The Web-based Inquiry Science Environment (WISE) is a free, available, open-source, inquiry learning and teaching platform. In WISE, students receive online guidance while working in pairs, supported by their teachers. In addition, the WISE software supports the design of inquiry activities informed by the knowledge integration framework. The community of WISE researchers, teachers, discipline experts, and software designers has created units addressing complex science topics, conducted comparison studies to refine instruction, and identified ways to promote knowledge integration. The WISE library (http://wise.berkeley.edu) houses classroom-tested and supported units on topics such as chemical reactions, photosynthesis, and global climate change, with each unit consisting of 5 to 10 days of activities (Figure 3.1).

This chapter illustrates how WISE research informs the design of instruction using Digital Teaching Platforms (DTPs). WISE offers users a full set of resources for design and implementation of inquiry teaching and learning, as well as design strategies that foster knowledge integration and are applicable to DTPs. WISE supports designers, researchers, discipline specialists, and classroom teachers to work in collaboration to create and refine inquiry science instruction.

Currently, WISE has over 250,000 student accounts with approximately 3,000 new student accounts being added each month. Each year, about 5,000 teachers use WISE. Design partnerships continuously author new WISE units specific to their state standards and contexts. Research by the WISE community has produced principles and patterns to guide future designers. The WISE open-source community has developed units in seven languages and added features to the learning environment. Readers are invited to participate in this effort.

Figure 3.1. Example of the Web-based Inquiry Science Environment (WISE): Chemical Reactions. WISE includes an inquiry map that guides students through a series of steps, an activity page (such as the Molecular Workbench interface shown here), auto-scored items, and explanation notes.

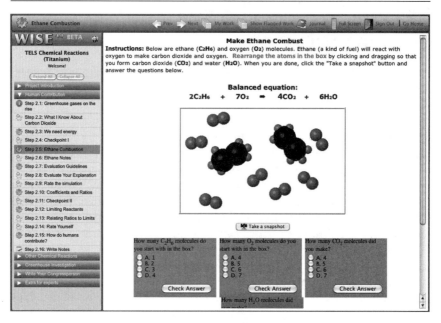

The goal of this chapter is to describe insights from WISE research that can help both teachers implementing DTPs and researchers designing DTPs. The value of technology-enhanced units is well established by WISE research and many other research programs (Greaves, Chapter 2 of this volume; Lee, Linn, Varma, & Liu, 2010). This chapter draws on evidence from comparison studies and iterative refinement studies to identify design principles and patterns synthesized in the knowledge integration framework. For example, studies have compared the impact of typical and WISE units for complex science topics such as thermodynamics, mitosis, and plate tectonics. In addition, refinement studies have increased the effectiveness of dynamic visualizations by incorporating knowledge integration guidance. These insights can facilitate the design process and guide customization.

INTRODUCTION TO WISE AS A DIGITAL TEACHING PLATFORM

WISE has many of the features of Digital Teaching Platforms, including interactive, feedback-rich units; an easy-to-use, expandable authoring environment; tools for inquiry teaching; and professional development activities.

Interactive, Feedback-Rich Units

WISE units log student actions continuously and support a variety of feedback and assessment methods for students and teachers. Assessments include short essays, science narratives, MySystem diagrams (a type of concept map), virtual experiments, graphing activities (including graphs generated by probeware), flipbook animations, and interactive visualizations. The WISE technology infrastructure can personalize guidance for students, support teachers in responding to students online, and enable researchers to collect detailed data from remote sites by logging and analyzing student actions and responses (see also Chapters 7 and 9 of this volume).

Easy-to-Use, Expandable Authoring Environment

WISE features easy-to-learn authoring tools, allowing teachers to customize instruction and design teams to prototype new activities quickly. WISE authors take advantage of powerful inquiry features, including embedded notes, virtual experiments, interactive visualizations, concept maps, collaborative activities, assessment formats, and tools for students to represent their ideas in drawings and animations. Since WISE is open source, it is easy to incorporate resources developed by others. Current WISE units incorporate probeware to graph motion and temperature, Concord Consortium's Molecular Workbench to provide atomic-scale visualizations, and NetLogo (Wilensky & Reisman, 2006) to simulate experiments on topics such as climate change and orbital motion.

Tools for Inquiry Teaching

To help teachers manage classes where students are working in small groups on inquiry units, WISE offers in-class, between-class, and end-of-year tools. During and between classes, teachers can review students' work, monitor class progress, send notes to individuals and groups, and assign grades. For example, teachers can flag student responses to use for class discussion, grade students using pre-made comments, and use an online gradebook to summarize their students' progress.

Professional Development Activities

WISE has developed professional development workshops to help teachers succeed with inquiry teaching. Teachers contrast strategies for approaching *inquiry dilemmas* such as asking inquiry questions, supporting instruction with visualizations, and guiding students to critique experiments. At end-of-unit and annual workshops, teachers customize inquiry instruction. Typically, teachers modify both the units and their strategies for guiding inquiry. Research shows that when teachers customize instruction based on evidence from student work, their next cohort of students gains more integrated and coherent understanding of science as compared to their prior cohort (Gerard, Spitulnik, & Linn, 2011).

KNOWLEDGE INTEGRATION FRAMEWORK

To achieve powerful, cumulative effects on student learning, the knowledge integration framework offers principles and patterns that synthesize findings from over 30 years of research in the learning sciences. This research shows the advantages of inquiry learning compared to knowledge telling (Buckley, Gobert, Kindfield, Horwitz, et al., 2004; Kali, Linn, & Roseman, 2008; Linn & Eylon, 2006, 2011; Mokros & Tinker, 1987; Quintana, Reiser, Davis, Krajcik, et al., 2004). In knowledge telling, students encounter a barrage of information in textbooks and lectures that they typically isolate from their existing ideas and ultimately forget (see Chapter 10, this volume). Knowledge integration, in contrast, respects and engages student ideas, helps students detect gaps in their knowledge, and supports students as they use new ideas to address compelling problems. With knowledge integration instruction, rather than providing information that is passively absorbed, students are empowered to guide their own learning (Linn & Hsi, 2000). Many research groups have investigated and refined the knowledge integration framework (Davis & Krajcik, 2005; Linn, Davis, & Bell, 2004; Sisk-Hilton, 2008).

The knowledge integration framework emphasizes that learners develop a repertoire of incoherent and fragmented ideas as a result of personal experience, observation of the natural world, cultural beliefs, social context, and instruction (diSessa, 1988; Driver, Asoko, Leach, Mortimer, & Scott, 1994; Eylon & Linn, 1988). Deep science learning requires students to integrate ideas from multiple sources and to determine the most fruitful, generative, and coherent perspectives.

Researchers have extracted principles from empirical studies of knowledge integration to guide designers of inquiry units. Linn et al. (2004) included principles and associated evidence in a book reporting extensive research. Kali (2006) developed a design principles database by engaging a broad community of designers in synthesizing their knowledge. Kali et al. (2008) led participants in two National Science Foundation–funded centers for learning and teaching to consolidate their ideas into principles and reported the findings. These findings can guide knowledge integration efforts in many types of DTPs.

Knowledge Integration Pattern

Researchers have identified a pattern consisting of four knowledge integration processes that jointly promote coherent science understanding and help students become lifelong learners: eliciting ideas, adding ideas, distinguishing ideas, and sorting out ideas (Linn & Eylon, 2006; 2011). This pattern has value not just for WISE, but also for all learning geared toward integrated understanding.

Elicit Ideas. Knowledge integration emphasizes eliciting and building on student ideas. Research shows that students develop a repertoire of ideas about scientific phenomena that reflects their observations, experiences, and intellectual efforts. Many studies show the benefit of eliciting ideas or making predictions (e.g., Gunstone & Champagne, 1990; Linn & Hsi, 2000). When students articulate their ideas, they often discover that they have multiple views of the same topic. When students identify their own ideas, they can test them against new ideas and get feedback on them from discussions with other students. Eliciting ideas also makes student thinking visible to teachers.

In the WISE Chemical Reactions unit, for example, eliciting ideas identified several intriguing views held by students. Many students expected the atomic model instantaneously to convert oxygen and hydrogen molecules into water without any intermediate stages, a process consistent with the symbolic formula. Others expected all the molecules to break into atoms and then reform. Some predicted that the molecules of oxygen and hydrogen would combine to form one huge molecule (Figure 3.2; Chiu & Linn, 2008; Zhang & Linn, 2008).

Add Ideas. Adding new ideas is the goal of every science activity. In knowledge integration activities, designers engage learners by contrasting their previously held ideas with the ones that are added. Interactive visualizations allow students to test their ideas about phenomena that are too small (chemical reactions), fast (collisions), or massive (the solar system) to explore in classroom investigations. Virtual experiments allow students to investigate situations that are complex (global climate change), dangerous (airbag deployment), or prolonged (genetic inheritance). For example, in the Chemical Reactions unit, researchers used a Molecular Workbench visualization to illustrate bond breaking and bond formation (see Figure 3.3).

WISE designers use *pivotal cases* to make new ideas generative and productive. When new ideas meet the criteria of pivotal cases, they are effective for promoting knowledge integration (Linn, 2005). Pivotal cases have three characteristics. First, pivotal cases typically *contrast two conditions* that form a controlled experiment. For example, based on numerous observations that

Figure 3.2. Eliciting ideas about chemical reactions. Examples of student prediction drawings from the WISE chemical reactions unit.

Instructions: Draw $2N_2 + 6H_2 \rightarrow 4NH_3$, starting with $2N_2$ and $6H_2$ molecules.

Sample response (Instantaneous View):

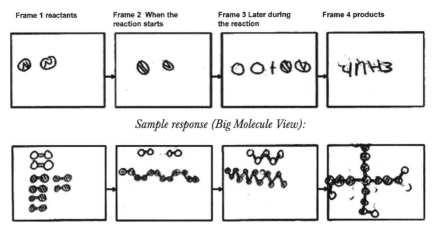

Sample response (Big Molecule View):

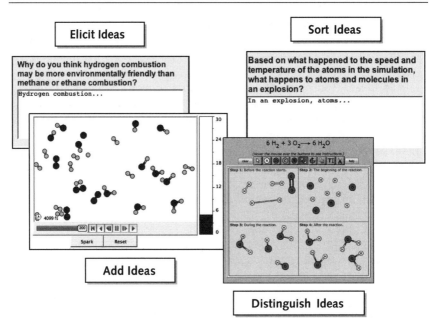

Figure 3.3. The Knowledge Integration pattern as implemented in the WISE chemical reactions unit.

metal objects feel colder to the touch than wooden objects when at room temperature, many students assert that metals are naturally cold and can be used to keep a soda cold. To help students interpret this idea, Mr. K., a collaborating teacher, added new ideas by asking students to contrast how metal and wood feel on a hot day at the beach and a cold day in the snow.

Second, pivotal cases are *personally relevant* and *elicit a narrative.* When he asked about how wood and metal feel on hot and cold days, Mr. K. found that many students immediately started describing their own experiences of getting into a hot car, walking barefoot on wooden or metal ramps, or freezing their fingers to a car door. This activity elicited valuable ideas students had not initially considered.

Third, pivotal cases *emphasize the language and methods of science.* Mr. K. used the WISE activity of having students compare the feel of objects in the classroom to their temperature as measured using a thermometer. He encouraged students to distinguish heat flow from temperature by using scientifically normative language to interpret the findings from their experiments.

Distinguish Ideas. Students tend to add new ideas in school and use them in the context where they were learned, rather than distinguishing them from their other ideas or using them in everyday life (Linn & Hsi, 2000). In the Chemical Reactions unit, students viewing an atomic-level visualization often believe that they understand the phenomena without connecting it to other ideas about chemistry (Chiu & Linn, 2011). This indicates that visualizations can be deceptively clear. To help students distinguish their ideas (as seen in Figure 3.2) from those in visualizations, WISE designers asked students to make drawings of their observations, represent their ideas using a sequence of drawings selected from a large set, or critique interpretations attributed to a hypothetical student. All of these approaches motivated students to return to the visualization to clarify their observations and resulted in improved student outcomes (Linn, Chang, Chiu, Zhang, & McElhaney, 2010).

Sort Out Ideas. Ultimately, students need to coordinate productive ideas, prior knowledge, and experience to achieve coherent and durable scientific understanding. WISE units guide students to organize their ideas in a narrative, explain their ideas to a peer, write a persuasive argument to a government official, or make a comprehensive representation of their knowledge to sort out their ideas. To pull their ideas together, the Chemical Reactions unit instructs students to write a letter to a policy maker about climate change using evidence from their experiments on limiting and excess reagents.

Together, these processes compose the knowledge integration pattern (see Figure 3.3). The pattern can be used to design, review, or critique curriculum materials. WISE features the implementation aspects of the pattern, making it easy for designers to create instruction that promotes scientific understanding. Most WISE features–such as interactive visualizations and virtual experiments–also log student activities, providing assessments of student progress and evidence for improving instructional designs. These are all strategies that generalize to many types of DTPs.

Assessments of Knowledge Integration

WISE assessments and rubrics are designed to measure knowledge integration. Knowledge integration items ask students to explain outcomes, critique experiments, and compare alternatives. They also contribute to instruction by asking students to apply their ideas to new situations. In contrast, most district, state, and national tests are poorly aligned with science standards and insensitive to instruction (Clark & Linn, 2003; Shepard, 2000).

To succeed on knowledge integration items, learners need to link, connect, or distinguish ideas and warrant their answers with evidence. For example, Linn and Hsi (2000) used an item that asked students to distinguish between heat and temperature and to use evidence to support their views. In the Global Climate unit, students distinguished between an actual greenhouse and the greenhouse effect. Rubrics for scoring items reward students for explanations that use evidence to distinguish among ideas (see Figure 3.4).

Analysis of over 100 items developed for grades 6 to 12 shows the benefits of WISE assessments. The items measure knowledge integration in a psychometrically rigorous manner, and constructed-response items scored with the knowledge integration rubric showed satisfactory reliability across units and years $(r > .74$; Liu, Lee, Hofstetter, Linn, 2008). In addition, a comparison between items that required student-selected and student-generated explanations showed that generating explanations, although significantly more difficult for students, was also more educationally valuable (Linn, Lee, Tinker, Husic, & Chiu, 2006; Liu et al., 2008).

To assess the impact of WISE units, researchers designed embedded assessments, pre- and post-unit tests, and annual assessments. WISE assessments can both strengthen instruction and establish student accomplishments. These types of assessment activities can fit into any DTP framework.

IMPACT OF KNOWLEDGE INTEGRATION UNITS

Studies on the impact of WISE units have used several methodologies. To demonstrate the overall advantage of knowledge integration units, researchers conducted both comparison studies that pit one instructional approach against another, and learning trajectory studies that follow students over

Figure 3.4. A Global Climate Change Assessment Item and Scoring Rubric

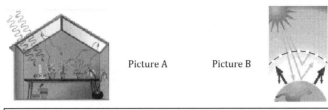

Picture A   Picture B

Picture "A" shows a real greenhouse where light from the sun passes through the glass panels and heats the inside. The glass panels of the greenhouse keep the heat energy from escaping.

Picture "B" shows the greenhouse effect on Earth.

Which part of picture B is like the glass of the greenhouse? (choose one)
__ Sun __ Space __ Atmosphere __ Earth

Explain your answer.

Knowledge Integration Scoring Rubric

	KI Level	Greenhouse Response Characteristics
0	**No Answer**	Blank
1	**Off task**	Response is irrelevant to the task or "I don't know."
2	**Incorrect** non-normative ideas. non-normative links.	Incorrect description of pictures. Inaccurate connections between greenhouse and earth's atmosphere. Repeat of the multiple choice answer.
3	**Partial** relevant ideas without elaborated links	Matches similar elements in two pictures. Describes one picture. Mentions that atmosphere reflects, absorbs, or receives sunlight and does not relate to other ideas.
4	**Basic** One scientifically valid link between two normative ideas.	Mentions atmosphere is like the glass on a greenhouse and lets heat in and traps it there or keeps most of heat inside
5	**Complex** Two or more scientifically valid links	Mentions atmosphere is like the glass on a greenhouse and says "receive sunlight energy and blocks earth's (radiation) energy (or IR) from escaping to the space"

months and years. To improve the units, researchers used design research methodologies to compare alternative versions of the instruction (Design-Based Research Collective, 2003; Linn et al., 2004). Both of these methods yield findings that can help refine design principles and patterns.

Overall WISE Impact

A series of studies shows that WISE units designed following the knowledge integration framework improve student understanding of complex science. A time-delayed cohort comparison study compared students who studied the typical curriculum to a group who studied WISE units taught by the same teachers. Students were tested in schools that served English language learners, students underrepresented in science, and students receiving free or reduced price lunches. The WISE cohort ($N = 4{,}520$) achieved almost one-third of a standard deviation improvement (effect size of .32, $p < .001$) compared to the typical cohort ($N = 3{,}712$). Traditional multiple-choice questions were unable to detect this gain. This finding demonstrates the value of constructed response items for assessing knowledge integration (Linn et al., 2006; Quellmalz & Pellegrino, 2009).

A learning trajectory study tracked students' development of coherent ideas on pre-test, post-test, and annual assessments. In one study, high school students learned about unseen processes involving molecules (chemical reactions), electrons (electrostatics), population-based genetics (evolution), and chromosomes (meiosis). WISE followed these students ($N = 764$), who were taught by 11 teachers from six schools in three states, as they completed pre-tests and post-tests immediately before and after the unit enactment, and annual assessments at the end of the school year. Analyses revealed that mean knowledge integration values significantly increased from pre-test to post-test and from post-test to delayed post-test across these four different WISE curriculum units, $F(2, 1867) = 73.75$, $p < .001$ (Linn & Eylon, 2011). For the Chemical Reactions unit, the delayed post-test was significantly higher than the immediate post-test (Chiu & Linn, 2011). For the Electrostatics unit, the delayed post-test was slightly, but not significantly, higher than the immediate post-test (Shen & Linn, 2011). Considering that typical lab-based studies show a consistent drop on delayed post-tests, these results indicate that a focus on coherent ideas helps students retain and even continue to develop their ideas.

Refining Instruction Using Visualizations

Demonstrating the overall advantages of WISE units does not clarify the contribution of specific features of the units. The most unique aspects of the units are the visualizations and virtual experiments. To illustrate the usefulness of refinement studies, this section focuses on visualizations.

Scientific visualizations are extremely valuable because they illustrate complex scientific ideas, but this also makes them difficult to design and interpret. Initial versions of educational visualizations typically reflect the designers' ideas about the discipline and benefit from refinement based on observations of users. WISE classroom refinement studies of visualizations reveal several guidelines for designers: simplify visualizations, connect to everyday phenomena, highlight disciplinary knowledge, and mitigate deceptive clarity.

Simplify Visualizations. All refinement studies show the benefit of simplifying the visualization and emphasizing the salient information. For example, Molecular Workbench visualizations (Figures 3.1, 3.2, 3.3) can illustrate the complex systemic nature of chemical reactions. In any given instructional sequence, only some aspects of that complexity are typically relevant.

Chiu and Linn (2008, 2011) grappled with the decision to display both kinetic energy and potential energy or to display only kinetic energy as the reactions occur. Analyses of student work and comparison studies showed that displaying both forms of energy was confusing to students. Teachers reported that the California standards for high school chemistry only required kinetic energy. These refinements improved student outcomes from the unit.

Connect to Everyday Phenomena. Connecting visualizations to phenomena students are likely to encounter in their lives illustrates the relevance of science, increases opportunities to use science ideas in the future, and strengthens the links between representations. In two WISE units where students explore visualizations of exothermic reactions, researchers found students benefited from linking their knowledge of the atomic-level reaction to an observable explosion in the form of a video of a hydrogen balloon exploding. By having students compare their interpretation of the balloon explosion and their interpretation of the explosion in Molecular Workbench, the units helped students connect observable and unseen molecular reactions. In both cases, students were encouraged to think about the implications of the results of their experiments for a science policy issue.

In the Hydrogen Fuel-Cell Cars unit, Zhang and Linn (2008) focused on the explosion of hydrogen and oxygen as a way to power a vehicle. In the Chemical Reactions unit, Chiu and Linn (2008) illustrated how burning of fuel connects to limiting and excess reactants (an important disciplinary topic). Chiu and Linn engaged students in conducting virtual experiments about emissions from power plants, where excess reactants contribute to the worldwide increase in carbon dioxide in the atmosphere. Students used a NetLogo climate change model to explore the impact of increases of carbon dioxide in the atmosphere on global temperature. By using the Molecular Workbench visualization to explore limiting and excess reagents and then using the NetLogo model to investigate the implications of excess pollutants, Chiu and Linn were able to tie the Chemical Reactions unit to climate change, a policy issue that students might encounter in news articles. In a culminating activity, students wrote a letter to a policy maker using their scientific evidence to discuss the issue of climate change.

Highlight Disciplinary Knowledge. Many studies illustrate the need to edit visualizations to highlight important disciplinary knowledge. For example, both

Chiu and Linn (2008) and Zhang and Linn (2008) found that students failed to recognize that energy was necessary in order to start a chemical reaction. One problem is that the importance of energy in chemical reactions is obscured in the symbolic representation of the reaction. Often, students interpret the arrow between the two sides of the equation to mean that the sides are equal. They do not recognize that chemical reactions can be endothermic or exothermic.

To strengthen the units, Chiu and Linn added two pivotal cases. The first pivotal case linked the chemical reaction to an observable phenomenon: a hydrogen balloon exploding (illustrated in a video). The pivotal case compared using a match to ignite a hydrogen balloon with the need to add energy for a molecular reaction to get started. Students were guided to map the flame igniting the balloon to the start of the chemical reaction. The comparison also illustrated that when the reaction started, an explosion occurred. Instruction ensured that students noted and interpreted these parallels. This pivotal case also supported students telling a story or developing a narrative around the events. Students were able to explain how the two situations were caused by the same underlying event: adding energy. Further, the pivotal case motivated intense class discussion. This pivotal case allowed students to compare two similar investigations. They could connect the observable phenomena to a molecular level representation.

The second pivotal case compared two versions of the Molecular Workbench visualization. In the first version, the molecules moved but no energy was added. Without adding energy, students observed that the molecules moved, but there was no change in the bonds represented in the visualization and no increase in kinetic energy. Bonds did not break and get reformed. Essentially, there was no spark, so the reaction between hydrogen and oxygen did not progress. In the second version, students hit a button that added energy by displaying a spark (shaped sort of like a lightning bolt). Students observed that when they added the spark the reaction sped up and the level of kinetic energy increased. They tracked the breaking and formation of bonds. Students were able to use multiple forms of evidence to support their arguments: bond breaking, bond formation, energy changes, rate of molecular movement, and movement of individual atoms.

These two comparisons qualify as pivotal cases (Linn, 2005). They compare two similar conditions; they clarify the symbolic equation by helping students visualize the contribution of energy; they allow learners to make an analogy between the match and the spark; and they enable students to develop a narrative about the role of energy in a chemical reaction. In addition, discussion of the cases provokes effective dialogue among students. Taken together, these cases clarify the connection between a chemical reaction and an explosion. Students conjectured a variety of different explanations concerning the role of the spark. For example, some students thought that the spark directly led to the increase in kinetic energy, and others argued that it took some time for the spark to initiate the reaction and for the reaction to produce increases in kinetic energy. Both Chiu and Linn (2008) and Zhang and Linn (2008) refined the instruction to help students make sense of the relationship between adding energy and the eventual release of energy.

The pivotal cases highlight important disciplinary knowledge that is neglected in typical instruction. Students often fail to connect bond breaking and bond formation to symbolic equations because they need to understand the role of energy more thoroughly. Refining instruction featuring visualizations by focusing on key disciplinary ideas can strengthen the impact of visualizations on learning.

Mitigate Deceptive Clarity. To assess students' perceptions of their ability to learn from scientific visualizations, Chiu and Linn (2011) studied students' assessments of their understanding of the chemical reactions visualization. They compared two conditions. One group rated their understanding immediately after they experimented with the chemical reactions visualization. The other group rated their understanding immediately after they had written an explanation of what they thought the chemical reactions visualization illustrated. They were interested in whether students would rate their understanding right after viewing the visualization higher or lower than their understanding after they wrote an explanation.

Chiu and Linn (2011) found that students rated themselves to have better understanding of chemical reactions after viewing the visualization than after writing an explanation about the visualization. This means that students either overestimate their understanding after viewing the visualization or underestimate their understanding after writing the explanation. Analysis of the data showed that students overestimate their understanding after viewing the visualization, supporting the claim that visualizations have deceptive clarity (Chiu & Linn, 2008). This overestimation of understanding may deter students from careful analysis of the visualization. Chiu and Linn (2008) found that students identify gaps in their understanding when they explain their observations. Prompts to explain their ideas motivate students to recognize gaps and go back to the visualization to refine their ideas.

These findings resonate with research on desirable difficulties (Linn et al., 2010). Desirable difficulties are learning activities that slow learning and often increase errors but ultimately improve outcomes. Several studies suggest that one of the principles of desirable difficulties—encouraging students to generate responses—ensures that students articulate the distinctions found in visualizations and develop sophisticated understanding of unseen processes illustrated in visualizations.

Conclusions on Visualizations Guidelines

In summary, these classroom comparison studies identify ways to improve the effectiveness of visualizations and suggest guidelines for designers. The studies show the value of adding pivotal cases. By simplifying the visualizations and focusing on essential points, the refinements direct student attention to key ideas. By presenting instruction in a sequence that allows students to make appropriate links across representations, including links between symbolic and observable representations of the phenomena, instruction increases the coherence of ideas. By adding desirable difficulties, instruction can overcome deceptive clarity and motivate students to monitor their own learning and detect gaps in their knowledge. Taken together, these iterative refinements substantially increase the effectiveness of instruction featuring visualizations (Linn & Eylon, 2011). To promote knowledge integration in DTPs, designers can add pivotal cases and emphasize desirable difficulties.

THE FUTURE OF DIGITAL TEACHING PLATFORMS

WISE research has powerful implications for the design and implementation of DTPs. Using the knowledge integration pattern and taking advantage of visualizations are likely to improve outcomes in most units. The first process of the pattern, eliciting ideas or asking for predictions, is particularly valuable for helping students integrate their ideas. Visualizations are valuable for the second process, adding ideas. Ensuring that students can distinguish ideas by comparing alternatives using scientific criteria, the third process, is also central to the success of instruction. Finally, encouraging students to reflect on their ideas helps students put their insights together into a coherent argument.

WISE research is beginning to focus on ways to combine units to create a full curriculum. This involves organizing student activities to support cumulative understanding (Confrey & Maloney, Chapter 8 of this volume; Linn & Eylon, 2011). Typical instruction is often fragmented and incoherent, reflecting standards that do not address the cumulative understanding needed in science. Using powerful visualizations and instruction based on the knowledge integration pattern has the potential to achieve this goal.

NOTE

This material is based upon work supported by the National Science Foundation under grant Nos. ESI 0334199 and ESI 0455877. Any opinions, findings, and conclusions or recommendations expressed in this material are those of the author and do not necessarily reflect the views of the National Science Foundation. The author appreciates comments and discussions with the Technology-Enhanced Learning in Science research group. Special thanks go to David I. Miller and Elissa Sato for helpful comments and suggestions. Help from Jon Breitbart and Michael O'Hara in preparing this chapter is greatly appreciated.

REFERENCES

Buckley, B., Gobert, J. D., Kindfield, A. C. H., Horwitz, P., Tinker, R. F., Gerlits, B., . . . Willett, J. (2004). Model-based teaching and learning with BioLogica: What do they learn? How do they learn? How do we know? *Journal of Science Education and Technology, 13*, 23–41.

Chiu, J. L., & Linn, M. C. (2008). Self-assessment and self-explanation for learning chemistry using dynamic molecular visualizations. In *International perspectives in the learning sciences: Creating a learning world: Proceedings of the 8th International Conference of the Learning Sciences: Vol. 3* (pp. 16–17). Utrecht, The Netherlands: International Society of the Learning Sciences, Inc.

Chiu, J. L., & Linn, M. C. (2011). The role of self-monitoring in learning chemistry with dynamic visualization. In A. Zohar & Y. J. Dori (Eds.), *Metacognition and science education: Trends in current research (Contemporary trends and issues in science education, 40)* (pp. 133–163). London: Springer-Verlag.

Clark, D. B., & Linn, M. C. (2003). Scaffolding knowledge integration through curricular depth. *Journal of the Learning Sciences, 12*, 451–494.

Davis, E. A., & Krajcik, J. S. (2005). Designing educative curriculum materials to promote teacher learning. *Educational Researcher, 34*, 3–14.

Design-Based Research Collective (2003). Design-based research: An emerging paradigm for educational inquiry. *Educational Researcher, 32*, 5–8.

diSessa, A. A. (1988). Knowledge in pieces. In G. Forman & P. Pufall (Eds.), *Constructivism in the computer age* (pp. 49–70). Hillsdale, NJ: Lawrence Erlbaum Associates.

Driver, R., Asoko, H., Leach, J., Mortimer, E., & Scott, P. (1994). Constructing scientific knowledge in the classroom. *Educational Researcher, 23*, 5–12.

Eylon, B. S., & Linn, M. C. (1988). Learning and instruction: An examination of four research perspectives in science education. *Review of Educational Research, 58*, 251–301.

Gerard, L. F., Spitulnik, M., & Linn, M. C. (2011). Teacher use of evidence to customize inquiry science instruction: A longitudinal investigation of the impacts on teacher and student learning. *Journal of Research in Science Teaching, 47*, 1037–1063.

Gunstone, R. F., & Champagne, A. B. (1990). Promoting conceptual change in the laboratory. In E. Hegarty-Hazel (Ed.), *The student laboratory and the science curriculum* (pp. 159–182). New York: Routledge.

Kali, Y. (2006). Collaborative knowledge-building using the Design Principles Database. *International Journal of Computer-Supported Collaborative Learning, 1*, 187–201.

Kali, Y., Linn, M. C., & Roseman, J. E. (Eds.). (2008). *Designing coherent science education.* New York: Teachers College Press.

Lee, H.-S., Linn, M. C., Varma, K., & Liu, O. L. (2010). How do technology-enhanced inquiry science units impact classroom learning? *Journal of Research in Science Teaching, 47,* 71–90.

Linn, M. C. (2005). WISE design for lifelong learning: Pivotal cases. In P. Gärdenfors & P. Johansson (Eds.), *Cognition, education and communication technology* (pp. 223–256). Mahwah, NJ: Lawrence Erlbaum Associates.

Linn, M. C., Chang, H.-Y., Chiu, J. L., Zhang, Z., & McElhaney, K. (2010). Can desirable difficulties overcome deceptive clarity in scientific visualizations? In A. Benjamin (Ed.), *Successful remembering and successful forgetting: A Festschrift in honor of Robert A. Bjork* (pp. 239–262). New York: Routledge.

Linn, M. C., Davis, E. A., & Bell, P. (Eds.). (2004). *Internet environments for science education.* Mahwah, NJ: Lawrence Erlbaum Associates.

Linn, M. C., & Eylon, B. S. (2006). Science education: Integrating views of learning and instruction. In P. A. Alexander & P. H. Winne (Eds.), *Handbook of educational psychology* (2nd ed., pp. 511–544). Mahwah, NJ: Lawrence Erlbaum.

Linn, M. C., & Eylon, B. S. (2011). *Science learning and instruction: Taking advantage of technology to promote knowledge integration.* New York: Routledge.

Linn, M. C., & Hsi, S. (2000). *Computers, teachers, peers: Science learning partners.* Mahwah, NJ: Lawrence Erlbaum Associates.

Linn, M. C., Lee, H.-S., Tinker, R., Husic, F., & Chiu, J. L. (2006). Teaching and assessing knowledge integration in science. *Science, 313,* 1049–1050.

Liu, O. L., Lee, H.-S., Hofstetter, C., & Linn, M. C. (2008). Assessing knowledge integration in science: Construct, measures and evidence. *Educational Assessment, 13,* 33–55.

Mokros, J. R., & Tinker, R. F. (1987). The impact of microcomputer-based labs on children's ability to interpret graphs. *Journal of Research in Science Teaching, 24,* 369–383.

Quellmalz, E., & Pellegrino, J. (2009). Technology and testing. *Science, 323,* 75–79.

Quintana, C., Reiser, B. J., Davis, E. A., Krajcik, J. S., Fretz, E., Golan, R. D., . . . Soloway, E. (2004). A scaffolding design framework for software to support science inquiry. *Journal of the Learning Sciences, 13,* 337–386.

Shen, J., & Linn, M. C. (2011). A technology-enhanced unit of modeling static electricity: Integrating scientific explanations and everyday observations. *International Journal of Science Education, 33,* 1597–1623.

Shepard, L. A. (2000). The role of assessment in a learning culture. *Educational Researcher, 29,* 4–14.

Sisk-Hilton, S. (2008). *Teaching and learning in public: Professional development through shared inquiry.* New York: Teachers College Press.

Wilensky, U., & Reisman, K. (2006). Thinking like a wolf, a sheep or a firefly: Learning biology through constructing and testing computational theories—An embodied modeling approach. *Cognition and Instruction, 24,* 171–209.

Zhang, Z., & Linn, M. C. (2008). *Using drawings to support learning from dynamic visualizations. International perspectives in the learning sciences: Creating a learning world. Proceedings of the 8th International Conference of the Learning Sciences: Vol. 3* (pp. 161–162). Utrecht, The Netherlands: International Society of the Learning Sciences, Inc.

CHAPTER 4

Reading Instruction
Technology-Based Supports for Classroom Instruction

Arthur C. Graesser
Danielle S. McNamara

This chapter provides a snapshot of technologies that support reading instruction in the context of Digital Teaching Platforms (DTPs). A DTP allows the teacher to track progress of individuals and groups of students in the classroom, and to use these student profiles to adaptively guide future learning activities. With respect to reading, progress is ideally tracked on a variety of skills and strategies across the multiple levels of language and discourse defined in the first section of this chapter. Such formative assessment is needed to inform the creation of dynamic and individualized plans for reading instruction. DTPs, in conjunction with the classroom teacher, optimize the learning environment by providing students with reasonable suggestions or options on what tasks, texts, tests, and subject-matter topics to conquer next. In classrooms featuring DTPs, students are also more motivated because they can track their own progress in the curriculum and their skill development.

Major advances have been made in recent years on computer analyses of texts on multiple levels of language and discourse. This presents the opportunity to diagnose reading problems at a more fine-grained level and to remediate these problems by judiciously selecting texts, tasks, tests, and topics for students. This chapter emphasizes technologies that help students comprehend text beyond the word and into the realm of sentence and discourse meaning. This is not to deny the importance of word decoding and vocabulary, both of which are addressed in this chapter. However, the more advanced levels of language and discourse have been particularly difficult to research, not to mention to teach, to evaluate, and to center educational policy around. It is these more-advanced levels that have been the primary focus of our own research and technology development.

All students are expected to read proficiently at multiple levels of language and discourse in order to pass high-stakes tests and to develop 21st-century skills. Proficient reading is a reasonable expectation of all students because it is well documented that reading literacy opens the doors to more rewarding professions, higher salaries, and an improved quality of life (Resnick, 2010). However, there are some salient challenges in today's world that make it more difficult to become a proficient reader. The reading experience in the mid-20th century was less complex in that children and adults had the opportunity to read books in a linear fashion, beginning to end, in a single sitting over long stretches of time. But today we live in a world of email, instant messaging, Facebook, chat rooms, portals, Google, Wikipedia, teleconferences, solitary and multiparty games, sensuously rich video, YouTube, Twitter, iPhones, and other technologies that break up our experiences into smaller packages of time and content. Texts are not only shorter, but the reading process is typically distributed over time and integrated with other media, tasks, and actions. Texts are read for the purpose of accomplishing short-term goals, solving problems, communicating with others, writing reports, and playing games.

This *distributed information ecology* forces students to abandon the long periods of sustained concentration on reading text, which is possibly a prerequisite for acquiring the skills of reading at deeper levels of comprehension. However, perhaps it is not a prerequisite. Perhaps deep comprehension can be achieved in a world where smaller, bite-size texts are interwoven with actions, tasks, and goals in today's world of multimedia, multitasking, and multi-communication. These types of skills are emblematic of the learning modalities required for students to receive the full benefits of DTPs.

This chapter is divided into four sections. The first section identifies the many levels of language and discourse that need to be considered in a comprehensive model of reading intervention. A reader may have deficits at one or more of these levels, so the technology needs to diagnose particular deficits for particular readers. Further, groups of readers or the entire class have distributions of deficits or skill levels that the teacher needs to observe and manage.

The second section presents some automated metrics for scaling texts on *text complexity* as it is defined in the first section. The assignment of texts to readers can be made in a fashion that fits the readers' proficiency profiles in addition to their self-regulated choice of materials to read.

The third section presents some examples of technology that can diagnose reading deficits and train students to rectify such deficits. These technologies typically follow a *diagnosis and remediation* framework that is tailored to particular readers in individualized training. However, these systems can also be integrated with DTPs to handle groups of readers in classroom environments.

The fourth section explores the reading process in more advanced digital environments that consider student motivation and that incorporate multiple media, tasks, and pedagogical objectives. In this case, students read in order to learn, act, solve problems, and communicate with others—activities that are at the heart of DTPs.

LEVELS OF LANGUAGE, DISCOURSE, AND READING COMPREHENSION

Psychological theories of reading comprehension have identified the representations, structures, strategies, and processes across various linguistic levels (Graesser & McNamara, 2011; Kintsch, 1998; McNamara, Graesser, & Louwerse, in press). This chapter considers six levels, as elaborated in Table 4.1: *words, syntax,* the explicit *textbase,* the referential *situation model* (sometimes called the mental model), the *discourse genre* and *rhetorical structure* (the type of discourse and its composition), and the *pragmatic communication level* (between speaker and listener, or writer and reader).

Three of these levels—words, syntax, and pragmatic communication—are self-explanatory. The textbase refers to explicit ideas in a text in a form that preserves the meaning but not the precise wording and syntax. The situation model refers to the subject matter that is being described in informational texts or the microworld that evolves in a story. This would include the people, objects, spatial setting, actions, events, processes, plans, thoughts, and emotions of people, and other referential content. The discourse genre is the type of text, such as a news story, a folk tale, a persuasive editorial, or a science text, that explains a causal mechanism. The rhetorical structure is the organization of the text at a macro level and the discourse function of particular excerpts. Table 4.1 lists key components of the six levels, but it is beyond the scope of this chapter to provide more detailed definitions. For a more detailed overview of the levels of language and discourse, see Graesser and McNamara, 2011.

Table 4.1 depicts components of each level that are constructed as a *result* of successful comprehension. This *compositional* viewpoint alone is insufficient for researchers who are interested in comprehension deficits and the interventions to remediate them. To guide this type of research, each component should also be considered via several viewpoints:

- *Knowledge.* The reader needs to have the prerequisite knowledge about the component through prior experience and/or training.
- *Process.* The reader needs to be able to process the component by recognizing patterns in the text and by executing relevant skills and strategies proficiently.

- *Diagnosis of deficit.* If the reader is not proficient in processing the component, the technology or teacher needs to diagnose the deficit.
- *Remediation of deficit.* The technology or teacher attempts to remediate the deficit by some form of training or intervention.
- *Compensation of deficit.* Some readers show no response to an intervention that attempts to remediate the deficit. In such cases, there needs to be compensation for the deficit through alternative reading components or augmented technologies.

Table 4.1. Levels of Language and Discourse

Level	Example Components of Level
Words	Word meaning representation
	Word composition (graphemes, phonemes, syllables, morphemes, lemmas)
	Parts of speech (noun, verb, adjective, adverb, determiner, connective)
Syntax	Syntax (noun-phrase, verb-phrase, prepositional phrase, clause)
	Linguistic style
Textbase	Semantic meaning
	Explicit propositions or clauses
	Referring expressions linked to other text constituents
Situation model	Situation conveyed in the text
	Agents, objects, and abstract entities
	Dimensions of temporality, spatiality, causality, intentionality
	Inferences that elaborate text and link to the reader's experiential knowledge
	Connectives that explicitly link events, actions, states, and goals
	Given versus new information
	Images and mental simulations of events
Genre & rhetorical structure	Discourse category (narrative, persuasive, expository, descriptive)
	Rhetorical composition (cause+effect, claim+evidence, problem+solution)
	Epistemological status of propositions and clauses (claim, evidence, warrant)
	Speech act categories (assertion, question, command, request, greeting, etc.)
	Theme, moral, or point of discourse
Pragmatic communication	Goals of author
	Attitudes and beliefs (humor, sarcasm, eulogy, deprecation)

Comprehension Scenarios

Readers can face reading obstacles at any of the levels in Table 4.1. There can be deficits in the reader (e.g., lack of knowledge or skill), the text (e.g., incoherent text; esoteric, irrelevant jargon), or the training (e.g., an emphasis on shallow levels of reading). The severity of an obstacle can range from a minor irregularity that adds some cost in processing time to a major impasse that results in a complete breakdown in comprehension. Attempts can be made to compensate for the problem by recruiting information from other levels of discourse, from prior knowledge, from external sources (e.g., other people or technologies), or from strategies. The scenarios below illustrate some obstacles and resulting consequences.

Scenario 1. A child has trouble recognizing letters in the alphabet, so there is an obstacle in lexical decoding at the word level (level 1 in Table 4.1). The word deficit blocks the child from understanding any of the text at levels two through six.

Scenario 2. A high school student reads a health insurance document that has lengthy sentences with embedded clauses, numerous quantifiers (e.g., all, many, rarely), and many logical operators (e.g., and, or, not, if). The student understands most words, but has only a vague idea what the document explicitly states because of complex syntax, a dense textbase, and an ungrounded situation model (i.e., deficits at levels two through four). Nevertheless, the student signs the contract because he or she understands its purpose and trusts the school. Levels 5 and 6 circumvent the need to understand levels two through four completely.

Scenario 3. Laboratory partners in an engineering course read the directions in order to assemble a new computer. They argue about how to hook up the cables on the dual monitors. They have no problem understanding the words and textbase in the directions (levels one through three) and no problem understanding the genre and purpose of the document (levels five and six), but they do have a deficit at the situation-model level (level four).

Scenario 4. A science student asks his roommate to proofread a term paper, but the roommate is a journalism major who knows little about science and complains that there is a problem with logical flow. The science major revises the text by adding connectives (e.g., because, so, therefore, before) and other words to improve the cohesion. The revised composition is more comprehensible. Improvements at levels one and three compensated for a deficit at level four.

Scenario 5. Parents take their children to a new Disney movie that has some adult themes. The children notice the parents laughing at different points in the movie than they are. The children are making it successfully through discourse levels one through four, but not levels five and six.

These scenarios illustrate how deficiencies at one or more discourse levels can have substantial repercussions on the processing at other levels. Reading researchers need to understand the processing mechanisms both *within* levels and *between* levels.

Comprehension Calibration and Levels

Obstacles to comprehension are often invisible to the reader. Research on metacognition has extensively documented that most adults have limited abilities to detect and monitor many cognitive states (Hacker, Dunlosky, & Graesser, 2009). Research on *comprehension calibration* has collected ratings from readers on how well they believe they have comprehended texts, and these ratings are correlated with objective tests of text comprehension. The comprehension calibration correlations are alarmingly low ($r = .27$) even among college students (Maki, 1998).

Readers often have an illusion of comprehension when they read text because they settle for shallow levels of analysis as a criterion for adequate comprehension. Shallow readers believe they have adequately comprehended text if they can recognize the content words and can understand most of the sentences, when in fact they are missing the deeper knowledge, occasional contradictions, and false claims. Linn, in Chapter 3, discusses similar shallow processing for visual media that are deceptively simple. Deep comprehension requires inferences, linking ideas coherently, scrutinizing the validity of claims, comparing content of different texts, and understanding the motives of authors (Rouet, 2006; Wiley et al., 2009). For most students, deep comprehension may only be selectively achieved in everyday reading experiences.

In studies conducted in our laboratory (Graesser et al., 2004; Van Lehn et al., 2007), college students read textbooks on technical topics such as computer literacy and Newtonian physics. They subsequently completed a test on deep knowledge with well-constructed multiple-choice questions similar to the Force Concept Inventory in physics (Hestenes, Wells, & Swackhamer, 1992) or essays that required deep reasoning. The results revealed that students had zero learning gains after reading the textbook, and that the post-test scores did not differ from a condition in which the students read nothing at all. In contrast, the learning gains were quite substantial in tests of shallow knowledge.

On the other hand, students experienced learning gains for deep knowledge from learning environments that challenged their comprehension of the material. For example, a computer system, AutoTutor, has an animated agent that has a collaborative discussion with the reader in natural language during the course of answering difficult questions.

The reading strategies of literate adults are typically aligned with shallow rather than deep comprehension, even when they have a nontrivial amount of world knowledge on the topics and when they have sufficient reading strategies to gain entrance to college. Readers need to be better challenged by the text, tasks, tests, technology, or teacher.

A fundamental question raised by this chapter is how teachers can manage DTPs to help students improve their reading and achieve deeper levels of comprehension. Quite clearly, the teachers will need to understand the many manifestations of meaning, such as the six levels in Table 4.1; this can be accomplished through professional development. Further, the DTP will need supports that address deficits at these various levels. The DTP needs diagnostic capabilities so that it can inform the teacher what problems are experienced by particular readers, and what supports can help to remediate the deficits. Individual technologies are now available that address these challenges. However, DTPs must integrate these technologies, and teachers need to understand how to use the DTP effectively.

COMPUTER TOOLS FOR ANALYZING TEXT AT MULTIPLE LEVELS

One way to challenge students is to assign them texts that are somewhat more complex than they can easily manage. The texts presumably should not be too difficult or too easy, but at the right zone of complexity—the students' *zone of proximal development* (Vygotsky, 1978). This requires the scaling of texts on complexity at multiple levels of comprehension.

This is a unique point in history because widespread access is available to computer tools that analyze specific texts and large text repositories (called *corpora*). The increase in automated text analyses can be attributed to landmark advances in computational linguistics (Jurafsky & Martin, 2008), statistical representations of world knowledge (Landauer, McNamara, Dennis, & Kintsch, 2007), and systematic corpus analyses (Biber, Conrad, & Reppen, 1998). Thousands of texts can be quickly accessed and analyzed on thousands of measures in a short amount of time.

A frequent approach to scaling texts is to have a single dimension of text complexity. This is the approach taken by metrics such as Degrees of Reading Power (DRP) (Koslin, Zeno, & Koslin, 1987). Word frequency, word length, and sentence length are strong predictors of these metrics of text difficulty. An overall metric of text difficulty is limited in its utility in helping students improve their reading, however. Assessments of text difficulty need to be pitched at particular levels of language and discourse in order to target remediation intelligently.

This challenge motivated an automated text analysis system called Coh-Metrix (Graesser & McNamara, 2011; Graesser, McNamara, Louwerse, & Cai, 2004; McNamara, Graesser, & Louwerse, in press). Coh-Metrix is a computer facility that analyzes texts on the discourse levels one through five in Table 4.1. Our goals in designing Coh-Metrix were to enhance standard text difficulty measures by providing scores on the levels in Table 4.1, as well as to determine the appropriateness of a text for a reader with a particular profile of cognitive characteristics. One version of Coh-Metrix is available to the public for free online at http://cohmetrix.memphis.edu.

Coh-Metrix Analysis

We explored nearly 1,000 measures of language and discourse with Coh-Metrix, but a relatively small number of dimensions can explain text variations. A Coh-Metrix analysis was performed on 37,520 texts in a corpus provided by Touchstone Applied Science Associates (TASA). This TASA corpus represents the texts that a typical senior in high school would have encountered throughout grades K-12. The texts are scaled on Degrees of Reading Power, which can approximately be translated into grade level (McNamara et al., in press). Most of the text genres were classified by TASA as being in language arts (narrative), science, and social studies/history, but other categories were business, health, home economics, and industrial arts.

We performed statistical analyses on the TASA text corpus in order to discover what aspects of texts account for text complexity. We discovered that eight dimensions accounted for an impressive 67% of the variability among texts. The five major dimensions of those eight were:

- *Narrativity.* Narrative text tells a story, with characters, events, places, and things that are familiar to the reader. Narrative is closely affiliated with everyday oral conversation.
- *Referential cohesion.* High-cohesion texts contain explicit words and ideas that overlap across sentences and the text.
- *Situation model cohesion.* Causal, intentional, and temporal connectives help the reader form a more coherent and deeper understanding of the text.
- *Syntactic simplicity.* Sentences with few words and simple, familiar syntactic structures are easier to understand. Complex sentences have structurally embedded syntax.
- *Word concreteness.* Concrete words evoke mental images and are more meaningful to the reader than abstract words.

These five dimensions are expressed in terms of ease of comprehension, but the scores could be reversed for measures of text difficulty.

We scaled the TASA corpus of 37,520 texts on their ease/difficulty with respect to particular components of discourse. More specifically, we computed a normalized z-score on each of the five principal components for each text. A z-score is a standardized metric in standard deviation units, with zero being the mean and higher scores being easier for a particular dimension. The scores are higher and positive when the texts are easier on the component and more negative when the texts are more difficult. As predicted, correlations with DRP grade level were negative: −.69, −.47, and −.23 for narrativity, syntactic simplicity, and word concreteness respectively.

However, the results for cohesion dimensions were quite different. Texts had slightly higher referential and causal cohesion at the higher grade levels, with correlations of .03 and .11, respectively. Text cohesion appears to be slightly higher for texts on the more difficult subject matters. One of many explanations for this result is that writers increase cohesion to compensate for the difficulty of the subject matter (McNamara et al., in press).

Coh-Metrix Conclusions

Our analysis of Coh-Metrix scores supports a number of conclusions. First, there are at least five dimensions of text difficulty that should be considered when analyzing texts. This is very different than that notion adopted throughout the United States that there is a unidimensional scale of text difficulty, such as DRP or Lexile scores, two commonly used programs that assess reading complexity and assign numbers to texts according to their difficulty. Second, in addition to explaining aspects of a large corpus of texts, the top five dimensions in the Principle Components Analysis (PCA) have a foundation in theories of reading comprehension that were described earlier (Graesser & McNamara, 2011; Kintsch, 1998). Indeed, the close alignment between theory and the inductive principal component analysis was a gratifying validation of the multilevel theoretical framework. Third, the DRP grade levels have the strongest negative correlations with narrativity, syntax, and word concreteness. Fourth, the cohesion measures tend to increase slightly as a function of DRP grade level, but the correlations were modest. Therefore, standard text difficulty measures such as DRP and Lexile do not highly correlate with these cohesion measures, which suggests that unidimensional measures are not tapping more global discourse meaning. The standard text complexity metrics handle word and sentence constraints, but not deeper and more global meaning.

The practical challenge is how these text difficulty dimensions can be communicated to teachers, students, and administrators who may not be highly trained in research methods. One approach is to convert the z-scores to percentile scores on text difficulty, making them more likely to be familiar to teachers and laypeople. A percentile score varies from 0 to 100, with higher scores meaning the text is more difficult. Percentile profiles on the Coh-Metrix dimensions can be viewed by teachers—including those using DTPs—when they suggest texts for students to read. The profiles can be viewed by principals and administrators when they select textbooks and other readings for students in different achievement clusters. The profiles may even be viewed by students when they choose what to read in digital libraries or in game environments that assign more points for texts that are more challenging.

For any text, the text complexity profiles can also be generated automatically by a DTP. This opens the door for an automated selection of texts to assign or suggest to readers, or to include in a library for readers to select on their own. The automated text selection mechanism should be sensitive to the reader's profile of reading proficiency at various levels. The texts would focus on the reader's challenge zone for the various components, based on what the computer knows about the reader and about the text. The computer algorithm can also consider motivational, emotional, and noncognitive characteristics of the reader. Readers with high self-efficacy (i.e., they are convinced they can perform well) and academic risk (i.e., they take on challenging tasks and do not get emotionally upset if they fail) can be encouraged to read texts that aggressively expand their challenge zone. In contrast, readers with low self-efficacy and low academic risk taking would receive different texts that are within their challenge zone.

COMPUTER INTERVENTIONS FOR READING INSTRUCTION

A *diagnosis and remediation* framework has always guided intervention programs for reading instruction, as well as programs for mathematics, science, and other subject matters. The first step in using a computer intervention is to assess how well the student has mastered particular skills, strategies, and knowledge relevant to reading. These reading proficiencies have traditionally been assessed annually or intermittently throughout the year by psychometric tests that are administered by professional testers or by computer. The more contemporary approach is formative assessment that tracks mastery of a large number skills and concepts very frequently so that the teacher can adjust the instruction dynamically and adaptively to the students' needs. Examples of formative assessments in mathematics are in Chapters 5 and 8 of this volume. Formative assessment in general is discussed in Chapter 9.

Reading assessments have traditionally addressed proficiencies that funnel into one of three categories: lexical decoding, vocabulary, and meaning. Lexical decoding includes such generic skills as the identification of alphabetic symbols, the association between speech sounds and letters, phonemic awareness, decomposition of words into syllables or morphemes, and speed (i.e., fluency) of accomplishing these subskills (Adams, 1990). Generic tests of vocabulary measure how many words a student knows. Sometimes particular texts have rare words that require pre-training before the student has a fair chance at comprehending a text.

Researchers have established that a word is not mastered by simply knowing its definition; a word needs to be experienced in multiple contexts of use before it is conceptually rich enough to guide the interpretation of sentence meanings and the generation of inferences (Perfetti, 2007). Regarding meaning, tests such as the Woodcock-Johnson and Gates-MacGinitie reading tests are routinely administered to readers in order to assess meaning comprehension. However, the analysis of meaning is not as fine-grained and theoretically grounded as we are proposing in this chapter.

Individualized student instruction is more effective than having all students in a classroom move at the same pace on the same materials (Connor, Morrison, Fishman, Schatschneider, & Underwood, 2007). One obvious reason is there are aptitude-treatment interactions: Some types of readers benefit from one instruction method, whereas other types of readers benefit from another. One powerful demonstration of this is reported by Connor et al. (2007). Connor developed and tested her Assessment to Instruction (A2i) web-based software. She compared students who were above versus below average in lexical decoding (i.e., letter- and word-reading skills) and students who were above versus below average in vocabulary. She discovered that the following instruction methods were appropriate for different types of students:

- IF (low lexical decoding) THEN (use explicit teacher-managed, code-focused instruction).
- IF (high lexical decoding) THEN (do not use explicit teacher-managed, code-focused instruction).
- IF (low vocabulary) THEN (use combination of explicit teacher-managed, code-focused instruction and explicit meaning-focused instruction).
- IF (high vocabulary) THEN (use explicit meaning-focused instruction or independent reading).

Students with high lexical decoding skills and vocabulary may best be left alone to conduct independent reading. Reading on topics that interest them would no doubt be a high priority, but sometimes in practice the teacher would be expected to nudge them toward topics that address state standards. In contrast, more explicit instruction is needed for the other groups of readers. This type of customization is the hallmark of a DTP.

There is an abundance of computer technologies available for instruction at the level of lexical decoding and vocabulary. For example, text-to-speech engines can produce spoken output as the words being spoken are highlighted on the computer display. Speech-to-text facilities involve the student reading words aloud and the system giving feedback on their errors (Mostow, 2008). Multimedia environments provide simultaneous presentations of printed words and their pictorial referents in the form of static images (e.g., a picture of a truck) or dynamic events (e.g., shooting a basketball). A healthy cottage industry is generating computer environments to train students to associate sounds, letters, words, and pictures; to decompose complex words into their syllables or morphemes; and to help students learn vocabulary. The bigger challenge has been to develop computer environments with instruction at the level of meaning. These learning environments have begun to emerge in the last decade (McNamara, 2007) and provide a foundation for integrating these capabilities into a DTP.

iSTART

One promising system that focuses on deeper levels of meaning is the iSTART system (McNamara, O'Reilly, Best, & Ozuru, 2006). iSTART is a web-based computer program that uses conversational agents to provide reading strategy training for deeper levels of comprehension. iSTART incorporates theoretically motivated Self-Explanation Reading Training (SERT) (McNamara, 2004), which has proven to be effective when used by teachers in classrooms. SERT and iSTART teach students to self-explain science texts by using active reading strategies that facilitate and enhance comprehension. These strategies include paraphrasing explicit text, generating elaborative inferences, generating bridging inferences that connect text elements, predicting what will happen next in the text, and monitoring one's comprehension.

The original version of iSTART had three modules. In the Introduction module, students watch the teacher-agent (avatar) explain the reading strategies to two student-agents; this is a form of vicarious learning where students learn by observing interactive agents. In the Demonstration module, students are quizzed on various aspects of the strategies as they communicate through interactions with agents. In the Practice module, students practice generating typed self-explanations, and the conversational agents provide feedback on performance. The practice section incorporates feedback that to some extent is adaptive to the level of student performance. For example, a paraphrase strategy is appropriate when the student has low ability and the self-explanations are not remotely related to the text. In contrast, bridging and elaborative inference strategies would be better suited to students with greater world knowledge and reading ability. Numerous experiments assessing the efficacy of iSTART have been conducted with over 1,000 middle school, high school, and college students. iSTART is effective in helping students use strategies to learn from texts. It also improves comprehension, particularly among low-knowledge readers (McNamara et al., 2006).

More recent versions of iSTART have added features to further improve learning and motivation. The strategy training is more adaptable to students' needs and rates of progress. The system has more intelligent mechanisms to track the reader's ability and to respond with appropriate instruction. There is a game version, called iSTART-ME (Motivationally Enhanced), that weaves in game elements to give the students an enhanced sense of control, performance-based feedback, reinforcement, challenges, and other features that optimize motivation.

One major challenge is to find ways to integrate these individualized computer learning environments into the classroom, given the many demands placed on teachers. Let us assume that the teachers have adequate computer resources and are convinced that that there is value in using intelligent computer technologies to remediate particular reading skills. If those hurdles can be cleared, systems like A2i (a web-based evaluation and instruction program) and iSTART can be integrated into classrooms and DTPs, as discussed in Chapters 1 and 10 of this volume. The DTP's suite of software tools must be easy for teachers to use in satisfying pedagogical and technological goals. Both A2i and iSTART have software modules that manage data on students' progress and that give instruction on effective use of the system. New texts can be added in iSTART so that teachers can use the system for different subject matter and at different points in the DTP curriculum. Unfortunately, most teachers are not currently trained to handle all of these levels of complexity. The major challenges will be to develop adequate authoring tools and to improve professional development to fill these gaps (see Chapter 1).

Reading for Learning and Doing

As a student progresses through kindergarten and primary school and on to high school, there is a shift from learning-to-read to reading-to-learn. Reading becomes more of a goal-driven activity (McCrudden & Schraw, 2007) that supports other activities. Sometimes the reader has passionate interests and intrinsic goals, such as a hobby, a pet project, or a multiparty game with a community of peers. More often, there are projects directed by the teacher, such as a writing assignment, a science exhibit, or the design of an artifact. In both cases, the student needs to hunt for reading materials that are relevant to the goals. When an article is accessed, the reader assesses the relevance of sections read, searches for answers to specific questions, and exits the text when it fails to deliver. The half-life of reading an article is very short unless it is particularly relevant, insightful, and helpful.

We can imagine the opportunity for researchers collecting data through DTPs on readers' patterns of reading activities throughout the day in both school and informal settings. An ecological profile of reading behavior would be tremendously insightful. There is some knowledge of how students read digital libraries and the Internet under limited contexts with goals forced upon the reader. For example, Wiley et al. (2009) collected eye-tracking data and/or think-aloud protocols as college students examined a set of websites on plate tectonics for the purpose of writing an essay on what caused the eruption of Mount St. Helens. The deeper comprehenders of plate tectonics spent more time on high-quality websites with rigorous science than on websites with pseudoscience (e.g., earthquakes are caused by oil drilling or by the alignment of planets in the solar system). They also spent more time on information on pages relevant to the goal and on explanations of the scientific mechanism.

Most readers have difficulty building *causal mental models* of topics in science and history, even after reading multiple texts (see Chapters 3 and 7, this volume; Rouet, 2006; Wiley et al., 2009). Sometimes there are simple linear causal chains of events, but more often there are complex enabling states, tradeoffs among causes, cycles of events, and dynamic systems that add considerable complexity. Students are prone to avoid such complex material unless there is a tremendous push or incentive in the learning environment.

Chapter 7 of this volume (see also Dede, 2009) describes a number of systems with immersive multiuser virtual environments (MUVEs), avatars, simulations, collaborative communication, multiparty serious games, and other motivating features that are explicitly designed to encourage deeper learning and to satisfy educational standards. A well-designed system periodically presents obstacles, system breakdowns, and apparent contradictions that put the student in *cognitive disequilibrium* (Graesser, Lu, Olde, Cooper-Pye, & Whitten, 2005); this requires problem solving, reasoning, and communication with peers to construct explanations, arguments, justifications, and clarifications on relevant subject matter content. All these are capabilities of DTPs (see Chapter 10, this volume).

THE FUTURE OF DIGITAL TEACHING PLATFORMS

There is tremendous potential for Digital Teaching Platforms to impact the teaching of literacy skills in grades K–12. A number of DTPs, such as iSTART, immersive MUVEs, and A2i, have been developed that are helping educators and researchers understand better how to tailor approaches to reading comprehension instruction to each individual student in ways that go beyond decoding and vocabulary, and teach more advanced areas of reading ability.

A host of questions remain about students' reading activities as they experience immersive MUVEs and other less standard curricular activities that will be incorporated into DTPs:

- Within an embedded digital library of articles, how much and what does a particular student read?
- What goals does that student pursue, and does she read articles that are relevant to her goals?
- When an article is fetched, what do students read, how much do they read, and when do they give up?
- How much of the information in an article gets incorporated in messages to peers, documents students write, arguments, and behavior?
- What deficits in reading components (see Table 4.1) present barriers to effective participation in the DTP curricular activities?

Answers to these questions can be explored by automatic tracking of the behavior and communication of the students who interact in DTPs. These data are available in log files and can be submitted to data-mining and data-farming analyses.

Quite clearly, the role of the teacher in immersive experiences like the EcoMUVE and other advanced learning environments will require some radical changes in professional development (see Chapter 10). If any deep learning is to occur, mentors are needed with expertise in pedagogy in addition to those with expert subject-matter knowledge (Shaffer, 2006). The teachers who manage these educational technologies will have a radically different skill set than the teachers of 50 years ago. It is easy to assign a book, prepare a test, and grade it, but it is difficult to understand and use the technologies discussed in this chapter. Sophisticated professional development is essential for teachers to realize the full value of DTPs in aiding student learning.

NOTE

This research was supported by the National Science Foundation (ALT-0834847, DRK-12-0918409), the Institute of Education Sciences (R305A080589, R305A080594), and the Department of Defense Counter Intelligence Field Activity (H9C104-07-0014). Any opinions, findings, and conclusions or recommendations expressed in this material are those of the authors and do not necessarily reflect the views of NSF, IES, or DoD.

REFERENCES

Adams, M. (1990). *Beginning to read: Thinking and learning about print.* Cambridge, MA: MIT Press.

Biber, D., Conrad, S., & Reppen, R. (1998). *Corpus linguistics: Investigating language structure and use.* Cambridge, UK: Cambridge University Press.

Connor, C. M., Morrison, F. J., Fishman, B. J., Schatschneider, C., & Underwood, P. (2007). The early years: Algorithm-guided individualized reading instruction. *Science, 315,* 464–465.

Dede, C. (2009). Immersive interfaces for engagement and learning. *Science, 323,* 66–69.

Graesser, A. C., Lu, S., Jackson, G. T., Mitchell, H., Ventura, M., Olney, A., & Louwerse, M. M. (2004). AutoTutor: A tutor with dialogue in natural language. *Behavioral Research Methods, Instruments, and Computers, 36,* 180–193.

Graesser, A. C., Lu, S., Olde, B. A., Cooper-Pye, E., & Whitten, S. (2005). Question asking and eye tracking during cognitive disequilibrium: Comprehending illustrated texts on devices when the devices break down. *Memory and Cognition, 33,* 1235–1247.

Graesser, A. C., & McNamara, D. S. (2011). Computational analyses of multilevel discourse comprehension. *Topics in Cognitive Science. 3,* 371–398.

Graesser, A. C., McNamara, D. S., Louwerse, M. M., & Cai, Z. (2004). Coh-Metrix: Analysis of text on cohesion and language. *Behavioral Research Methods, Instruments, and Computers, 36,* 193–202.

Hacker, D. J., Dunlosky, J., & Graesser, A. C. (Eds.). (2009). *Handbook of metacognition in education.* Mahwah, NJ: Erlbaum/Taylor & Francis.

Hestenes, D., Wells, M., & Swackhamer, G. (1992). Force concept inventory. *The Physics Teacher, 30,* 141–158.

Jurafsky, D., & Martin, J. (2008). *Speech and language processing.* Englewood, NJ: Prentice Hall.

Kintsch, W. (1998). *Comprehension: A paradigm for cognition.* Cambridge, UK: Cambridge University Press.

Koslin, B. I., Zeno, S., & Koslin, S. (1987). *The DRP: An effective measure in reading.* New York: College Entrance Examination Board.

Landauer, T., McNamara, D. S., Dennis, S., & Kintsch, W. (Eds.). (2007). *Handbook of latent semantic analysis.* Mahwah, NJ: Erlbaum.

Maki, R. H. (1998). Test predictions over text material. In D. J. Hacker, J. Dunlosky, & A. C. Graesser (Eds.), *Metacognition in educational theory and practice* (pp. 117–144). Mahwah, NJ: Erlbaum.

McCrudden, M. T., & Schraw, G. (2007). Relevance and goal-focusing in text processing. *Educational Psychology Review, 19,* 113–139.

McNamara, D. S. (2004). SERT: Self-explanation reading training. *Discourse Processes, 38,* 1–30.

McNamara, D. S. (Ed.). (2007). *Reading comprehension strategies: Theories, interventions, and technologies.* Mahwah, NJ: Erlbaum.

McNamara, D. S., Graesser, A., & Louwerse, M. M. (in press). Sources of text difficulty: Across the ages and genres. In J. P. Sabatini & E. Albro (Eds.), *Assessing reading in the 21st century: Aligning and applying advances in the reading and measurement sciences.* Lanham, MD: R&L Education.

McNamara, D. S., O'Reilly, T., Best, R., & Ozuru, Y. (2006). Improving adolescent students' reading comprehension with iSTART. *Journal of Educational Computing Research, 34,* 147–171.

Mostow, J. (2008). Experience from a reading tutor that listens: Evaluation purposes, excuses, and methods. In C. K. Kinzer & L. Verhoeven (Eds.), *Interactive literacy education: Facilitating literacy environments through technology* (pp. 117–148). Mahwah, NJ: Erlbaum.

Perfetti, C. A. (2007). Reading ability: Lexical quality to comprehension. *Scientific Studies of Reading, 11,* 357–383.

Resnick, L. B. (2010). Nested learning systems for the thinking curriculum. *Educational Researcher, 39,* 183–197.

Rouet, J. (2006). *The skills of document use: From text comprehension to web-based learning.* Mahwah, NJ: Erlbaum.

Shaffer, D. W. (2006). *How computer games help children learn.* New York: Palgrave Macmillan.

VanLehn, K., Graesser, A. C., Jackson, G. T., Jordan, P., Olney, A., & Rose, C. P. (2007). When are tutorial dialogues more effective than reading? *Cognitive Science, 31,* 3–62.

Vygotsky, L. S. (1978). *Mind in society.* Cambridge, MA: Harvard University Press.

Wiley, J., Goldman, S. R., Graesser, A. C., Sanchez, C. A., Ash, I. K., & Hemmerich, J. A. (2009). Source evaluation, comprehension, and learning in Internet science inquiry tasks. *American Educational Research Journal, 46,* 1060–1106.

CHAPTER 5

Effective and Meaningful
Use of Educational Technology
Three Cases from the Classroom

Neil T. Heffernan, Cristina L. Heffernan,
Michele Bennett Decoteau, & Matthew Militello

> The shift from steam to electric power was gradual and costly,
> not just because of the required investments in technology, but
> because the technology enabled and required fundamentally new
> ways of organizing and conducting work. (King, 1996, p. 248)

Technology in schools today is ubiquitous. Educational technology makes bold claims of efficiency, interactivity, and the ability to provide instantaneous, useful information for teachers to teach better and for students to learn more. Unfortunately, like many educational reformation predecessors, the research, development, and legislative policies that anchor 21st-century reform in technology remain largely underutilized and unrealized (see Cuban, 1993, 2001; Ravitch, 2000; Tyack & Cuban, 1995). Nonetheless, Digital Teaching Platforms (DTPs) have a unique opportunity to meet the social and economic demand to use educational technologies effectively.

This chapter describes a specific DTP that is designed to extend and transform current teaching practices. Specifically, relative advantage for teachers using this technology is garnered through ease of use, efficiency, and the ability to observe and document improvements in student engagement.

ASSISTments

ASSISTments is a web-based assessment system that provides tutoring based on student responses. The system is so named because it is a blend of assess*ment* and instructional *assist*ance. This system collects data efficiently and provides student-level diagnostic results (what we call *cognitively diagnostic*), allowing teachers to monitor students' progressions through the cognitive model. It has many features, including content, Mastery Learning, an advanced student-response system, teacher authoring, and assessment and data collection. This is a tool that can be adapted and used in a variety of manners with different cognitive models and content libraries. The most well-known library is middle school mathematics, and this is the library used here as an example. Nonetheless, it is important to remember that ASSISTments has many libraries of content, including statistics, science, and language arts.

The middle school-mathematics cognitive model is based on 130 specific mathematics skills. Examples of the skills are Venn Diagram, Percent of, Area of a Circle, and Area of an Irregular Figure. (A list of knowledge components is available at www.assistments.org/.) The system is not designed to teacher-proof the classroom. In fact, ASSISTments is designed to augment, replicate, and promote good teaching practices, including uncovering detailed diagnosis of misconceptions; providing immediate, specific feedback; and monitoring student practice.

ASSISTments has over 1,000 tutored items in middle school mathematics. *Tutored* means that if a student gets the problem wrong, he or she is given scaffolding questions, associated hints, and messages that provide guidance related to problem-solving heuristics, or *buggy* messages. Figure 5.1 shows a screen shot of a single ASSISTment. For this ASSISTment, the student must know two skills: Venn Diagram and Percent of. A student who gets the main problem right will move on to another problem. If not, as in this example, they will get tutoring.

Figure 5.1 shows that the student incorrectly typed 8, and the system responded, "Hmm, no. Let me break this down for you." The tutor then asked the student a scaffolding question: "Find the percent of students in Biology, Algebra, and Band." The student had to look at one hint to answer this question. This hint consisted of an image to show that the student had to add up the percents in gray. The next scaffolding question followed up, and this student got it right. The last question re-asked the original question.

The student typed in 23,400 and was given a buggy message, reminding the student to check to see that the answer was reasonable (i.e., less than 900). The system then reminded the student that when multiplying by 0.27, to move the decimal over two places to the left. Once a student actually types in the correct answer of 234, he or she can proceed to the next ASSISTment. The original question is tagged with two skills where the individual scaffolding questions are tagged, allowing the teacher to assign problems with more than one skill. Then, individual skills can be diagnosed by looking at the results of the scaffold questions.

Figure 5.1. Screen shot of a single ASSISTments question with associated scaffolding, tutoring, and buggy messages.

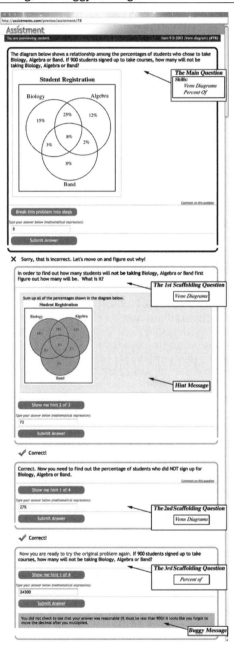

Note how this student received individualized, context-sensitive, just-in-time-help, while the teacher did not have to "do" any grading. By breaking questions into steps, the tutor is able to provide cognitively diagnostic information to teachers: items students get right, scaffolding questions they get right, and common wrong answers. If the teacher looks at a report of this student's work on this problem, he would see the student had a little trouble with the first Venn Diagram question, had no trouble on the second question, and had a little trouble with the Percent of skill in the third scaffolding question.

Figure 5.2 shows a teacher's item report where students have done four ASSISTments in a row (item numbers 4517, 8842, 4674, and 78). The teacher can see that over half of the students got the first question wrong on their first attempt (if the student has to ask for a hint, they are marked wrong). However, students seem to have learned from the tutoring and generally got the next two questions correct. On the fourth item, ASSISTment number 78, only 29% of students could get the item correct. The teacher sees that ASSISTment 78 also has the knowledge component of Percent of in addition to Venn Diagram. The teacher can see the common answers for the original question: Eighteen percent of the students answered "0" while 12% answered "657."

Figure 5.2. Teacher report for the last four ASSISTments completed by students.

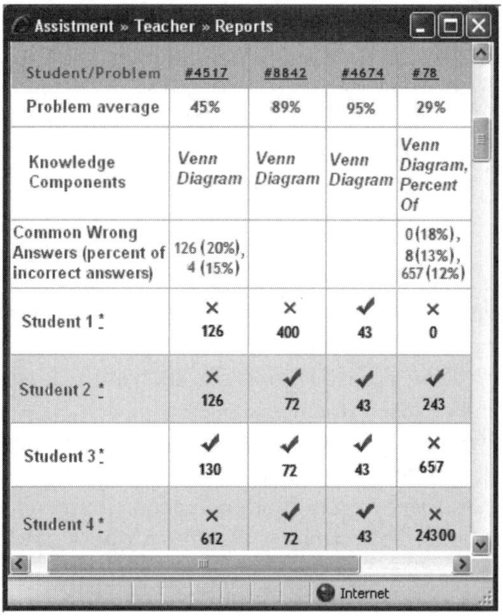

Student/Problem	#4517	#8842	#4674	#78
Problem average	45%	89%	95%	29%
Knowledge Components	Venn Diagram	Venn Diagram	Venn Diagram	Venn Diagram, Percent Of
Common Wrong Answers (percent of incorrect answers)	126 (20%), 4 (15%)			0 (18%), 8 (13%), 657 (12%)
Student 1	✗ 126	✗ 400	✓ 43	✗ 0
Student 2	✗ 126	✓ 72	✓ 43	✓ 243
Student 3	✓ 130	✓ 72	✓ 43	✗ 657
Student 4	✗ 612	✓ 72	✓ 43	✗ 24300

In addition to this cognitively diagnostic data as seen in Figure 5.2, ASSISTments can be used for Mastery Learning (an assessment feature) and nightly homework. While the digital divide is a genuine concern, many communities have public computers that, if given a few days, students can access outside of school. Parental notification is a feature that allows teachers to easily inform parents about how their child is performing and what they have, and have not, mastered. This saves the teacher tremendous amounts of time and enhances communication between the teacher and the student or parent. All of these features are designed to enhance what the teacher is already doing, but they also allow them to do it in a more efficient manner.

An innovative use of ASSISTments is the Advanced Student Response System. This feature allows teachers to create their questions (on the fly or prepared), ask the students to respond to them, anonymously post the answers using a projector or interactive whiteboard, and generate rich, meaningful discussions. This provides instantaneous feedback by students to questions teachers provide or to others students' work shown to the class.

The system comes with a student response system that also includes essay grading and provides a teacher-friendly presentation system. As more and more teachers who use ASSISTments have projectors or interactive whiteboards in their classrooms (see Chapter 2, this volume), the advantages of sharing data with students in class have emerged. In fact, when students have simultaneous access to computers, the teacher can project the results on the screen. We have seen the classroom light up with discussion in such situations. The resulting discussions can be instantly followed up by more data collection, creating a dialogue loop that involves every student responding to the teacher's questions online, and having their answers recorded on ASSISTments and projected for everyone to see. This feature is critical for DTP effectiveness in the classroom, as discussed in Chapter 10 of this volume.

In summary, this DTP can be used at multiple points in a teacher's routine:

- *Planning a lesson.* ASSISTments can help a teacher look at a scope and sequence, retrieve past lesson-plan data, and modify lesson plans based on current data.
- *Delivering a lesson.* ASSISTments can deliver the lesson with more focus on the coached practice aspect.
- *Evaluating the lesson.* ASSISTments can help a teacher determine the success or retention of a lesson.
- *Providing homework support.* Students receive immediate feedback on their actions. This provides assistance where needed and gives teachers immediate feedback on students' work.

ASSISTments IN ACTION IN REAL CLASSROOMS

This section closely examines the work of a number of teachers who are using ASSISTments to inform their teaching and help their students achieve success. They use it for nightly homework, Mastery Learning, and an advanced student response system. Together, these teachers demonstrate how the flexibility and responsiveness of these features help them build on what they already do in order to teach more effectively.

Homework

Nightly homework is an important part of extended classroom learning. With ASSISTments, teachers are able to streamline grading, the help they provide to students, and diagnostic assessments that are all part of the homework process. One teacher noted, "When I look at my emailed report (regarding ASSISTments homework) in the morning, I can save time and use the information to drive my instruction for that morning" (Christine O'Connor in Heffernan, 2010).

The traditional homework routine involves sending a set number of problems home with students; they do their best and come in the next day to see what they got wrong and to have questions answered. With ASSISTments, teachers select the problems for homework, students get feedback in the form of correct responses and sometimes tutoring, and the teachers review and plan around the emailed reports they get in the morning before class. One teacher noted, "When I look at my emailed report (regarding ASSISTments homework) in the morning, I can save time and use the information to drive my instruction for that morning" (Christine O'Connor in Heffernan, 2010). The teacher can even share the data with the class by pulling up and projecting the item report (see Figure 5.2) from the homework. For students without Internet access, teachers have the option of printing a handout.

Simply completing nightly homework on ASSISTments produces more learning than paper and pencil alone (Mendicino, Razzaq, & Heffernan, 2009). This echoes what other researchers have found in other disciplines (Warnakulasooriya & Pritchard, 2006). This section describes how one teacher, Ms. Tignor, uses these pre-made problems with tutoring, and how another teacher, Ms. O'Connor, uses ASSISTments along with her normal homework.

Ms. Tignor. Ms. Tignor works at a technical school, where she assigns a challenging problem set (with ASSISTments tutoring) from the high-stakes statewide assessment test for her students to solve online, outside of class. Each student must score "proficient," or take review mathematics classes and retake the exam. Ms. Tignor's goals for homework are for students to: work on problems to practice for the exam, get help in the form of ASSISTments tutoring on any problem they get wrong, and write up solutions for the problems they get wrong. With these three goals in mind, she gets her students involved in assessing how well prepared they are for the state exam. Students get help, and they also have to show her what they understand after working through the tutoring.

Ms. Tignor reinforces the need for students to show their work and gives them a worksheet to fill out if they get the problem wrong. She knows that the open response portion of the state test, where students must explain their work, is the most challenging. She collects their explanations and gives all students a rubric designed to focus on their ability to explain their work and to help her in assessing their work.

All students who get a problem wrong initially see ASSISTments tutoring to help them work through the problem (see Figure 5.1). The problem stays open on the screen, so students can refer back to the tutoring to help them write their explanations. Ms. Tignor has to look only at the work of students who could not solve the problem and need to be monitored.

One great benefit of assigning homework online is that Ms. Tignor does not have to wait until the next day to monitor how the whole class is doing. She explains that "[t]he ability to view student results in 'real-time' is invaluable and has had a profound effect on my teaching style" (Donna Lee Tignor in Heffernan, 2010). As seen in Figure 5.2, Ms. Tignor can get data instantaneously or first thing in the morning before she plans her daily lessons. She then uses these data to assess her students and make instructional plans for the next week.

Ms. Tignor has two routines that she uses to respond to the data she collects. First, she adds one or two of the problems from the previous week's homework to classwork as a warm-up problem. For example, one week only a third of the students get a problem correct. Ms. Tignor finds it beneficial to have a discussion about a topic that was clearly confusing to many students. Second, once a month during the weekly exam, Ms. Tignor confers with each student on their progress, during which their work on ASSISTments is discussed. During these meetings Ms. Tignor offers suggestions on students' writing of explanatory responses. This activity involves a lot of training the students to write about their mathematics, show their work, and manage their time.

Ms. O'Connor. Another teacher, Ms. O'Connor, who works at a suburban middle school, sends home regular nightly homework as ASSISTments, and has written additional ASSISTments that allow students to input their answers online and get correct feedback. Students are told which problem to do in their text. They start by doing the problem on paper because Ms. O'Connor values having the work organized and referenced in class. Then they input the answer in the system, click submit, and are instantly told if they need to try again if it is wrong, or move on to the next problem if correct. Ms. O'Connor can write hints or other support for these problems as she wishes.

These examples illustrate how teachers use this authoring feature differently. They also highlight how this feature harnesses technology that links the home and school and involves parents integrally in student work; creates efficiency in the teacher's ability to understand individual student learning prior to the next class meeting; and allows students to engage in homework in an electronic manner–capturing today's adolescents' desire to work in a technological environment.

Mastery Learning

Mastery Learning, similar to the first steps in Graesser's diagnosis and remediation framework (see Chapter 4, this volume), is a feature of ASSISTments that assesses a student's knowledge level on a single skill from the ASSISTments list of 130 skills. A major challenge of Mastery Learning is the bookkeeping. Keeping track of skill development is a time-consuming and detail-oriented task. Teachers need to keep track of the skills each student has and has not mastered, who is having trouble mastering a skill, and what the prerequisites are for each skill.

ASSISTments keeps track of all of these things for teachers, students, and parents. The Mastery Learning feature focuses on single skill items, like solving an equation or adding fractions–unlike most problems in ASSISTments, which require students to use multiple skills (e.g., ASSISTment number 78 that requires two skills, Figure 5.1). Different students need varying amounts of practice to demonstrate mastery of a skill to themselves and their teachers.

Building enough content for this sort of practice is the most important part of Mastery Learning. ASSISTments uses variables in the problem definitions, allowing each problem developed to become a set of problems measuring the same skill but with different numbers or names. This keeps the students practicing. In addition, of the 130 knowledge components tracked, there is a prerequisite structure already in place. For example, for a student to master the Pythagorean Theorem, she needs to have mastered equation solving and square roots. This tagging allows a student who is struggling in a knowledge component to move back to a prerequisite skill before continuing with the original skill.

If a problem set in ASSISTments is tagged with Mastery Learning, it automatically tracks the amount of practice students get, depending on how well they are answering the questions. Most of the problem sets determine that a student "masters" the skill once he gets a set number of problems correct in a row. Students who know the skill can demonstrate that quickly. Students who do not know the skill must work until they reach mastery. Students who are getting problems wrong can get help from the ASSISTments tutoring, or they can seek help from other sources. Teachers can monitor students using a simple report (see Figure 5.3) and seek out students who are struggling.

Ms. Mulcahey. Ms. Mulcahey gives out one Mastery Learning problem set each night to her suburban 8th-grade students. At the beginning of the year she selected skills that they should have mastered in 7th grade and monitored their progress. Many students made errors, but were able to attain mastery quickly. Ms. Mulcahey monitored and addressed the students who did not reach mastery. Later in the year, she selects skills that she has covered. This simple problem set just adds a few minutes to her students' nightly homework, and is an important part of her ability to give her students the practice they need.

Mr. Burnett. Mr. Burnett is a suburban middle school teacher who uses ASSISTments exclusively for Mastery Learning. His students start their work in the computer lab and then have to finish the work at home during the week. Mr. Burnett uses Mastery Learning in this way:

> I use Mastery Learning to reinforce learning from the classroom and to pinpoint any problems or weaknesses. I use ASSISTments as a two-tiered system: (1) it allows me to have students work independently using hints when they struggle and to come to me when they just cannot get over that hump on their own, and (2) it works as a great motivator to some students—they really work hard to see that word 'mastered' next to the assignment. (Mr. Andrew Burnett, personal communication to M. B. Decoteau, May 25, 2010)

Mr. Burnett monitors the students' progress by referencing a Mastery Learning progress report. The report tells the teacher if the student mastered a skill or is still working. It tells how many problems the student did and how long he spent in his quest to master a skill.

Like Ms. Mulcahey, Mr. Burnett reviewed content at the beginning of the year. This allowed him an efficient way to give practice only to those who needed it. As a conclusion to the Mastery Learning activity, he put together a regular ASSISTments problem set with one problem per skill to help him and the students monitor their overall progress on those review skills.

One extension of the Mastery Learning feature is the Automatic Reassessment and Retention System. This assesses students' retention of skills and

Figure 5.3. Teacher report showing Mastery Status of six students.

Student	Mastery Status	Amount of time that he/she has been working on this assignment	Problems seen
Student 1	Mastered	00:03:26	2
Student 2	Still Working	00:30:08	26
Student 3	Mastered	00:17:02	11
Student 4	Mastered	00:08:37	18
Student 5	Never Started		
Student 6	Mastered	00:00:34	2

forces students to revisit topics after mastery so they can demonstrate retention over many days. Typically, students are reassessed on a topic 1 week, 2 weeks, and 1 month later. If a class has retention rates less than 50%, this is a strong indicator of shallow learning and a topic the teacher needs to revisit.

The Mastery Learning feature provides a platform for teachers to allow students to practice as much as they need on a skill-by-skill basis. As students practice, the reports help the teacher monitor their strengths and weaknesses in these skills. The technology allows for templates with variables to build large sets of problems. ASSISTments also has an authoring tool available that, with training, allows anyone to build these problem sets on any skill they want.

ADVANCED STUDENT RESPONSE SYSTEM

This section shows how ASSISTments handles the important task of writing and reading explanations of solution strategies. The National Council of Teachers of Mathematics (NCTM) standards include communication in mathematics as one of the standards that can improve student understanding of mathematical concepts. Today's mathematics teachers are being asked to get students to explain their work verbally and in writing. They are also asked to include writing in their mathematics classrooms.

ASSISTments helps teachers orchestrate discussions and assess students' explanations of their work. Beyond declarative, factual knowledge and memorization, the Advanced Student Response System in ASSISTments provides students with procedural knowledge attainment and communication in mathematics. Procedural knowledge is a vital component to the deep understanding of mathematical knowledge and skills (NCTM, 2000).

When a teacher wants a student to provide an explanation in ASSISTments, the question type Open Response is selected, in contrast to the question types Fill In [the blank] or Multiple Choice. In this question type, a box is provided for students to type their explanations. The one drawback to this answer type is that, unlike the others, ASSISTments cannot grade these items. To facilitate these responses, there is a special link to a feature called Essay Grading. Once teachers link to this page, they see the question and the selection of explanations written by the students next to their names. They are then able to grade the essay on a scale from one to four.

Once this is done, the grade changes from "ungraded" to the percentage in the regular item report (see Figure 5.2), and the students' averages change. If a teacher wants to review the essays with the class, she can select just a few exemplary essays and only have them show up for the discussion. This allows the teacher to focus the discussion on the essays that move the learning objectives forward.

Ms. O'Connor. In the final days of a unit on linear equations, Ms. O'Connor gave an ASSISTments problem set that included regular Fill In [the blank] ASSISTments and one Open Response ASSISTments. The numerical answers are graded automatically, freeing up Ms. O'Connor's time to review and reflect on the students' written explanations. Once she collected all the explanations and read through them on ASSISTments, she selected a few of the explanations to use in class. She wants students to know their explanations will be read and possibly shared with other students, and to read other students' explanations. In reading one another's explanations, students both learn the mathematics by being exposed to another student's solution strategy and also how to write better explanations themselves.

Ms. O'Connor learned a lot by looking at the data that came in from this activity. First, all but one of her students got the right answers to A–D, so she knew they all had a strong understanding of the procedural parts of this problem. Armed with that information, Ms. O'Connor began to review the responses to question E. This question asked students to justify their answer by explaining how the number of club members going on the trip should affect their decision. Ms. O'Connor had been working on explanations with her students. She was looking for accurate vocabulary, the right answer, and a clear explanation of how students got their answers. She found the best way to improve explanations like this was to have students read and discuss one another's work.

To prepare for this, Ms. O'Connor carefully selected the five essays shown in Figure 5.4 to show a variety of levels of understanding and

Figure 5.4. ASSISTment question (shown to students) and an item report for Open Response questions from Ms. O'Connor's class.

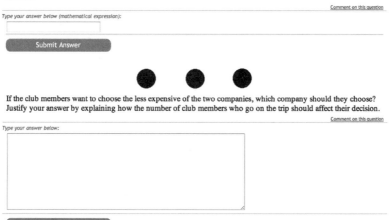

A local ski club plans to charter transportation for a ski trip. Two different companies are available for charter services.

SNOWBIRD CHARTER	**MOUNTAIN CHARTER**
Roundtrips depart daily 6 and 8:00am	Roundtrips daily at 6 and 8:00am
$300, plus $12 per person	$15 per person
Reservations are required	*Call for reservations*

If 72 club members sign up for the trip, what would be the total transportation cost for Snowbird Charter?

Comment on this question

Type your answer below (mathematical expression):

Submit Answer

If the club members want to choose the less expensive of the two companies, which company should they choose? Justify your answer by explaining how the number of club members who go on the trip should affect their decision.

Comment on this question

Type your answer below:

Submit Answer

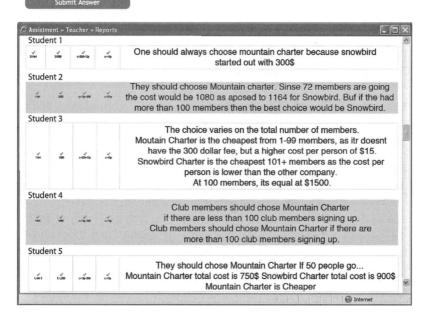

Student 1
One should always choose mountain charter because snowbird started out with 300$

Student 2
They should choose Mountain charter. Sinse 72 members are going the cost would be 1080 as aposed to 1164 for Snowbird. Buf if the had more than 100 members then the best choice would be Snowbird.

Student 3
The choice varies on the total number of members.
Moutain Charter is the cheapest from 1-99 members, as itr doesnt have the 300 dollar fee, but a higher cost per person of $15.
Snowbird Charter is the cheapest 101+ members as the cost per person is lower than the other company.
At 100 members, its equal at $1500.

Student 4
Club members should chose Mountain Charter if there are less than 100 club members signing up.
Club members should chose Mountain Charter if there are more than 100 club members signing up.

Student 5
They should chose Mountain Charter If 50 people go...
Mountain Charter total cost is 750$ Snowbird Charter total cost is 900$
Mountain Charter is Cheaper

misunderstanding. For example, Student 1 made an error in looking only at the *y*-intercept and not taking note of the per-person rate. Student 2 answered the question as 72 (which is the number calculated in A and B). The student also mentioned the break-even point of 100 skiers, but did not explain how this number affects the decision. Student 3 gave a very nice explanation clearly articulating what number of students should choose each company. The student was clear that at 100, either company could be chosen and also explained how the set fee and the rate per person affected this. Student 4 must have done some work to find 100, but did not clarify anything in the explanation. Student 5 did not even understand that there was a point where the two companies would be equal. The student just selected 50 students and argued that for that number Mountain Charter would be cheaper. All of these points and more were discussed in class as Ms. O'Connor went over the responses.

In this case, the Advance Student Response system allowed Ms. O'Connor to be more efficient and more effective as a teacher. The activity described here allowed students to give explanations that were easily read and graded by the teacher, and also allowed the teacher to share selected explanations with the rest of the class and have them discuss those responses. As a result, accountability of a lesson was no longer between the teacher and the student. With these types of advanced technologies, work becomes more public or more like the "gallery" described in Chapter 10 of this volume. In essence, student work becomes interactive with the teacher and peers. Making student work more public, while safeguarding student anonymity, is a powerful tool in advancing student learning.

THE FUTURE OF DIGITAL TEACHING PLATFORMS

The evolution of technology and of education have proceeded at different rates. Technology has revolutionized offices, stores, airlines, steel plants, hospitals, and the military (Tyack & Cuban, 1995). Yet schools have remained largely unaffected. The innovations that had staying power in schools were simple to manipulate, easy to access, and efficient for teachers (Cuban, 1986, 2001). Chalkboards, textbooks, the duplicating machine, and now the interactive whiteboard have captured these important characteristics.

Educational reforms have promised much and delivered very little for several reasons, including: reform designers are often noneducators; professionals are risk-averse; the school and district organization is highly bureaucratic and often dysfunctional; and education as an institution has a tradition of morphing reform to mirror current practices and routines. As a result, one should not be surprised that technologies have not had as pronounced an impact in education as they have had in other aspects of our lives.

So how do we get actual, sustainable technological advances in schools? The examples provided in this chapter offer a glimpse of what these new practices offer and how they may look:

- Teachers are freed of routine and mundane administrative tasks such as grading and organizing data in a way that can be quickly used;
- Students are asked to reflect on their own work as well as the work of fellow students;
- Students are asked to work alone and to collaborate with fellow students;
- Teachers are able view summaries of learning as well as specific aspect of possible problem areas;
- Students and teachers are able to articulate learning through examinations of both declarative and procedural knowledge;
- Students are presented with problem sets similar to future testing efforts;
- The platform is web- or cloud-based, making access in the new digital divide based only on connectivity.

Instructional technologies such as ASSISTments have powerful implications for policy, practice, and research. To begin, policy experts continue to emphasize student assessment and technology in discussions of school reformation. There is a clear and present press to use student achievement data to improve teaching and learning in the same way that the teachers described above are using data to inform their instruction.

In addition, this work has major implications for the current and future practice of teachers and those who lead and train them. If practice is to change to keep pace with the development of new technologies and the expectation of students, then pre- and in-service teacher development efforts must be altered. Moreover, more cloud-based, interactive instructional technologies must be developed and implemented in our schools.

Finally, further research is warranted to understand the utility of instructional technologies like ASSISTments. This research should not only consist of experimental and quasi-experimental studies of student achievement, but should also include more robust, detailed examinations of school-level educator development, implementation, and student engagement.

Digital Teaching Platforms are well situated to be the next educational innovation that can impact teaching and learning. Those who implement this new technology should be well versed in the history of technological innovations of the past. Kling (1996) stated, "We do not simply replace horses and mules with cars and trucks. We have configured an elaborate system of motorized transport, including new roads, traffic regulations, gas stations, repair shops, insurance and so on" (p. 44). Similarly, systems, structures, and technologies must be developed, implemented, supported, and sustained in schools. The road to the effective and meaningful use of educational technology must be paved with the right technology and the right people, support, and resources. If technologies are to have powerful, lasting impacts on the way teachers teach and how much students learn, then the technologies that are developed and the way they are used matter. Instructional technologies like ASSISTments have the potential to fundamentally alter the normative practices of the teaching profession, and thus the potential to improve student learning.

REFERENCES

Cuban, L. (1986). *Teachers and machines: The classroom use of technology since 1920.* New York: Teachers College Press.

Cuban, L. (1993). Computer meets classroom: Computer wins. *Teachers College Record, 95,* 185–210.

Cuban, L. (2001). *Oversold and underused: Computers in the classroom.* Cambridge, MA: Harvard University Press.

Heffernan, C. (2010). *Reville.* Accessed from http://teacherwiki.assistment.org/wiki/Reville.

King, J. L. (1996). Where are the payoffs from computerization? Technology, learning, and organizational change. In R. Kling (Ed.), *Computerization and controversy: Value, conflict and social choices* (pp. 239–260). New York: Academic Press.

Kling, R. (1996). Hopes and horrors: Technology utopianism and anti-utopianism in narratives of computerization. In R. Kling (Ed.), *Computerization and controversy: Value, conflict and social choices* (pp. 40–59). New York: Academic Press.

Mendicino, M., Razzaq, L., & Heffernan, N. T. (2009). Comparison of traditional homework with computer supported homework: Improving learning from homework using intelligent tutoring systems. *Journal of Research on Technology in Education, 41,* 331–359.

National Council of Teachers of Mathematics. (2000). *Principals and standards for school mathematics.* Reston, VA: Author.

Ravitch, D. (2000). *Leftback: A century of battles over school reform.* New York: Touchstone.

Tyack, D., & Cuban, L. (1995). *Tinkering toward utopia: A century of public school reform.* Cambridge, MA: Harvard University Press.

Warnakulasooriya, R., & Pritchard, D. E. (2006). Learning and problem-solving transfer between physics problems using web-based homework tutor. In P. Kommers & G. Richards (Eds.), *EdMedia 2005: World Conference on Educational Multimedia, Hypermedia, and Telecommunications, Montreal, Canada* (pp. 2976–2983). Chesapeake, VA: Association for the Advancement of Computing in Education.

CHAPTER 6

Highly Adaptive, Interactive Instruction
Insights for the Networked Classroom

Stephen J. Hegedus
Jeremy Roschelle

This chapter introduces a new form of Digital Teaching Platform (DTP) that has begun to prove important in addressing how to teach mathematics and science in engaging and motivating ways. Networked classrooms make use of the ever-increasing ubiquity of wireless networks in combination with dynamic, representationally rich software applications and highly adaptive curriculum. Networked classrooms are increasingly feasible given the prevalence of educational technologies in schools today.

This chapter offers some descriptions of what the elements of a networked classroom look like in terms of the connectivity used in classrooms, the curriculum, and the interactions between students and teachers. To support our claims for how the networked classroom can transform student learning and motivation, we outline what is necessary to effectively integrate networked environments and translate some 10 years of research and development into core implementation principles applicable to a wide range of DTPs. We conclude with recommendations for future use in terms of technology design, learning, and teaching.

CLASSROOM TECHNOLOGY:
ESTABLISHED INFRASTRUCTURES
AND NEW DIRECTIONS

To frame the discussion of classroom connectivity technology, this section outlines some established infrastructures that exist in classrooms today and contrasts them with new directions in classroom connectivity technology.

Established Infrastructures

There are three broad categories of technology in mathematics and science classrooms today: technology as tool, technology as tutor, and technology as media.

Technology as Tool. Technology in the form of hardware (e.g., graphing calculators, computers) or software (e.g., dynamic geometry applications) in mathematics and science classrooms has classically been referred to as a tool. This implies that the technology serves a specific purpose or a set of focused purposes. These can be cognitive in terms of creating accessible routes for students of various abilities to see things they may not have seen before, or affective to motivate learners to engage in a specific activity. In general, tools refer to computational purposes where the user can input a specific task and retrieve output. Increasingly faster graphing and computational routines have fueled the usage of these tools.

Technology as Tutor. Computers with sophisticated programs can create an interactive and responsive environment to serve as a virtual tutor (e.g., online or software-based interactive tutors). Excellent examples in this book are iSTART in Chapter 4 and ASSISTments in Chapter 5. These environments can provide feedback to users in supportive ways, present user response patterns, and offer progressively more supportive prompts that are aligned with what the user inputs. In a sense, these systems are personal and support one-to-one interactions.

Technology as Media. With the advent of increasingly more powerful personal computers and the availability of simple editing tools, the use of creative media has become a technology not only in professional settings, but also for students in schools. Editing photos, movies, and audio from personal sources of data can provide a motivating learning experience for students through compelling presentations. This is another example of using technology as a tool, but in this case, it is a tool used through the affordances of other ubiquitous technologies (e.g., digital cameras).

New Directions: Intersection of Digital and Representational Infrastructure

Our conception of a DTP is an infrastructure that incorporates both generic and content-specific tools, offers pedagogical support to control and monitor user input, and provides feedback loops. In this conception, DTPs are generative, allowing easy authoring of additional experiences so that teaching and learning can be creative.

In each of the established infrastructure cases, the strongest similarity they share with the types of technology available in connected classrooms is the importance of representation. Whether it is a representation of a beautiful scene, a form of expressive dance captured in video, a representation of assessment or inquiry as an interactive tutor, or the digital representation of a computational procedure in the form of a graph, representations matter. These various representations form a *representational infrastructure* for the DTP.

The connections of computational and visual affordances offer a deep and wide infrastructure that can be defined as a complex bedrock of functionalities based on expressive and operational affordances (Hoyles, Morgan, & Woodhouse, 1998). In contemporary society, infrastructure has become not only a material concept, but also a social one. The affordances of such a representational infrastructure allow the possibility to create a social learning network via enhanced communication (Kaput, Noss, & Hoyles, 2001; Kaput & Roschelle, 1998; Kaput & Schorr, 2007). The implementations of these representational elements emphasize flexibility, in the sense that the various elements can be used in huge varieties of combinations tuned to specific curricular objectives, student needs, and pedagogical approaches. (See http://www.kaputcenter.umassd.edu/products/software/ for more details on the software we have designed and implemented in a wide variety of classrooms.) This approach is analogous to other historical encapsulations of structure into a notation system. For example, the standard placeholder system for whole numbers embodies, in extraordinarily compact form, a hierarchical exponential structure in a way that democratizes access to computation with almost arbitrarily large numbers (Kaput & Shaffer, 2002).

Similarly, infrastructure that supports the evolution and growth of communication, *digital infrastructure*, has had a profound impact on society. These changes have been evolving simultaneously with representational infrastructures. The profound impact that a co-evolution of such infrastructures can have on classroom-based education is now becoming clear. A digital infrastructure is composed of networks, wires, and servers to allow information to flow through communication acts and services to various populations. Similar to representational infrastructures, digital infrastructures have largely been material in nature, but they are also social in their constitution. To date, the primary development trajectories have been in terms of their physical implementation into society (e.g., installation of broadband connectivity across a whole town or country).

A DTP allows for both digital and representational infrastructures to intersect in a classroom, and meaning-making is therefore enhanced as traditional forms of expression are transformed or enabled. At the heart of this convergence is a transformation of expression where learners can express themselves through the representational layers of software and where a participatory structure enables learners to express themselves in natural ways through both speech acts (e.g., metaphors, informal registers, deixis) and physical actions (e.g., gesture or large body movements) (see Moreno-Armella & Hegedus, 2009, for a concrete introduction).

Within such an environment, the thought processes of math and science students, not the technology, are at the heart of the classroom. The technology offers a structure to sustain communication and argumentation, and the teacher uses a DTP to structure activities for individuals and to generate whole-class discussion. Further, the teacher can establish a playing field for the classroom as a whole through legitimate peripheral participation. All students can contribute in mathematically meaningful ways by personally constructing mathematical functions or models of natural phenomenon. This enhances motivation by supporting a sense of personal agency, where students are more willing to participate because their contributions have meaning and relevance. Such individual to whole-group dynamics can establish an immersive experience (as developed in Chapter 7, this volume), which has been shown to cause changes in children's learning and, equally as important, in their willingness to continue to study mathematics.

HIGHLY ADAPTIVE, INTERACTIVE INSTRUCTION

To illustrate the principles of a classroom based on both representational and digital infrastructures, we examine the software environment SimCalc Math-Worlds, a curriculum and teaching platform that emphasizes a similar flow-dynamic to Time To Know (as described in Chapter 10 of this volume). The information comes from work conducted over a 4-year program of research and development (2007–2011) that included four cluster randomized trials and one quasi-experimental study implementing SimCalc MathWorlds in Algebra 1 and Algebra 2 classrooms across seven districts in Massachusetts. Software and curriculum were developed at the University of Massachusetts at Dartmouth, with external advisors at SRI International and the evaluation team based at the University of Massachusetts Donahue Institute. The examples come from the Algebra 1 curriculum, which can be found at: http://www.kaputcenter .umassd.edu/products/curriculum/.

SimCalc MathWorlds

SimCalc MathWorlds (SimCalc) allows for an investigation into students' use of dynamic, executable mathematical inscriptions. SimCalc also focuses attention, fosters personal identity, and provides opportunities for situating individual constructions in larger structures, such as parameterized families of functions.

SimCalc software is freely available for Texas Instruments (TI) graphing calculators for use with the TI Navigator Learning System. It is also available as a commercial, cross-platform software application for larger-scale adoption in schools and districts. The computer version of SimCalc software can talk directly to the TI graphing calculator version, collect student work, and interpret and re-display data.

Alternatively, another version of the software allows students to use computers and share constructions with the teacher on a wireless or wired network. The most powerful instantiation in terms of learning opportunities and ease of implementation is the computer version of the software made available on a wireless cart of laptops. This is the ideal infrastructure for a DTP.

Networked classrooms not only allow for efficient methods of collating the work of students from their calculators or personal computers, but they also allow for the aggregating of student work in some mathematically meaningful way via the teacher's computer (see Chapter 8, this volume). New mathematical activity structures, which utilize the potential of the networked classroom, enable the student to develop a personal mathematical object on his or her calculator or computer. This becomes invested with additional mathematical meaning when it becomes part of a larger public display, including the constructions of their own classmates that are further enhanced by classroom discussion (see also Chapter 10).

The SimCalc software provides learning environments where students can interact with animated objects whose motion is controlled by visually editable pieces or algebraically defined position and velocity functions. Also, motion-data from the physical motion of a student can be imported into SimCalc and displayed both as a function in the usual ways and (re)animated as well. The activity structures of a SimCalc classroom can help develop the meaning of linear functions and equations at three different levels of organization: individual, small group, and whole class.

In activities emphasizing parametrically varying mathematical objects (coefficients of linear functions in this case), individual students act as indices for the parameters (so each student has his or her own function), and the family of linear functions for classroom discussion is aggregated on a computer with classroom display. The functions are dynamic position versus time functions that drive motion simulations. Hence, not only do algebraic coefficients and the resulting coordinate graphs of the functions vary, but their motions do as well. As a result, an individual student is personally identified both with a formal mathematical function (in algebraic and graphical form) and with an object moving in a simulation. The student's construction thus moves from the private place of their own personal device or computer to a common and public location in front of the class.

Each student can have a unique numerical identifier supplied through the software and structured by the teacher by modifying a graphical map of the class prior to the activity's start. This identifier is a mixture of a student's group number and count-off within that group, e.g., 0105 is group 1, count-off 5.

One ideal activity is Staggered Start–Simultaneous Finish, in which the students must write a linear function ($y = mx + b$) for their actor in one of Sim-Calc's virtual worlds. Each student must start at three times their group number and all students end in a tie with a target actor. This activity can be done in SimCalc's Fishy World (see Figure 6.1), where the target actor is the Teacher Fishy and is represented by the function $y = 2x$ [0, 6], or a motion of 2 meters per second for 6 seconds. The Staggered Start-Simultaneous Finish activity yields multiple solution strategies. Students need to determine, depending on their point of view, the velocity of their fish, the slope of their fish's Position versus Time graph, or the coefficient of x in the algebraic description of the Position versus *Time* function, $y = mx + b$. The teacher can configure the activity within the software to be completed graphically (i.e., students can drag pieces of graphs via hotspots) or can require students to define the function algebraically by inputting parameters for the function and its domain.

Some students computed the needed slope systematically based on their starting point and target ending point; others reasoned from a distance-time relationship; and still others used trial and error based on the motions or the graphs. The focus here is on how connectivity in combination with the social organization of the class influenced their strategy and how it enabled forms of discussion that would not otherwise easily be achieved. It should also be stressed that this example is really an exemplar of a highly configurable curricular activity system, as it is so easily manipulatable to generate many other activities. For example, the teacher can change the speed of Teacher Fishy or the amount of time it swims. There are numerous mathematical variations and differing types of computational complexity in changing the multiplier of the start-off number, or offsetting the race in time, or even creating a two-piece race. All these variations have analogous counterparts in science classrooms.

This algebraic structure emerges at the whole-class level and has attributes of the Digital Teaching Platform. In Figure 6.1, the work of 14 students has been collected (within 1 to 2 seconds) alongside the Teacher Fishy (the hammer-headed shaped one). Groups (of fish) are lined up vertically. In this case, after 3 seconds of animating the world, Group One has collectively moved 7.5 meters. The work of each student in Group One is independent in the world, but their graphical representations are identical and "piled up" on top of one another. These can be cycled through by clicking on the graphs. Multiple representations (e.g., graphs, tables, and algebraic expressions) can be displayed at once and progressively displayed group by group.

This activity leads to a constructive classroom discussion regarding the role of the starting position in the $y = mx + b$ expression, the individual role of each student in this part of the expression, and the location of each student.

Figure 6.1. SimCalc's Fishy World.

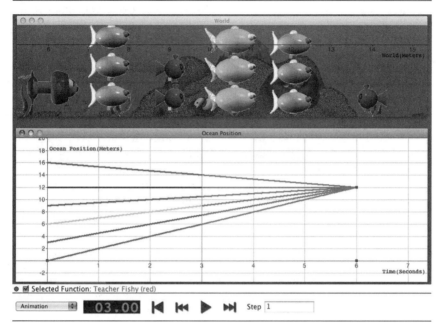

Consistently, students impute personal identity to the entities in the display, referring to them either in terms of their numerical-identifier origins or by the name of the student who produced them. For example, students may say, "0201 is steeper than 0203," or "Jon is faster than Benny," and students may also refer to the objects in terms of their relationship to their origins or their "owner" (e.g., "the function that Jon made" or "Jon's function"). In first-person situations, students often referred to the objects as if they were themselves. For example, they might say, "I'm going backward," rather than, "my fish is going backward," even though the latter itself indicates personal ownership and identity with the object produced.

Participatory Learning Reflects Real-World Situations

Donald (2001) describes how humans accomplish the extraordinarily complex tasks of managing their mental resources and communication in everyday social contexts using the cultural tools of language and, as needed, other representational tools. Most mathematical activity ignores these resources despite unanimous scholarly recognition of the power of classroom talk and norms that support inquiry and purposeful discussion. The kinds of aggregation activity structures described in SimCalc deliberately build systematic mathematical variation, personal identity, and ownership into a functional classroom role by making them an intrinsic part of the activity structure itself at one or another level of group organization. Used in this way, a DTP is a synergistic integration of software affordances and participatory-infused curriculum, which yields highly adaptable interactive instruction.

This type of instruction affords a flexible, rapid, and intensified form of classroom-based discourse and activity. As illustrated in SimCalc, mathematical discourse is infused with personal attributes and requires students to listen to one another. SimCalc as a DTP supports a sustained and deep focus on improving mathematical thinking, as it builds on the contributions of participants in expressive ways.

Technology is transforming learning both inside and outside the classroom. However, there is a distinction between networks that exist outside the classroom but are still used inside the classroom (e.g., social networks and Wikipedia) and the types of networked classrooms presented in this chapter. A main difference between distributed cognition inside a classroom and social networks outside is the potential lack of personal agency for the participants because individual identities can be concealed in a social network. Participants do not necessarily know which people are contributing to the discussion, whereas in the networked classroom thoughts and ideas are infused with personal identity. Such notions link to participatory learning for both students and teachers and can aid in transforming their roles inside the classroom.

The transformation of teaching within a DTP centers on the perception that learning is active within the technological environment, and this enables students to articulate and to challenge ideas in ways not possible without the technology.

Dynamic Representations

Functions or models are dynamic and not static objects. They describe dynamic relationships, such as how salaries might change over time, how someone's height increases relative to their arm span, or how the position of a car varies with respect to time as it is driven from home to school. Static graphs have historically been used to represent co-varying data (i.e., how two sets of data vary with each other), yet they are quite abstract systems to interpret. What does it mean to "read a graph"? Most days, one can observe a graph on the front page of *USA Today*, a widely read newspaper aimed at a wide background of readers, so one can expect the average citizen to interpret what this representation means.

Static graphs are limited, however, in the representation of dynamic processes. For example, piecewise graphs, which look like someone has joined a collection of dots with straight edges, tend to represent discrete movements in the cost of some commodity or index (e.g., the Dow Jones index) from day to day. There are also curvy graphs that represent rapid change. Other graphs represent rates against time (e.g., the membership rate of an institution over time), which expresses how something is changing per day. A membership rate might be 100 new members per day for January and then 50 new members per day for February. How many total members are there at the end of February? Does the graph adequately represent these numbers?

The answer, invariably, is no, and other computational techniques are necessary to annotate this abstract representation. In contrast to static graphs, dynamic representations allow smooth and continuous animations of what these graphs represent as well as interactions that can yield changes in an informative way. Through such a medium, children and adults can access the complexities of functions and models and the underlying principles of change and variation.

Structuring Pedagogy

Instruction that is interactive and highly adaptive can be a generative structure that formulates one specific question or mode of directing the attention of a whole classroom of children through digital or physical media. Given the multitude of pieces of information that can be flowing around a networked classroom, it is imperative that teachers can direct attention to specific participants and their contributions. For example, a teacher might direct the attention of the class to observe the contribution of one student by pointing at a particular feature of the motion of the character that this student created.

Highly adaptive, interactive instruction needs new forms of digital management. Within SimCalc, the teacher can control and modify a student's working environment by sending the activity in that individual SimCalc environment to every student working within the same problem-space. The teacher can then focus students' attention on this particular illustration by freezing each student's SimCalc environment. This is a useful, generic feature for DTPs.

Another attribute of the SimCalc DTP is that the teacher can manage student work and, hence, the flow of interaction by using a compact table and collecting, showing, or hiding each student's contribution at the click of a button. It is useful to contrast this atemporal management at a representational level (e.g., "I can show Billy's position whenever I choose") with a temporal snapshot of the status of the classroom with the Time To Know Platform, as illustrated in Chapter 10 of this volume.

Such methodologies or *control panels* are vital to create efficient and effective implementation. Technology should simplify and not add to the complexity of a classroom. Teachers need the power to format the discursive space; yet, if they are faced with too many buttons, menus, or data, teachers quickly reject the system, feeling a lack of ownership and value.

Simple analysis tools allow teachers to click and show a student's work, a group's work, or the work of the whole class in one or two clicks with a transparent interface. This is not only important from a usability perspective, but also from a highly adaptive, interactive instruction perspective. Making a subtle change in what can be visible supports reflection and conjecture. Hiding the set of graphs or animated characters that belong to one group, and asking the rest of the class what they expect to see before showing these, creates a space for students to make conjectures based upon their own work or by observing attributes of the representations.

In summary, SimCalc as a DTP is dynamic, interactive, and generative. It supports collaboration by infusing personal identity within the environment and executability to test reasoning. This modifies traditional ideas about the roles of students and teachers; SimCalc instruction features students generating knowledge and the teacher serving as a guide.

LEVERAGING DTPs FOR MAXIMUM LEARNING

There are three essential ingredients necessary to implement networked classroom DTPs. First, the infrastructural aspects of the environment must be well understood to enable a sophisticated Digital Teaching Platform. Central is the provision of both a representational and a communication infrastructure. As such, the DTP is both a cognitive and a social resource in the classroom. Wireless technology and computers are beginning to approach ubiquitous presence in schools either through district investments or at the hands of students (e.g., cell phones, PDAs, iPhones).

Second, professional development is essential. Today, only a few educators see transforming learning experiences to shape students' perceptions of the world as a key element of instruction. Curriculum that has a purposeful design to support both coherent content and creativity allows for adaptive instruction (Roseman, Linn, & Koppal, 2008). To use SimCalc well, teachers must learn how to transform their pedagogy to include enhancing students' contributions, orchestrating the timing of individual and group input, and enabling the integration of new and diverse ideas into the collective learning process.

Teaching that moves beyond lectures and structured activities to include open discourse and interplay of varying ideas among teachers and students fosters independent thinking and motivates students to want to learn more. As such, DTPs may redefine the concept of enhancing student productivity in ways that affect structured activities and encourage collaboration among students and teachers to construct new types of academic deliverables. Teachers and students can join in experiences that not only shape exploration, but also scaffold the understanding of more complex ideas. Professional development needs to focus on these new aspects of how technology modifies the interactions and norms of classroom discourse.

Third, for highly adaptive, interactive instruction to occur within a DTP, curricular activity systems that are both flexible and generative—and that organize the dynamic affordances of the representational systems—must be developed. The impact of classroom connectivity on pedagogy is rapidly evolving. Consequently, reforms are needed for traditional practices in classroom structure, student-to-teacher relationships, the role of the teacher, access to resources, and student participation. In particular, DTPs enable teachers to alter their instruction to accommodate participatory learning designs: teachers can have additional flexibility in the order and times an activity is presented to a class, a group of students, or individual students.

Classroom connectivity supports and enhances curricular activity systems. These systems are generative and provide a field for interactive teaching. Such adaptive designs can empower individual students to take action to interact, value identity, and challenge others' ideas. As agency shifts, the teacher becomes less a *sage on the stage* and more a *guide on the side*. Networked technology and intimate forms of pedagogy can amplify the centrality of the student voice; this, in turn, empowers the voice of the teacher.

Some students prefer studying and communicating their ideas in a group. Collaborative efforts such as broadcasting resources for others, accessing peer work, and posting feedback in online interactive-type environments provide a similar model of open learning. In this environment, teachers may elucidate reactions from students or draw out contradictory explanations related to the topic, thus promoting clarification of individual and group ideas. Beyond discursive practices, there is the profound impact that personal, in-the-moment physical actions can have in generating momentum in argument and debate.

In classes of students with diverse learning preferences, dynamic software and adaptive curricula allow students to navigate and investigate ideas in ways that meet their individual pace and style. With this approach, teachers facilitate the learning process by redirecting the students to the learning objectives of the curriculum and offering greater control of the learning process to the students themselves.

SimCalc, when used with highly adaptive curriculum, can transform the student-teacher relationship. Teachers can seek effective methods to foster instructional expertise that moderate a learning environment that is not bound by a single resource but instead advantageously adapts to open access of information provided by classroom connectivity.

A lack of personal confidence, social or cultural norms, or learning disabilities may keep some students from accessing opportunities to participate in class or may discourage interest in seeking resources that offer multiple viewpoints. However, motivational attributes of these students change over time as they see their work and identity valued within a collective environment. In a sense, mathematics turns out to be a safe haven to explore ideas as soon as it is seen as going well beyond answering either "right" or "wrong" when responding to a "mathematical" question.

THE FUTURE OF DIGITAL TEACHING PLATFORMS

The following questions look to the future and are provided here to encourage different ways of thinking about technology, learning, and teaching. Even though SimCalc is a DTP representing just one technological environment, many of the issues addressed here are germane to a wider variety of educational settings integrating technology and apply to many different types of DTPs.

What's Different About Technology?

Technology does not always need to be a tool that provides some functional input to a mathematics or science classroom. It can also support and organize curricular intentions sustained over periods of time that create the possibility for enhanced classroom interactivity. The environments described in this chapter illustrate highly adaptive interactive instruction. Three main design principles of such environments are examples of DTPs with integrated curriculum.

The first principle is to create a *distributed interactive interface* with many students and the teacher. Such an interface allows students to build mathematical models that are executable; they allow students to test their conjectures about their work. In addition, the interface allows students to share their constructions; empowers the teacher to manage contributions in mathematically meaningful ways; and, most important, distributes and collects a wide range of varying activities.

Second, the ability to have *multiple representations* that are re-presented over multiple hardware platforms allows different devices (e.g., PDAs, smartphones, and calculators) to be connected to computationally faster and higher-resolution platforms that extend the pedagogical opportunities of the teacher.

Finally, the technology described in this chapter allows people to *express themselves* in ways not possible (or maybe not even allowed) previously. This technology may cause a student to jump out of his or her seat, use expressive language, or even make personal connections to artifacts of the system by encouraging students to experience being a variable or an equal sign in an equation. These are learning events that no normal graphing calculator could provide.

What's Different About Learning?

Children need to be at the heart of the activity. Therefore, the primary learning objective is for each child to own his or her constructions or mathematical objects. Such ownership can infuse emotion and personality into the artifact that is then shared and referred to using personal identifiers. Creating a participatory structure that is both mathematically meaningful and easily supported by the technology supports expressive actions and fosters the development in a public context of skills that are critical to mathematical and scientific literacy, including reasoning, defending arguments, and building generalizations (Hegedus & Penuel, 2008).

What's Different About Teaching?

Teachers need to be aware of both the affordances of the DTP and the enhanced expressive modes of interaction that can occur within DTP classrooms. This in turn impacts the preparation and continuing professional development of teachers. Specifically, more time and space should be allowed for students' work both within the technology environment and with one another in whole-class discussion. In turn, teaching becomes a mutual and respectful development of a student's voice.

This chapter has illustrated one potential manifestation of a DTP, one that involves presenting and listening to each student's contributions, analyzing and orchestrating mathematical discussions, and thinking through iteratively more sophisticated and abstract conversations and dialogue. The flow of interaction between children exploring one another's thinking will give rise to a deeper and sustained reasoning process if based on respect given to the expressive contributions of all participants in the classroom. Thus, teachers need to value the identity of each student.

These recommendations can help structure thinking about the growth, use, and effective implementation of SimCalc and classroom connectivity as a new type of Digital Teaching Platform.

NOTE

This work is based upon work supported by the U.S. Department of Education, Institute of Education Sciences Grant No. R305B070430. Any opinions, findings, and conclusions or recommendations expressed in this chapter are those of the authors and do not necessarily reflect the views of these agencies. We thank Brenda Berube for her input on earlier versions of this chapter.

REFERENCES

Donald, M. (2001). *A mind so rare: The evolution of human consciousness.* New York: W.W. Norton & Company.

Hegedus, S., & Penuel, W. R. (2008). Studying new forms of participation and identity in mathematics classrooms with integrated communication and representational infrastructures. *Educational Studies in Mathematics, 68*(2), 171–183.

Hoyles, C., Morgan, C., & Woodhouse, G. (Eds.). (1998). *Rethinking the mathematics curriculum.* London: Springer-Verlag.

Kaput, J., Noss, R., & Hoyles, C. (2001). Developing new notations for learnable mathematics in the computational era. In L. D. English (Ed.), *The handbook of international research in mathematics* (pp. 51–73). London: Kluwer Academic Publishers.

Kaput, J., & Roschelle, J. (1998). The mathematics of change and variation from a millennial perspective: New content, new context. In C. Hoyles, C. Morgan, & G. Woodhouse (Eds.), *Rethinking the mathematics curriculum* (pp. 155–170). London: Springer-Verlag.

Kaput, J., & Schorr, R. (2007). Changing representational infrastructures changes most everything: The case of SimCalc, algebra and calculus. In M. K. Heid & G. Blume (Eds.), *Research on technology in the learning and teaching of mathematics: Vol. 2: Case studies* (pp. 211–253). Charlotte, NC: Information Age Publishing.

Kaput, J., & Shaffer, D. W. (2002). On the development of human representational competence from an evolutionary point of view: From episodic to virtual culture. In K. Gravemeijer, R. Lehrer, B. van Oers, & L. Verschaffel (Eds.), *Symbolizing, modeling and tool use in mathematics education* (pp. 277–293). London: Kluwer Academic Publishers.

Moreno-Armella, L., & Hegedus, S. (2009). Co-action with digital technologies. *ZDM: The International Journal on Mathematics Education: Transforming Mathematics Education through the Use of Dynamic Mathematics Technologies, 41,* 505–519.

Roseman, J. E., Linn, M. C., & Koppal, M. (2008). Characterizing curriculum coherence. In Y. Kali, M. C. Linn, & J. E. Roseman (Eds.), *Designing coherent science education: Implications for curriculum, instruction, and policy* (pp. 13–36). New York: Teachers College Press.

PERSONALIZATION

Part III examines various affordances for customization that DTPs offer, including various forms of teacher-guided peer collaboration. This customization enables adjusting learning to the specific needs of each individual, using embedded diagnostic assessments to provide guidance for instruction. Authors articulate the deep connections DTPs provide between formative assessment and content mapping, as well as how one-to-one classrooms present unique opportunities for evaluation.

Chapter 7 examines the opportunities posed by immersive learning environments and addresses the challenges of using the DTP to integrate them into regular classrooms with one-to-one computing. Immersive learning environments offer unique opportunities to meet the challenge of customizing learning to individuals in a group-teaching situation. These rich, digital contexts have affordances different from any other interactive media: they enable participants, their collaborators, and the environment itself to shape a personal educational experience tailored to individual desires and needs. The chapter explores how the DTP infrastructure provides scaffolding for immersive learning that enables teacher support and how it can gather data on student performance and contribute to diagnostic feedback for students and teachers.

Chapter 8 outlines a proposal for a comprehensive, integrated, classroom assessment system that serves multiple functions of assessment and is targeted to provide improvements in instructional guidance to teachers. The development and design of Digital Teaching Platforms brings with it changes to the character, purpose, and possibilities for assessment. The authors demonstrate how diagnostic assessments designed around learning trajectories that document the growth of student knowledge can be folded seamlessly into curriculum and instruction. They report on current work to produce the first generation of such assessments and close the chapter with a description of how they can enhance a teacher's work flow of instruction.

Chapter 9 examines various forms of assessment. The chapter explores some recently developed and unexplored ways in which computer-based technologies can support formative assessment. The chapter also explores cognitive diagnostic assessment, examining two projects that are developing cognitive diagnostic assessment systems for algebra and geometry. The third section explores potential uses of computer-based technology to improve the efficiency of collecting and analyzing student work, and the final section reflects on the purpose of formative assessment and the importance of validity.

CHAPTER 7

Customization in Immersive Learning Environments
Implications for Digital Teaching Platforms

Chris Dede

For more than a decade, my research team has studied immersive learning environments, which offer unique opportunities to meet the challenge of customizing instruction to individuals in a group-teaching situation. These rich digital contexts have features different from any other interactive media: They enable participants, their collaborators, and the environment itself to shape an engaging, immersive educational experience tailored to individual preferences and needs. However, realizing the full potential for customization of these emerging media will require resolving difficult technical and conceptual issues, as well as integrating immersive learning environments within both Digital Teaching Platforms (DTPs) and regular classrooms with one-to-one computing. Progress made in achieving these objectives may provide insights into designing other forms of customization for DTPs. Further, customized virtual environments can produce formative diagnostic data for teachers, allowing them to personalize instruction for each individual student.

VARIOUS TYPES OF IMMERSIVE LEARNING ENVIRONMENTS

Regardless of the interface used to achieve it, *immersion* is the subjective impression that one is participating in a comprehensive, realistic experience (Lessiter, Freeman, Keogh, & Davidoff, 2001). Immersion in a mediated, simulated experience (such as a virtual environment or an augmented reality) involves the willing suspension of disbelief. Two types of immersive interfaces underlie a growing number of formal and informal learning experiences (Dede, 2009): multiuser virtual environments and augmented reality interfaces.

Multiuser virtual environment (MUVE) interfaces offer students an engaging *Alice in Wonderland* experience in which their digital emissaries in a graphical, virtual context actively engage in experiences with the avatars of other participants and with computerized agents. MUVEs provide rich environments in which participants interact with digital objects and tools, such as historical photographs or virtual microscopes (Ketelhut, Nelson, Clarke, & Dede, 2010).

Augmented reality (AR) interfaces enable ubiquitous computing models; students carrying mobile wireless devices through real-world contexts engage with virtual information superimposed on physical landscapes (such as a tree describing its botanical characteristics, a historic photograph offering a contrast with the present scene, or a "cloaked" alien spaceship visible only through the mobile device). This type of mediated immersion infuses digital resources throughout the real world, augmenting students' experiences and interactions (Klopfer, 2008).

This chapter focuses on the customization of MUVEs and their implications for the personalization of DTPs; however, similar opportunities apply across the spectrum of immersive interfaces and social media.

The Educational Value of Situated Learning

The capability of computer interfaces to foster psychological immersion enables technology-intensive educational experiences that draw on a powerful pedagogy—situated learning. Situated learning requires authentic contexts, activities, and assessment coupled with guidance from expert modeling, mentoring, and legitimate peripheral participation (Dede, 2008). As an example of legitimate peripheral participation, graduate students work within the laboratories of expert researchers who model the practice of scholarship. These students interact with experts in research as well as with other members of the research team who understand the complex processes of scholarship to varying degrees. While in these laboratories, students gradually move from novice researchers to more advanced roles with evolving skills and expectations.

Potentially quite powerful, situated learning is seldom used in formal instruction because creating tacit, relatively unstructured learning in complex real-world settings is difficult. However, virtual environments and augmented realities can draw on the power of situated learning by creating immersive, extended experiences with problems and contexts similar to the real world (Dede, 2009). In particular, MUVEs and ARs provide the capability to create problem-solving communities in which participants can gain knowledge and skills through interacting with other people who have varied levels of skills, thus enabling legitimate peripheral participation.

The Educational Value of Transfer

Situated learning is important in part because of the crucial issue of *transfer.* Transfer is defined as the application of knowledge learned in one situation to another situation and is demonstrated if instruction on a learning task leads to improved performance on a transfer task, ideally a skilled performance in a real-world setting (Mestre, 2002). The *preparations for future learning* approach to measuring transfer focuses on extended performances where students learn how to learn in a rich environment and then solve related problems in real-world contexts (Schwartz, Sears, & Bransford, 2005). With conventional instruction and problem solving, attaining preparation for future learning requires *far* transfer: applying knowledge learned in a situation to a quite different context whose underlying semantics are associated but distinct. One of the major criticisms of instruction today is the low rate of far transfer generated by presentational instruction; even students who excel in educational settings often are unable to apply what they have learned to similar real-world contexts (Mestre, 2002).

The potential advantage of immersive interfaces for situated learning is that their simulation of real-world problems and contexts means that students must attain only *near* transfer to achieve preparation for future learning: applying knowledge learned in a situation to a similar context whose surface features and underlying semantics are closely related. Flight and surgical simulators demonstrate near transfer of psychomotor skills from digital simulations to real-world settings. A variety of studies are currently under way to assess whether similar transfer results to the real world are possible for other types of immersive learning.

Integration of Situated Learning Experiences into Digital Teaching Platforms

As discussed in Chapter 10 of this volume, the Time To Know curriculum, which is representative of current state-of-the-art DTPs, includes a variety of learning experiences. Some of these are highly structured, others are more open-ended; some are guided by the teacher, others by the technology infrastructure that provides customized instruction for each student; some are individual, others are collaborative. These instructional interventions draw primarily on three theories about learning and teaching: behaviorism, cognitivism, and constructivism (Dede, 2008).

Behaviorists believe that since learning is based on experience, instruction should center on manipulating environmental factors to create instructional events inculcating content and procedures in ways that alter students' behaviors. Cognitivists believe that since learning involves both experience and thinking, instruction should center on helping learners develop interrelated, symbolic mental constructs that form the basis of knowledge and skills. Constructivists believe that since learning involves constructing one's own knowledge, instruction should center on helping learners actively invent individual meaning from experience. All three approaches are of value for certain types of students, content, and instructional goals.

DTPs should incorporate as many evidence-based theories of learning as possible into their instruction because no single way of teaching is effective for all students. As described earlier, what immersive interfaces can add to current DTPs is instructional experiences based on situated learning. The inclusion of this pedagogical approach in DTPs would expand their repertoire and enable greater customization to each student, subject, and set of instructional objectives. In particular, the embedded assessments in the immersive modules provide information to help teachers make better decisions regarding the rest of the curriculum.

OPPORTUNITIES FOR CUSTOMIZATION IN IMMERSIVE LEARNING ENVIRONMENTS

Immersive interfaces offer a variety of affordances for customizing an individual participant's experiences. Some of these capabilities involve personalization by the user, while others require sophisticated actions by the immersive system itself. Neither of these is well understood from a research perspective, and the automatic personalization of the environment to the user involves substantial technical challenges.

User-Based Personalization of Immersive Learning Experiences

An individual participant in an immersive learning environment has two major opportunities for personalizing that experience. The first of these is to customize the appearance and the capabilities of one's avatar. Many virtual worlds offer detailed ways in which users can carefully hone the appearance of their digital selves. Frequently, these involve choices not available in the real world, such as selection of gender, ethnicity, height, body structure, and even species (e.g., dwarf, elf, etc.). These selections may also result in unique strengths and weaknesses (e.g., dwarves may have an advantage in fighting, while elves are adept in magic), and typically the designers of the virtual environment have set up complex tradeoffs, such as increasing intelligence at the expense of strength.

In immersive learning environments, this type of personalization has thus far been used primarily to enhance users' psychological immersion. If one's avatar looks like oneself (or some inner version of oneself not physically expressed in the real world, or one's desired, imagined self), then the individual will feel more invested in the experiences of that avatar (Kafai, Quintero, & Felton, 2010). Researchers have studied the positive effects of how virtual characters resembling oneself aid engagement and learning (Cassell, Tartaro, Rankin, Oza, & Tse, 2007; Kim, Baylor, & Shen, 2007).

Another dimension of avatar customization is to use the tradeoffs of role choices as ways to manipulate dimensions of the educational simulation. For example, in *Alien Contact!*, the AR-based curriculum (http://isites.harvard.edu/icb/icb.do?keyword=harp), each of the four roles students on a team can assume (chemist, cryptologist, computer hacker, and FBI agent) has unique capabilities that provide access to a special type of data (Dunleavy, Dede, & Mitchell, 2009). These tradeoffs can mirror real-world dynamics (reporters and scientists have different opportunities and strengths in data collection) and also may allow the user tacitly to manipulate variables in the educational simulation as a means of learning (e.g., in a game in which experiences and accomplishments lead to attaining new *powers*, one may select capabilities for one's avatar to maximize performance in a particular set of experiences).

A second way in which an individual participant in an immersive learning environment can personalize that experience is by selecting what options are available as experiential features. For example, in the River City MUVE-based curriculum (http://muve.gse.harvard.edu /rivercityproject/), participants had access to embedded hints of various types and could select whether to activate or ignore these (Nelson, 2007). Of course, user selection of options is a feature of many instructional applications, but the effects of those choices are more pervasive in immersive learning environments than in other types of educational experiences because they shape every aspect of the virtual world.

Customization of Immersive Learning Experiences by the System Itself

From a technical standpoint, MUVEs are unique in their ability to keep minutely detailed records of the moment-by-moment movements, actions, and utterances of each participant in the environment. This "audit trail" of individual performances potentially enables customization to individual learners through interpreting, based on behavior, what the participant does and does not know. (Semi-immersive interfaces, such as augmented realities, capture some of this information, as do all social media.) Current research in an assessment project and a curriculum project can be used to illustrate how event logs, chat logs, and similar student-generated server data can provide insights for customizing learning experiences to individual pupils.

Customized Virtual Performance Assessments. With funding from the Institute of Education Sciences (IES), our research team is developing and studying the feasibility of using virtual performance assessments to assess scientific inquiry for use in middle school settings (grades 7 and 8) as a standardized component of an accountability program (http://vpa.gse.harvard.edu/). The results from these virtual performance assessments also provide a potential basis for diagnostic understandings of what individual students need next in terms of learning experiences, leading to formative changes that customize instruction.

According to White and Fredrickson (1998), scientific inquiry is an active process comprising four primary components: theorizing, questioning and hypothesizing, investigating, and analyzing and synthesizing. Measuring these inquiry processes, as well as the products that result from them, has long been a challenge for educators and researchers (Marx, Blumenfeld, Krajcik, et al., 2004). We have reframed White and Fredrickson's four categories into knowledge, skills, and abilities that we want to assess. We linked these skills and abilities back to the National Science Education Standards and the National Assessment of Educational Progress (NAEP) framework.

We started with a long list of inquiry skills and narrowed them down by working through the Evidence-Centered Design (ECD) framework (Mislevy & Haertel, 2006) to develop tasks that elicit evidence students are identifying a problem, collecting data through observation, making inferences about information to form a hypothesis, and drawing conclusions based on experimental results. Frameworks such as the Assessment Triangle (National Research Council, 2001) and ECD provide rigorous procedures for linking theories of learning and knowing to pupils' performances in assessment situations, as well as for developing interpretations of what each student knows and does not know.

The assessments we are creating are simulations of real ecosystems with underlying causal models (Clarke & Dede, 2010). In these immersive simulations, we can vary our causal models or can set the variables to create alternative conditions under which students can conduct an experiment. Our first assessment is based on a high-fidelity, immersive virtual simulation of an Alaskan bay with a kelp forest (see Figure 7.1).

In this assessment, students investigate the marine ecosystem and must discover why the kelp forest is becoming depleted. They take on the identity of a scientist and have an avatar they move around the virtual world. Their avatar can interact with nonplayer characters (NPCs) we programmed, walk around and observe visual clues, and use tools of scientists to measure

Figure 7.1. Virtual Alaskan Bay.

salinity, nitrates, and temperature anywhere in the world. The first part of the assessment borrows from game design and sends students on quests that lead them to making observations and inferences about the kelp. They spend time gathering information and then are asked to identify the problem. These early stages of inquiry, such as data gathering and problem identification, are difficult to capture in a multiple-choice test, but are easily portrayed via a student's movement and actions in the world. Students also talk to the NPCs in the world, making decisions about questions to ask them and selecting the type of tests necessary to gather data related to forming and articulating a hypothesis about why kelp are dying.

Everything the students do in the world is captured, from the moment they enter the environment until the moment they leave. These data streams are recorded in XML in a back-end architecture that allows for real-time analysis of student paths in the ecosystem, as well as logging for later analysis. However, we are not simply capturing and counting clicks. We are creating ways to triangulate performances by having students provide feedback on why they collected data or why they made a particular choice. For example, we are developing interfaces that do not require composing text (see Figure 7.2) as an interactive method for assessing student products and performances. These utilize technologies that allow us to rely less on text (so that students' difficulties

Figure 7.2. Theory Builder Interface.

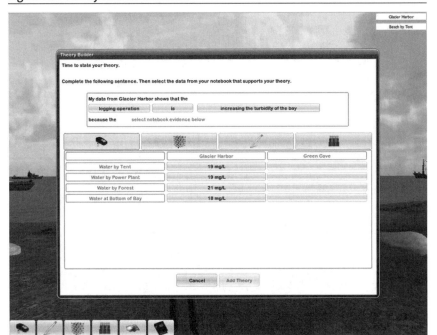

with reading/writing do not confound the assessment), and more on interactive representations such as drag-and-drop interfaces, symbolic representations, and audio queries. As Chapter 9 of this volume describes, these types of Universal Design for Learning (UDL) strategies can help customize immersive interfaces to special learning needs, both sensory and cognitive (Meyer & Rose, 2005).

Unlike physical performance assessments, which are vulnerable to a student making a mistake in the early stages of a task that then invalidates later work on the problem, we use event logs and other data to ensure each student always has the accurate information needed to frame and perform the task at hand. Through narrative, we can continually update students with valid information to remediate problems in immediate prior performance, thereby ensuring various phases of assessing their understanding are independent, not interdependent.

Other chapters in this volume discuss at greater length the importance of DTPs using assessments interwoven with instruction to aid customization. For example, Chapter 5 of this volume describes how making these assessments adaptive is a powerful way of minimizing the amount of time they consume in reaching an accurate picture of what students know and do not know. As discussed later, designers can develop immersive virtual performance assessments that are adaptive through real-time analysis of event logs. Chapter 9 depicts how formative diagnostic assessments for instruction are crucial in guiding the interventions of a DTP, both for the system and the teacher. As described below, developers can interweave immersive virtual performance assessments into curricula to perform this type of embedded diagnosis.

Customizing Curricula through Tracking Student Actions. Beyond improving the validity and authenticity of assessments, the strategy of analyzing pupils' audit trails potentially provides a rich basis for diagnosing what each individual student needs next as a learning experience, enabling formative shifts in instruction. As an illustration, we have developed and are studying EcoMUVE (www.ecomuve.org): a MUVE-based curriculum that addresses grades 6 through 8 life science National Science Education Standards (Metcalf, Clarke, & Dede, 2009). EcoMUVE is an inquiry-based, 4-week curriculum that incorporates student experiences in immersive, simulated virtual ecosystems to enhance student understanding of ecosystem science, the inquiry process, and the complex causality inherent in ecosystem dynamics. One of our two digital ecosystems is a pond (see Figure 7.3) in which students use their avatars to explore the environment, observe realistic organisms in their natural habitats, talk to the local residents, and collect water, weather, and population data.

Figure 7.3. Measuring the Pond Ecosystem.

EcoMUVE's submarine tool (see Figure 7.4) allows students to see and identify microscopic organisms, allowing the realization that organisms invisible at the macro level, such as algae and bacteria, play critical roles in the pond ecosystem. Students visit the pond over a number of virtual days, eventually making the surprising discovery that many fish have suddenly died. Students work in teams to collect and analyze data, solving the mystery through learning about complex causality.

EcoMUVE provides new ways of accessing the causal structures inherent in ecosystem relationships via immersive simulation. For example, moving through the virtual world can help students understand spatially distributed ecological phenomena. The EcoMUVE world models the pond and its surroundings, including a nearby golf course and a housing development. Students walk their avatars uphill to the housing development and down along a drainage ditch to see how water flows into the pond. Through exploration, students discover that fertilizer runoff from the development is the distant cause of an algae bloom at the local pond.

Linked visual representations reinforce student learning about abstract ecosystem concepts. For example, students see the surface of the pond become greener during the algae bloom. They measure pond turbidity and

Figure 7.4. Beetle Viewed from Submarine.

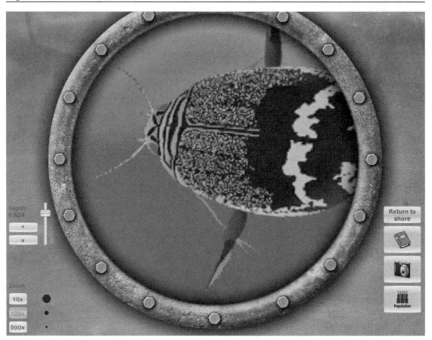

can link the measurements to their experiences by walking under the water of the pond and seeing how murky it looks on different days. The EcoMUVE curriculum uses a jigsaw pedagogy in which each student plays a different role (Water Quality Specialist, Naturalist, Microscopic Specialist, Investigator) in collecting the full range of data vital to the success of the team. This builds on the types of collaborative strategies that Chapter 4 of this volume describes, and also emphasizes the types of mediated communication, using multiple representations, that Chapter 6 advocates for customizing in DTPs.

Using the event logs and chat logs from MUVEs, as well as other types of student-generated data, we plan to develop formative, immersive virtual assessments to evaluate the learning progression of students' complex science reasoning in the context of 4th- through 6th-grade ecology. Chapter 8 of this volume describes the value of DTPs centering both instruction and assessment on students' trajectories through subject-specific learning progressions. We believe these diagnostic assessments, taken periodically during learning rather than at the end of the curriculum, will provide teachers with insights into student learning not possible with pencil and paper tests. Further, these diagnostic assessments will provide customized feedback to each student during the instructional process—a task that is not feasible for teachers to do during instruction.

Customized feedback to students allows them to regulate their individual learning and promotes the development of personal agency. Self-regulated learning by nature is an active, effortful process in which learners set goals for their learning and then attempt to monitor, regulate, and control their cognition, motivation, and behavior (Pintrich, 2000). To develop a sense of agency for their learning, students need to have the ability to consciously choose, influence, and structure their actions in order to achieve their learning goals (Code, 2010). This is another type of personalization enabled by immersive interfaces and other media that generate audit-trails.

Real-Time Customized Modification of Immersive Learning Environments. As discussed above, immersive learning environments could potentially have back-end systems that customize the experience in a variety of ways for individual students. Based on a model of the student derived from audit-trail analysis, these back-end systems would typically involve presenting some specially configured version of the simulation: unique buildings, resources, paths, and so on. In immersive learning environments such as America's Army, which is a virtual world used as a recruiting method by the U.S. Army, companies such as Pragmatics, Inc., have demonstrated automated analysis of user actions with real-time modification of the virtual world in response (Underwood, Kruse, & Jakl, 2009).

This chapter describes only one such set of modifications illustrative of the other possibilities: Animated Pedagogical Agents (APAs). An APA can ask and answer questions, provide guidance, and help students feel connected to the activity at hand (Bowman, 2008). Research suggests that APAs can fill various roles of mentorship, including expert, motivator, collaborator, and learning companion (Chou, Chan, & Lin, 2003). This parallels the work with agents described in Chapter 4 of this volume.

For example, Baylor and Kim (2005) created three versions of an APA: the Expert, designed as older than the participants, formal in appearance and language, and providing domain-specific information; the Motivator, casual in appearance and language, providing encouragement; and the Mentor, less formal than the Expert yet older than the Motivator, providing a mix of information and encouragement (Bowman, 2008). The results from the Baylor and Kim study confirmed that the agent roles were not only perceived by the students to reflect their intended purposes, but also led to significant changes in learning and motivation as intended by their design. Specifically, the Expert agent led to increased information acquisition, the Motivator led to increased self-efficacy, and the Mentor led to overall improved learning and motivation (Baylor & Kim, 2005, p. 1).

One can imagine tailoring a wide range of APAs to various student needs and embedding these in a customized manner inside of immersive learning environments.

Designers can manipulate APAs in sophisticated ways that customize and enhance individual learning. As an illustration, Bailenson, Beall, Blascovich, Loomis, and Turk (2005) discuss how immersive virtual environments enable productively transcending real-world limits on social interaction; all interactions (verbal and nonverbal) can be strategically filtered or manipulated by the system (Transformed Social Interaction–TSI) without the interactants' awareness. For example, given that eye gaze influences persuasion in social interaction, one could engineer a virtual world where a digital teacher could maintain eye contact with every digital student in a virtual classroom at the same time. This is possible because every student sees the virtual world from their own computer display, and these versions of reality need not be congruent.

Another intriguing example of TSI related to learning includes identity capture–morphing one's face to appear similar to another's (Bailenson et al., 2008). For example, when personalizing digital teachers to make them more similar to their students, students whose teachers resemble them pay more attention compared to control conditions. Likewise, participants who interacted with virtual humans that looked just like them, but who performed novel actions that those individuals had never done, had dramatic results in their learning (Fox & Bailenson, 2008). As an illustration, participants demonstrated behavioral changes in exercise based on watching the virtual self lose weight through physical activity and in eating habits by watching their virtual self gain weight by eating unhealthy foods. Further research is needed to demonstrate a spectrum of ways in which APAs can be customized to enhance individual motivation and learning.

One other point to note is that virtual learning companions need not be smarter than the student in order to foster engagement and educational gains. Schwartz et al. have developed a computer-based agent, Betty's Brain, that capitalizes on the social aspects of learning. Students instruct a character called a Teachable Agent (TA) that can reason based on how it is taught; this provides an environment in which knowledge can be improved through revision. Their learners demonstrate the *protégé effect*: students make greater effort to learn for their TAs than they do for themselves (Chase, Chin, Oppezzo, & Schwartz, 2009). The researchers speculate that having a personal TA may invoke a sense of responsibility that motivates learning and also may protect students' egos from the psychological ramifications of failure.

Overall, back-end analysis of logfiles from immersive learning environments may lead to a rich set of interventions that can customize each student's experiences to their desires and needs. Much research remains to be done both on the technical issues involved in analysis and on the full range of interventions that can personalize learning.

THE FUTURE OF DIGITAL TEACHING PLATFORMS

Immersive learning environments offer unique opportunities to meet the challenge of customizing learning to individuals in a group teaching situation. These rich digital contexts have affordances different than any other interactive media, capabilities that enable participants, their collaborators, and the environment itself to shape a personal educational experience tailored to individual desires and needs. However, realizing the full potential of these learning media for customization will require resolving difficult technical and conceptual issues.

Customized virtual environments can produce formative diagnostic data for teachers that are valuable in personalizing instruction for each individual student. Understanding how best to weave these immersive experiences into the full array of instructional modalities delivered by DTPs will require research, as will providing effective professional development that enables teachers to achieve the full benefit of virtual environments. To date, findings from early studies of this sophisticated pedagogical intervention are encouraging, and DTPs provide a promising vehicle for integrating immersive interfaces into the classroom.

NOTE

My research referenced in this chapter was supported by several grants from the National Science Foundation and from the U.S. Department of Education's Institute for Education Sciences. The views expressed in this chapter are mine and do not necessarily represent perspectives of these funders.

REFERENCES

Bailenson, J., Beall, A., Blascovich, J., Loomis, J., & Turk, M. (2005). Transformed social interaction, augmented gaze, and social influence in immersive virtual environments. *Human Communication Research, 31*, 511–537.

Bailenson, J., Yee, N., Blascovich, J., Beall, A., Lundblad, N., & Jin, M. (2008). The use of immersive virtual reality in the learning sciences: Digital transformations of teachers, students, and social context. *The Journal of the Learning Sciences, 17*, 102–141.

Baylor, A. L., & Kim, Y. (2005). Simulating instructional roles through pedagogical agents. *International Journal of Artificial Intelligence in Education, 15*, 95–115.

Bowman, C. (2008). *Measured and perceived effects of computerized scientist mentors.* Unpublished doctoral dissertation, Harvard University, Graduate School of Education, Cambridge, MA.

Cassell, J., Tartaro, A., Rankin, Y., Oza, V., & Tse, C. (2007). Virtual peers for literacy learning. *Educational Technology, 47*(1), 39–43.

Chase, C., Chin, D. B., Oppezzo, M., & Schwartz, D. S. (2009). Teachable agents and the protégé effect. *Journal of Science Education and Technology, 18*, 334–352.

Chou, C., Chan, T., & Lin, C. (2003). Redefining the learning companion: The past, present, and future of educational agents. *Computers and Education, 40*, 255–269.

Clarke, J., & Dede, C. (2010). Assessment, technology, and change. *Journal of Research on Technology in Education, 42*, 309–328.

Code, J. (2010). *Agency for learning.* Unpublished doctoral dissertation, Simon Fraser University, Burnaby, British Columbia, Canada.

Dede, C. (2008). Theoretical perspectives influencing the use of information technology in teaching and learning. In J. Voogt & G. Knezek (Eds.), *International handbook of information technology in primary and secondary education* (pp. 43–62). New York: Springer.

Dede, C. (2009). Immersive interfaces for engagement and learning. *Science, 323*, 66–69.

Dunleavy, M., Dede, C., & Mitchell, R. (2009). Affordances and limitations of immersive participatory augmented reality simulations for teaching and learning. *Journal of Science Education and Technology, 18*, 7–22.

Fox, J., & Bailenson, J. (2008, May). *Virtual exercise in the third person: Identification, physical similarity, and behavioral modeling.* Paper presented at the Annual Conference of the International Communication Association, Montreal, Quebec, Canada.

Kafai, Y. M., Quintero, M., & Felton, D. (2010.) Investigating the "why" in Whypox: Casual and systematic explorations of a virtual epidemic. *Games and Culture, 5*, 116–135.

Ketelhut, D. J., Nelson, B. C., Clarke, J., & Dede, C. (2010). A multi-user virtual environment for building and assessing higher order inquiry skills in science. *British Journal of Educational Technology, 41*, 56–68.

Kim, Y., Baylor, A. L., & Shen, E. (2007). Pedagogical agents as learning companions: The impact of agent affect and gender. *Journal of Computer-Assisted Learning, 23*, 220–232.

Klopfer, E. (2008). *Augmented reality: Research and design of mobile educational games.* Cambridge, MA: MIT Press.

Lessiter, J., Freeman, J., Keogh, E., & Davidoff, J. (2001). A cross-media presence questionnaire: The ITC-sense of presence inventory. *Presence: Teleoperators and Virtual Environments, 10*, 282–297.

Marx, R. W., Blumenfeld, P. C., Krajcik, J. S., Fishman, B., Soloway, E., Geier, R., & Revital, T. T. (2004). Inquiry-based science in the middle grades: Assessment of learning in urban systemic reform. *Journal of Research in Science Teaching, 41*, 1063–1080.

Metcalf, S. J., Clarke, J., & Dede, C. (2009, April). *Virtual worlds for education: River City and EcoMUVE.* Paper presented at Media in Transition international conference, MIT, Cambridge, MA.

Mestre, J. (2002). *Transfer of learning: Issues and a research agenda.* Washington, DC: National Science Foundation.

Meyer, A., & Rose, D. H. (2005). The future is in the margins: The role of technology and disability in educational reform. In D. H. Rose, A. Meyer, & C. Hitchcock (Eds.), *The universally designed classroom: Accessible curriculum and digital technologies* (pp. 13–35). Cambridge, MA: Harvard Education Press.

Mislevy, R. J., & Haertel, G. D. (2006). *Implications of evidence-centered design for educational testing* (PADI Tech. Rep. No. 17). Menlo Park, CA: SRI International.

National Research Council. (2001). *Knowing what students know: The science and design of educational assessment.* Washington, DC: National Academies Press.

Nelson, B. C. (2007). Exploring the use of individualized, reflective guidance in an educational multi-user virtual environment. *Journal of Science Education and Technology, 16*, 83–97.

Pintrich, P. (2000). The role of goal orientation in self-regulated learning. In M. Boekaerts, P. Pintrich, & M. Zeidner (Eds.), *Handbook of self-regulation* (pp. 451–502). San Diego, CA: Academic Press.

Schwartz, D. L., Sears, D., & Bransford, J. D. (2005). Efficiency and innovation in transfer. In J. Mestre (Ed.), *Transfer of learning from a modern multidisciplinary perspective* (pp. 1–51). Charlotte, NC: Information Age Publishing.

Underwood, J. S., Kruse, S., & Jakl, P. (2009). Moving to the next level: Designing embedded assessments into educational games. In P. Zemliansky & D. Wilcox (Eds.), *Design and implementation of educational games: Theoretical and practical perspectives* (pp. 126–140). Hershey, PA: Information Science Reference.

White, B., & Fredrickson, J. (1998). Inquiry, modeling, and metacognition: Making science accessible to all students. *Cognition and Instruction, 16*, 3–118.

CHAPTER 8

Next-Generation Digital Classroom Assessment Based on Learning Trajectories

Jere Confrey
Alan Maloney

The design and development of Digital Teaching Platforms (DTPs) bring changes to the character, purpose, and possibilities for *classroom* (as distinct from *summative* or *high-stakes*) assessment. This chapter develops a conceptual framework for the design of digital platforms for classroom assessment.

Classroom assessment refers here to the combination of assessment practices needed to guide instructional decision-making. This chapter locates classroom assessment within an overall configuration of curriculum, instruction, and assessment. Three key functions of classroom assessment are outlined: curricular monitoring, formative or embedded assessment, and diagnostic assessments. The design elements of an assessment platform to support each of these functions, which are crucial to the effectiveness of DTPs, are also identified. The chapter then reports in more detail on our own progress in building diagnostic assessments designed around learning trajectories that foster the growth of student knowledge. This is followed by a discussion of how to design and deploy diagnostic assessments in classroom practice. Finally, the chapter revisits the integration of the design elements and learning trajectories in a shared classroom assessment platform.

THE CHALLENGES OF CLASSROOM ASSESSMENT

Optimizing the positive effects of classroom assessment on student achievement depends on meeting three key challenges. The first challenge is to

Digital Teaching Platforms, edited by Chris Dede and John Richards. Copyright © 2012 by Teachers College, Columbia University. All rights reserved. Prior to photocopying items for classroom use, please contact the Copyright Clearance Center, Customer Service, 222 Rosewood Dr., Danvers, MA 01923, USA, tel. (978) 750-8400, www.copyright.com.

ensure that before being subjected to high-stakes assessments, *all students have the opportunity to learn* the curricular material associated with the standards that are assessed in summative tests. The second challenge is to *generate and support more articulation, elaboration, and engagement among students and teachers, and to foster students in becoming more aware of and taking responsibility for their own learning on a day-to-day basis.* The third challenge is to *document student growth in learning and understanding* (content *and* process) by using students' own responses efficiently and effectively to promote growth from initial states to more powerful, coherent, and aligned conceptions along empirically validated learning trajectories. The first challenge is linked primarily to *curriculum monitoring,* the second to *formative assessment,* and the third to *diagnostic assessment.*

As part of a larger DTP concept, this chapter argues for the careful and intentional design of an assessment platform that supports the articulation, collection, accumulation, and analysis of assessment data on student learning. We suggest that to fully realize the potential of classroom assessment to guide instructional improvement (teaching and learning), the construct of *learning trajectories* can be used as a unifying foundation for all three types of classroom assessment.

THE RELATIONSHIP AMONG CLASSROOM ASSESSMENT, INSTRUCTION, AND CURRICULUM

Productive classroom assessment seamlessly melds instruction and assessment, using evidence of student learning as feedback to drive instructional decision-making and improvement. Figure 8.1 models how the intended curriculum (including curricular program theory, choice of materials, and teacher planning) informs the cycle of interactions comprising the implemented curriculum, instructional practices, and classroom assessment, all of which are situated between the bookends of standards and high-stakes assessment (Confrey & Maloney, 2011).

This chapter specifically highlights the portion of the cycle of interactions involving direct interplay between classroom assessment and instructional practice or actions (while acknowledging that instruction entails practices in addition to those that can be adjusted or adapted in direct response to assessment feedback, such as the intentional introduction of curricular material or new assignments), and emphasizes the need for assessment that has a degree of independence from particular curricula. The central role assigned to the third focus, learning trajectories, at the heart of the interactive cycle (see Figure 8.1), will also be further considered.

Figure 8.1. Components and interactions within a standards-based instruction and
assessment system.

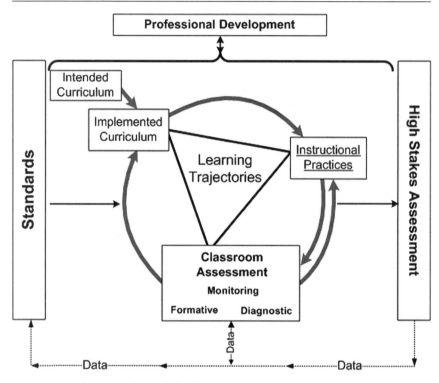

THREE-PART CLASSROOM ASSESSMENT
FOR INSTRUCTIONAL IMPROVEMENT

Curriculum monitoring refers to a coarse-grained means of documenting which
parts of a curriculum have been taught, and of providing opportunities for
teachers to share periodically administered instruments such as chapter or
unit tests. *Formative* or *embedded* assessment, in contrast, refers to fine-grained
practices used by teachers to adapt or adjust instruction daily, based on their
observations, student responses, and analyses of students' work. *Diagnostic*
(*dia*, to split apart, and *gnosi*, to learn, or knowledge) assessments are instruments designed for the major goal of providing teachers and students with
explicit descriptions of the progress students make on key concepts.

    We distinguish between an informal use of a diagnostic perspective (as a
part of formative assessment practice) and *diagnostic assessments* that produce

learning profiles. We use diagnostic assessment to refer to particular arrays of assessment items, along with the configurations of behaviors and responses that indicate what a student has learned and what remains missing in relation to an underlying theory of learning of particular concepts.

In our own work, that underlying theory is the learning trajectory construct. Learning trajectories are one way of articulating the "big ideas" that are increasingly important as organizing concepts for standards, cognitive development, instruction, and assessment. The structure of a learning trajectory is a progression from less to more sophisticated reasoning about a set of concepts that lead one to the other—a structure that permits one to differentiate the elements of learning that influence the development of skills and reasoning in particular subject matter (Clements & Sarama, 2004; Confrey, Maloney, Nguyen, Mojica, & Myers, 2009; Corcoran, Mosher, & Rogat, 2009). While learning trajectories are assumed to be influenced by curriculum when it supports progress on big ideas, it is also assumed that learning trajectories support diagnosis of student progress across multiple curricula.

The delineation of three components of classroom assessment is based on prior work on learning trajectories to inform state standards (Confrey & Maloney, in press), North Carolina's Accountability and Curriculum Reform Effort (North Carolina Department of Public Instruction, 2008), and the National Research Council's study of the evaluation of curricular effectiveness (Confrey & Stohl, 2004). In practice, these three assessment components would draw upon a common database of assessment items.

CURRICULUM MONITORING AND OPPORTUNITY TO LEARN

Curriculum monitoring addresses the first challenge above, namely, the *opportunity to learn* an intended curriculum (Porter, 2005). It focuses on what parts of an intended curriculum are covered, how well the curriculum is implemented, and facilitation of teacher collaboration and exchange of curriculum-based measures of student achievement (such as chapter tests).

Methods of monitoring students' exposure and access to curricular topics could range from documenting the extent to which a teacher complies with a district's scope and sequence, to the decisions individual teachers make to adapt or supplement a curriculum in light of their individual circumstances and students' needs. Recent attention to documentation and monitoring of students' opportunities to learn has led to examining curricular implementation in relation to standards-based practices, curricular coverage, written and enacted lessons, and textbook integrity (see Krupa & Confrey, 2010; Tarr, McNaught, & Grouws, in press). A curricular monitoring tool should therefore incorporate a variety of methods for educational practitioners to communicate and coordinate their curriculum-related instructional coverage.

To support new approaches to curricular and implementation monitoring, a DTP should include design elements for capturing teachers' curricular coverage, pacing, and documentation of students' performance on related curriculum-based assessments. The platform could promote an adaptive approach to curricular use by creating a record of expert teachers' choices and commentary, and making those records available for review and discussion by others. Overall, the curricular monitoring component would support ongoing teacher reflection and teacher-teacher and teacher-administrator communication, as well as related opportunities for reciprocal professional development with regard to curriculum implementation. Embedded in a rich network design, the curriculum monitoring component could become a fundamental means of professional development and an important frontier for the evolution of a DTP.

FORMATIVE ASSESSMENT

The second challenge in optimizing the benefits of classroom assessment—generating and supporting more articulation, elaboration, and engagement among students and teachers; and fostering students in becoming more aware of and taking responsibility for their own learning on a day-to-day basis—charges us to realize more fully the potential of formative assessment. The Council of Chief State School Officers (CCSSO) defined formative assessment as "a process used by teachers and students during instruction that provides feedback to adjust ongoing teaching and learning to improve students' achievement of intended instructional outcomes" (McManus, 2008, p. 22).

The CCSSO identified five key features of formative assessment: reliance on learning progressions; explicit learning goals and success criteria; descriptive feedback to students; collaboration; and student, peer, and self-assessments (McManus, 2008).

Formative assessment is a key element for increasing student achievement. It aims to reveal student thinking via classroom interactions (peer-to-peer and peer-to-teacher exchanges) for use in shaping instruction (Black & Wiliam, 1998; Heritage, 2007; Shepard, 2000). Teachers build on student ideas that become visible through student utterances, questions, explanations, or work samples elicited by prompts, tasks, or elicitation questions (Popham, 2008; Stiggins, 2005). Formative assessment aims, among other things, to illustrate how various concepts evolve, and to support their refinement through eliciting the variety of student ideas, sequencing of student responses, and early and actionable identification of student misconceptions and errors. Research syntheses indicate that such formative assessment activities have proven benefits to student achievement (Black & Wiliam, 1998), provided that formative assessment is carefully defined and uses efficient methodologies (Dunn & Mulvenon, 2009; Shute, 2008).

The success of eliciting student thinking for formative assessment purposes depends on a teacher's ability to interpret student responses in real time, foster peer-to-peer interactions, and adjust instructional activities to support their students' learning day to day. While formative assessment comprises a set of practices rather than instruments, and episodes are ephemeral rather than enduring, DTPs can help to capture data on these practices. Developing a deeper understanding of documented and validated learning trajectories and systematically gathering valid and reliable data on student performance will complement and strengthen these other essential classroom assessment practices.

Formative assessment practices are taking multiple forms as digital classroom technologies are developed. Support for formative assessment in technology-rich environments is described in Chapter 9 of this volume. The use of formative assessment practices has also led to the development of *contingent pedagogies* that support adapting instruction based on the rapid gathering and evaluation of student responses to instruction (DeBarger, Penuel, Harris, & Schank, 2010)—which in turn directly generate and respond to (i.e., interpret, act on) student behaviors. For example, many students already rely informally on available social networking technology (texting, internet chat, emailing, in addition to the telephone) to collaborate on homework and project assignments; DTPs potentially provide a means to scaffold, extend, and document such collaboration.

All these approaches to formative assessment practice can be supported by digital tools, including clickers, student work galleries, and systems supporting reflection and peer review. Formative assessment can be richly enhanced by fast, flexible networked devices, as well as by environments and network architectures that promote rich, artifact-driven interactions among students.

A DTP should incorporate a number of design elements (affordances) to support the formative component of a classroom assessment system. These design elements are informed by a rich variety of social networking, search engines, communication devices, and multiuser games (as in Chapter 7), as well as by educational experience and computer science theory. Chief among these design elements are

1. A database for assessment resources and artifacts
2. Peer-to-peer and peer-to-mentor communication

3. Capability for peer and mentor commenting
4. Capability to display and sequence artifacts and inscriptions
5. Selection, accumulation, display, and summaries of data, evidence, and observations
6. Next-steps tools for interpreting exchanges and evidence and deciding on follow-up, whether directive, prescriptive, or facilitative (engendering student action)

Resource and Artifact Database

This first design element for the formative component of classroom assessment in a DTP is a structural one: a dynamic and extensible library in which to construct, record, configure, and store a rich variety of assessment resources and artifacts (items, measures, scoring rubrics, simulations, prompts, and projects) and to tag them flexibly for use in a variety of circumstances. For instance, some items (or assessments) could be sequestered securely, leaving others, such as rubrics, scoring methods, and item and artifact history, more broadly accessible.

Peer-to-Peer and Peer-to-Mentor Communication

Because the DTP must support artifact generation, responses, and collaboration, this second design element includes tools to support classroom discourse: demonstrating, explaining, representing, modeling, questioning, and responding. Most students already communicate directly through cell phone text messaging, instant messaging, video exchange, and/or applications such as Skype and iChat. Classroom discourse in a digital environment requires the three basic modalities of audio, texting, and video. Effective formative assessment in mathematics also requires tools to support the communication of subject area–specific information (graphers, spreadsheets, data displays) and a spectrum of other resources vital to mathematical inscription (web pages, pictures, simulations, etc.).

Commenting

Closely related to but distinct from communication capabilities, the capability to comment on one's own and others' work requires supports that allow the layering of discourse for feedback, collaboration, and peer- and self-assessment. This element includes resources to post notes; mark positions or locations; show emphasis, ratings, or preferences; and share affective responses.

Display of Participants' Artifacts and Inscriptions

One of the most effective instructional strategies in formative assessment is the construction of narratives of student approaches via the intentional sequencing of student artifacts. The corresponding design element is a means to manage the selective sequestering and display of student contributions. This element leverages the principles of moderator-driven *gallery* functionality in some web-based meeting applications (see Chapter 10, this volume). To support multiple layers of collaboration (small-group and whole-class) in a formative assessment context, it is important to design for both teacher and student control, and to promote students' agency in presenting, demonstrating, and discussing their own work.

Selection, Accumulation, Display, and Summaries of Artifacts, Data, Evidence, and Observations

DTPs offer the promise of flexible means to select, retain, re-use, and catalogue resources and artifacts, providing teachers with ways to extend and refine formative assessment resources and discourse over time and in collaboration with colleagues. For example, teachers could select student inscriptions for sharing "in the moment." They could also select enduring records of individual students' work to serve multiple longer-term purposes (e.g., review of work with student and parents, or reflecting on and revising instructional approaches with colleagues).

The capability to collect, display, accumulate, and recall the products of student contributions, and to summarize and evaluate them, will also allow teachers to utilize a spectrum of student groupings and data, as well as individual and group evaluations, to support instruction. Collectively, these features can foster increased systematicity in the use of data and observations as evidence of student learning. Teachers will require professional development to assist them in learning varieties of ways to examine the data available to them, to develop deeper understanding of descriptive statistics (including key concepts of central tendency, distribution and variation, change over time, and ways to compare groups), and to use other data sources (such as attendance data or end-of-course exam results) (Dede, Honan, & Peters, 2005; Mandinach & Honey, 2008; Means, Padilla, DeBarger, & Bakia, 2009).

Next-Steps Tools

Formative assessment is not complete unless it leads to decisions and actions based on the information generated. The final design elements for formative assessment is *next-steps* tools, by which a teacher (or student) interprets the summarized data and determines a course of action.

The next steps depend on the expertise of the teacher–based on the teacher's prior experience, knowledge of the content, and pedagogy–and are enhanced when possible by data, observations, and other evidence engendered by formative assessment. Black and Wiliam (1998) distinguished two general types of instructional responses: *directive*, in which a precise set of actions is prescribed, and *facilitative*, in which the intended actions involve expectation of student action, reaction, critique, or reflection.

For the design of a classroom assessment system within a DTP, to what extent can the system support interpretation and decision-making in formative assessment? Presumably, many models could be imagined, but we suggest that an adaptively responsive system centered on learners and instruction requires an underlying model of learning. The classroom assessment system is not a content-independent suite of software, but a system of software functionality and resources configured in relation to an underlying learning model that defines the envelope of instructional affordances and next steps. As will be argued below, learning trajectories provide a model that can support this role for both formative and diagnostic assessment approaches.

DIAGNOSTIC ASSESSMENTS AND LEARNING TRAJECTORIES

The third challenge of classroom assessment–*documenting student growth in learning and understanding* (content *and* process), from initial states to more powerful, coherent, and aligned conceptions–explicitly foregrounds learning trajectories. Across the United States, interest has been growing in the concept of learning trajectories (or learning progressions) as a framework for delineating students' learning over time. Learning trajectories are the spine of the classroom assessment system. This component of assessment can drive instructional decision making and facilitate *instructional customization*, potentially leading to paradigmatic shifts in how learning and teaching are viewed in a digital world.

Learning trajectories are the learning model best suited to anchor diagnostic assessment in mathematics education and for learning the big ideas of mathematics over extended periods of time (K–8, for instance). Learning trajectories are also one of the five major features called for in formative assessment (Heritage, 2010).

A learning trajectory incorporates mathematical concepts, instruction, student reasoning, and openness to revision in ways that are responsive to progress in research on learning and teaching. We define a learning trajectory as

[a] researcher-conjectured, empirically-supported description of the ordered network of constructs a student encounters through instruction (i.e., activities, tasks, tools, forms of interaction, and methods of evaluation), in order to move from informal ideas, through successive refinements of representation, articulation, and reflection, towards increasingly complex concepts over time. (Confrey et al., 2009, p. 346)

All treatments of learning trajectories share five common assumptions:

1. Learning trajectories are based on synthesis of existing research, further research to complete the sequences, and a validation method based on empirical study.
2. Learning trajectories identify a particular domain and a goal level of understanding.
3. Learning trajectories recognize that children enter instruction with relevant yet diverse experiences, which serve as effective starting points.
4. Learning trajectories assume a progression of cognitive states from simple to complex. While such a progression is not linear, neither is it random, and it can be sequenced and ordered as *expected tendencies* or *likely probabilities*.
5. Progress through a learning trajectory assumes a well-ordered set of tasks (curriculum), instructional activities, interactions, tools, and reflection. (Confrey, Maloney, Nguyen, & Rupp, in press)

In science and mathematics, efforts to systematically link learning progressions and associated assessments are beginning to emerge. Clements and Sarama have developed curriculum, including assessments for grades K–2, based on their learning trajectory for composition and decomposition of geometric shapes (Clements & Sarama, in press; Clements, Wilson, & Sarama, 2004). Battista (2004, 2007) has developed a conceptual framework for measurement of area and volume, along with cognition-based assessments for elementary grades. Lehrer, Schauble, and colleagues have developed learning progressions on topics of mathematical modeling, the construction of measure, and statistical reasoning (Lehrer, Kim, & Schauble, 2007; Lehrer & Schauble, 2006). Minstrell (2001) pioneered the use of assessments to link to specific cognitive behaviors including partial beliefs and misconceptions with theoretical constructs of facets and Diagnoser, a web-based assessment program for math and science (Thissen-Roe, Hunt, & Minstrell, 2004). DeBarger, Penuel, Harris, and Schank (2010) are linking Minstrell's diagnostic tools to the use of specific curricular treatments in earth science and investigating teachers' use of contingent pedagogies with classroom technologies (e.g., clickers) in light of student responses to elicitation questions using Minstrell's facets approach.

The Diagnostic E-Learning Trajectories Approach (DELTA) directly approaches assessment using the learning trajectory model. The goals of the DELTA project are as follows:

1. Identify, by synthesis of existing research, the key levels of learning trajectories associated with particular mathematics concepts.
2. Validate the learning trajectory and describe initial outcome spaces through clinical interviews and teaching experiments.
3. Construct and field-test assessment items across diverse populations of students.
4. Develop prototype diagnostic assessment instruments.
5. Develop and test a use model for deploying the assessments in classrooms. We seek to revitalize the concept of diagnostics in mathematics education as a means of identifying and supporting healthy and productive student progress along learning trajectories.

Our methodology, outlined in Figure 8.2 (Maloney & Confrey, 2010), has been informed by the principles of evidence-based design (Mislevy, Steinberg, Almond, & Lucas, 2006; Wilson, 2005). It begins with the identification of a learning trajectory that is supported by research synthesis. We then undertake clinical interviews to iteratively extend and fill in any necessary levels of the initial learning trajectory. From these interviews, we also outline the outcome space, the variety of possible responses to a set of tasks at each level. We then construct a set of assessment items and pilot these with students to determine the extent to which they elicit configurations of responses similar to those of the interview tasks. To more broadly examine item and learning trajectory validity in relation to each other, we conduct field tests of the items across diverse student populations, construct item rubrics based on the student responses, and check for consistency of item responses in relation to the learning trajectory proficiency levels. Score data are analyzed with various measurement models, such as Item Response Theory, and interpreted in relation to the learning trajectory proficiency levels and task classes. Once sets of items seem to adequately assess the levels of the learning trajectory, these must be assembled into diagnostic assessments. The final stages of the DELTA project methodology are to design a means of collecting diagnostic information within classroom instruction and to accumulate and interpret the results for students and teachers in Diagnostic Learning Profiles.

The content focus of the DELTA project is six conceptual clusters within rational number reasoning: equipartitioning; division and multiplication; fractions, ratio, and rate; decimals and percent; similarity and scaling; and measurement of length and area (Confrey, 2008). These rational number reasoning conceptual clusters are critical to student success in algebra (and beyond) and

Figure 8.2. Methodology for building diagnostic assessments based on a learning trajectory.

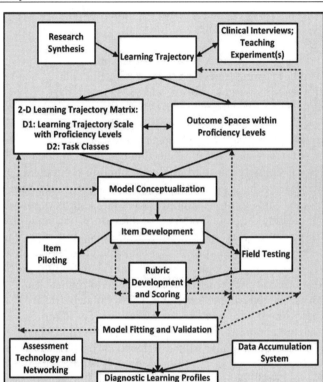

are the topics in which students who fail to succeed in algebra and higher mathematics tend to be weakest. Synthesis of the research in the field led us to propose a conceptual map of rational number reasoning and to identify three essential core meanings for the expression a/b that students must master and among which they must distinguish: a/b as a number located on the number line, a/b as a multiplicative operator, and a/b as a ratio (Confrey, 2008).

To illustrate what is meant by a learning trajectory, the learning trajectory for the concept of equipartitioning is described in some detail here:

- Equipartitioning/Splitting indicates cognitive behaviors that have the goal of producing equal-sized groups (from collections) or pieces (from continuous wholes) as "fair shares" for each of a set of individuals.

- Equipartitioning/Splitting is not breaking, fracturing, fragmenting, or segmenting in which there is the creation of unequal parts.
- Equipartitioning/Splitting is the foundation of division and multiplication, ratio, rate, and fraction.

A two-dimensional matrix represents the conceptual framework of the equipartitioning learning trajectory (Figure 8.3); this matrix also serves as a scaffold for assessment items, rubrics, and video exemplars.

The vertical axis (read from bottom to top) defines the learning trajectory's proficiency scale. Proficiency levels correspond to numerous research findings, for instance that young children will most readily learn to share collections (for numbers of recipients such that the collection can be shared fairly). They then learn to share a single whole, and gradually build to competency in sharing multiple wholes among a set of recipients to produce noninteger solutions. Students quickly come to understand the three key criteria of successful equipartitioning: creating the proper number of shares, creating equal-sized shares, and exhausting the original quantity. The trajectory's proficiency levels also incorporate key mathematical practices, such as naming and justifying results, as well as strategies that strengthen overall student reasoning, such as mathematical relations and properties that lead to generalized results.

The horizontal axis of the learning trajectory matrix (Figure 8.3) lists categories of assessment item contexts, or *task classes*. These represent the types of objects that are equipartitioned (collections versus single wholes, rectangles versus circles) and the numeric values of the splits, both of which cause items to vary in difficulty for students. The progression of difficulty in task classes is somewhat nonintuitive; it does not correspond to the counting order of the number of persons sharing. For instance, most young children can readily and fairly share a collection or a rectangle or circle between two people, but they can share among four much more readily than among three. It is common for children to successfully share a circular whole fairly among six before they can operationalize sharing among three.

DESIGNING AND IMPLEMENTING DIAGNOSTIC ASSESSMENTS

Developing and validating the assessments is only one part of enacting a diagnostic assessment system. For diagnostic assessments to be effective, delivery technologies that fit the instructional activity flow must be identified or engineered. The design elements outlined above for the formative assessment component apply also to diagnostic assessment, with some shifts in emphasis: methods of accumulating, storing, and retrieving student response

Figure 8.3. Equipartitioning Learning Trajectory Matrix. Proficiency levels form the vertical scale. Task classes, listed along the top row, form the horizontal dimension.

Equipartitioning Learning Trajectory Matrix (grades K-8) Task Classes→ Proficiency Levels	A Collections	B 2-split (Rect/Circle)	C 2^n split (Rect)	D 2^n split (Circle)	E Even split (Rect)	F Odd split (Rect)	G Even split (Circle)	H Odd split (Circle)	I Arbitrary integer split	J $p = n+1$; $p = n-1$	K p is odd, and $n = 2^i$	L $p \gg n$, p close to n	M all p, all n (integers)
16 *Generalize*: *a* among *b* = *a*/*b*													
15 *Distributive property*, multiple wholes													
14 *Direct-, Inverse- and Co-variation*													
13 *Compositions* of splits, mult. wholes													
12 Equipartition *multiple wholes*													
11 Assert *Continuity principle*													
10 *Transitivity* arguments													
9 Redistribution of shares (*quantitative*)													
8 Factor-based changes (*quantitative*)													
7 *Compositions* of splits; *factor-pairs*													
6 *Qualitative compensation*													
5 *Re-assemble*: *n* times as much													
4 *Name* a share w.r.t. the referent unit													
3 *Justify* the results of equipartitioning													
2 *Equipartition single wholes*													
1 *Equipartition Collections*													

data; reports and next steps; flexible use of the resources within the cycle of classroom interactions (see Figure 8.1) and beyond the classroom; smartphones, iPads, and tablet computers as candidate devices; robust networking capabilities that anticipate heavy demand, and so forth.

Our use-model of diagnostic assessment comprises two phases, one involving formal assessment of students' proficiency and progress, and the other supporting student exploration based on feedback in relation to their responses. Students and teachers would shift between these two modes within the diagnostic context. Reporting would clearly indicate the mode in which an assessment measure had been undertaken.

A crucial design requirement is that the diagnostic system not simply report numeric scores on individual items, but also enable insight into student progress. The *diagnostic* value of the system resides in the extent to which it provides teachers with information that specifically improves their understanding of their students' reasoning in relation to a learning trajectory, and, subsequently, facilitates their instructional planning. The diagnostic assessment should support student learning of concepts over time by providing insight into the strengths and weaknesses of individual students and groups across task classes, assessing progress across multiple proficiency levels in relation to ongoing instruction, and signaling possible misconceptions.

Another design element in the diagnostic assessment system reporting is the creation of records that document the exchange and collaboration, via social networking tools, in which students engage as they share work, solicit assistance, collaborate, review, and comment on each other's work (see Chapters 10 and 6, this volume).

Finally, diagnostic information must be accessible to students and parents. By linking parents with teachers through the diagnostic system, with recommendations for appropriate instructional materials and practices from the curriculum, parents will be supported to assist their children in pursuing additional study.

THE FUTURE OF DIGITAL TEACHING PLATFORMS

Design elements that support formative assessment overlap considerably with those of diagnostic assessment. The environment on the whole must support practice, collaboration with peers, and communication with mentors (teachers, parents, and others). Resources that support formative assessment practices, such as multiple communication modalities, commenting, juxtaposition of student work, and reporting at various levels of organization (individual, group, and whole-class), not only amount to an integrated continuum of technological supports for the entire classroom assessment system, but also mitigate against an overly narrow conceptualization of diagnostic approaches.

Likewise, the diagnostic assessment system based on learning trajectories, with reports and explicit suggestions of next steps in relation to big ideas of education, will provide a firmer cognitive foundation for formative assessment approaches. We have experimented with influencing instruction in both pre-service and in-service settings by engaging teachers in the concept of learning trajectories (Mojica, 2010; Wilson, 2009) and are continuing this line of research in developing the concept of learning trajectory-based instruction

(Sztajn & Confrey, 2010). A robust platform that facilitates both formative and diagnostic approaches could accelerate the pace of incorporating validated learning trajectories into schooling.

Ultimately, the configuration of such a DTP would combine the formative and diagnostic assessment components of classroom assessment and resources for teachers to monitor curriculum implementation and curriculum-centered tests. The combination of these components will synergistically address all three challenges posed at the outset: improving classroom interactions and students' awareness of and responsibility for their own learning; documenting growth in student learning; and improving opportunity to learn. By accessing all three components from a single intuitive dashboard interface, teachers, students, and parents can all take part in a communication and monitoring system that supports rich interactions, data-driven decision making, and over-all improved classroom teaching and learning.

We predict that this approach can usher in a resurgence of attention to instruction as a learning-teaching dyad. Instead of laboring with the ineffective assumption that instruction is merely about the delivery of chunks of content, education could begin with eliciting activities based in the learning trajectories and the assessment protocols. Students could be challenged from the outset to work on rich authentic tasks and be encouraged to move beyond their initial understanding, based on just-in-time introduction of new ideas, and mini-lessons aimed at developing proficiency in structured content segments. Curriculum monitoring would ensure that teachers attend more closely to students' opportunity to learn content, and diagnostic assessments would promote student progress on the big ideas. In such learning-teaching approaches, finding one's way around in curricular resources is an essential skill for teachers, and teachers would be supported in improving their instructional decision making and dynamically customizing curriculum for diverse groups of students.

Learning and teaching are thus fundamentally conceived of as a responsive, adaptive feedback system based on rich use of assessment materials in concert with structured curricular pieces. Student outcomes are evaluated in relation to the variety of artifact productions, discourse, and performances, including the assessment practices and measures used during and for instruction. We note that this perspective is similar to the way an experienced coach fosters expert performance, ensuring that core elements are fully developed, building on unique strengths and styles, and identifying weakness that need increased attention. The overall result of these innovations is to use rich classroom assessment to foster growth in individuals, build on the needs and abilities of groups, and develop a whole class's sense of identity and confidence.

REFERENCES

Battista, M. T. (2004). Applying cognition-based assessment to elementary school students' development of understanding of area and volume measurement. *Mathematical Thinking and Learning, 6*, 185–204.

Battista, M. T. (2007). The development of geometric and spatial thinking. In F. K. Lester (Ed.), *Second handbook of research on mathematics teaching and learning* (pp. 843–908). Charlotte, NC: Information Age Publishing.

Black, P., & Wiliam, D. (1998). Assessment and classroom learning. *Assessment in Education, 5*, 7–74.

Clements, D. H., & Sarama, J. (2004). Learning trajectories in mathematics education. *Mathematical Thinking and Learning, 6*, 81–89.

Clements, D. H., & Sarama, J. (in press). Learning trajectories: Foundations for effective, research-based education. In Maloney, A., Confrey, J., & Nguyen, K. H. (Eds.), *Learning over time: Learning trajectories in mathematics education.* Charlotte, NC: Information Age Publishing.

Clements, D. H., Wilson, D. C., & Sarama, J. (2004). Young children's composition of geometric figures: A learning trajectory. *Mathematical Thinking and Learning, 6*, 163–184.

Confrey, J. (2008, July). *A synthesis of the research on rational number reasoning: A learning progressions approach to synthesis.* Paper presented at the 11th International Congress of Mathematics Instruction, Monterrey, Mexico.

Confrey, J., & Maloney, A. P. (2011). *Engineering [for] effectiveness in mathematics education: Intervention at the instructional core in an era of Common Core Standards.* Paper prepared for the National Academies Board on Science Education and Board on Testing and Assessment for "Highly Successful STEM Schools or Programs for K–12 STEM Education: A Workshop."

Confrey, J., & Maloney, A. P. (in press). Linking mathematics standards to learning trajectories: Boundary Objects and Representations. In J. Confrey, A. Maloney, & K. H. Nguyen (Eds.), *Learning over time: Learning trajectories in mathematics education.* Charlotte, NC: Information Age Publishing.

Confrey, J., Maloney, A. P., Nguyen, K., Mojica, G., & Myers, M. (2009, July). *Equipartitioning/splitting as a foundation of rational number reasoning using learning trajecories.* Paper presented at the 33rd Conference of the International Group for the Psychology of Mathematics Education, Thessaloniki, Greece.

Confrey, J., Maloney, A., Nguyen, K. H., & Rupp, A. A. (in press). Equipartitioning, a foundation for rational number reasoning: Elucidation of a learning trajectory. In Maloney, A., Confrey, J., & Nguyen, K. H. (Eds.), *Learning over time: Learning trajectories in mathematics education.* Charlotte, NC: Information Age Publishing.

Confrey, J., & Stohl, V. (Eds.). (2004). On evaluating curricular effectiveness: Judging the quality of K–12 mathematics evaluations. Washington, DC: National Academy Press.

Corcoran, T., Mosher, F. A., & Rogat, A. (2009). *Learning progressions in science: An evidence-based approach to reform.* New York: Center on Continuous Instructional Improvement, Teachers College, Columbia University.

DeBarger, A. H., Penuel, W. R., Harris, C. J., & Schank, P. (2010). Teaching routines to enhance collaboration using classroom network technology. In F. Pozzi & D. Persico (Eds.), *Techniques for fostering collaboration in online learning communities: Theoretical and practical perspectives* (pp. 224–244). Hershey, PA: IGI Global.

Dede, C., Honan, J., & Peters, L. (Eds.). (2005). *Scaling up success: Lessons learned from technology-based educational innovation.* New York: Jossey-Bass.

Dunn, K., & Mulvenon, S. (2009). A critical review of research on formative assessment: The limited scientific evidence of the impact of formative assessment in education. *Practical Assessment, Research and Evaluation, 14*(7), 1–11.

Heritage, M. (2007). Formative assessment: What do teachers need to know and do? *Phi Delta Kappan, 89*(2), 140–145.

Heritage, M. (2010). *Formative assessment and next-generation assessment systems: Are we losing an opportunity?* Washington, DC: Council of Chief State School Officers.

Krupa, E. E., & Confrey, J. (2010). *Teacher change facilitated by instructional coaches: A customized approach to professional development.* Paper presented at the Annual Conference of North American Chapter of the International Group for the Psychology of Mathematics Education.

Lehrer, R., Kim, M., & Schauble, L. (2007). Supporting the development of conceptions of statistics by engaging students in measuring and modeling variability. *International Journal of Computers for Mathematical Learning, 12*, 195–216.

Lehrer, R., & Schauble, L. (2006). Cultivating model-based reasoning in science education. In R. K. Sawyer (Ed.), *Cambridge handbook of the learning sciences* (pp. 371–388). Cambridge, UK: Cambridge University Press.

Maloney, A. P., & Confrey, J. (2010, July). *The construction, refinement, and early validation of the equipartitioning learning trajectory.* Paper presented at the 9th International Conference of the Learning Sciences, Chicago, IL.

Mandinach, E. B., & Honey, M. (Eds.). (2008). *Data-driven school improvement: Linking data and learning.* New York: Teachers College Press.

McManus, S. (2008). *Attributes of effective formative assessment.* Washington, DC: Council of Chief State School Officers.

Means, B., Padilla, C., DeBarger, A. H., & Bakia, M. (2009). *Implementing data-informed decision-making in schools—Teacher access, supports and use.* Menlo Park, CA: SRI International.

Minstrell, J. (2001). Facets of students' thinking: Designing to cross the gap from research to standards-based practice. In K. Crowley, C. D. Schunn, & T. Okada (Eds.), *Designing for science: Implications from everyday, classroom, and professional settings* (pp. 369–393). Mahwah, NJ: Lawrence Erlbaum Associates.

Mislevy, R. J., Steinberg, L. S., Almond, R. A., & Lukas, J. F. (2006). Concepts, terminology, and basic models of evidence-centered design. In D. M. Williamson, I. I. Bejar, & R. J. Mislevy (Eds.), *Automated scoring of complex tasks in computer-based testing* (pp. 15–47). Mahwah, NJ: Lawrence Erlbaum Associates.

Mojica, G. (2010). *Preparing pre-service elementary teachers to teach mathematics with learning trajectories.* Unpublished doctoral dissertation, North Carolina State University, Raleigh, NC.

North Carolina Department of Public Instruction (NCDPI). (n.d.). *Accountability and curriculum reform effort.* Retrieved from http://www.ncpublicschools.org/acre/

Popham, W. J. (2008). *Transformative assessment.* Alexandria, VA: Association for Supervision and Curriculum Development.

Porter, A. C. (2005). Prospects for school reform and closing the achievement gap. In C. A. Dwyer (Ed.), *Measurement and research in the accountability era* (pp. 59–95). Mahwah, NJ: Lawrence Erlbaum.

Shepard, L. A. (2000). The role of assessment in a learning culture. *Educational Researcher, 29,* 4–14.

Shute, V. J. (2008). Focus on normative feedback. *Review of Educational Research, 78,* 153–189.

Sztajn, P., & Confrey, J. 2010. *Building a conceptual model of learning-trajectory based instruction.* Grant proposal funded by U. S. National Science Foundation.

Stiggins, R. J. (2005). From formative assessment to assessment FOR learning: A path to success in standards-based schools. *Phi Delta Kappan, 87,* 324–328.

Tarr, J. E., McNaught, M. D., & Grouws, D. A. (in press). The development of multiple measures of curriculum implementation in secondary mathematics classrooms: Insights from a three-year curriculumevaluation study. In I. Weiss, D. Heck, K. Chval, & S. Zeibarth (Eds.), *Approaches to studying the enacted curriculum.* Greenwich, CT: Information Age Publishing.

Thissen-Roe, A., Hunt, E., & Minstrell, J. (2004). The DIAGNOSER project: Combining assessment and learning. *Behavior Research Methods, Instruments, & Computers, 36*(2), 234–240.

Wilson, M. (2005). *Constructing measures: An item response modeling approach.* Mahwah, NJ: Lawrence Erlbaum.

Wilson, P. H. (2009). *Teachers' uses of a learning trajectory for equipartitioning.* Unpublished doctoral dissertation, North Carolina State University, Raleigh.

CHAPTER 9

Formative Assessment
A Key Component of Digital Teaching Platforms

Michael Russell

Formative assessment is the process of collecting and analyzing information about students' knowledge and understanding prior to or during instruction for the purpose of informing instruction or assisting students in improving their work (see Chapter 8, this volume). There are at least three characteristics of formative assessment that influence its effectiveness for supporting student learning in Digital Teaching Platforms (DTPs) and other types of classroom instruction. First, the information provided to educators must be linked to current learning goals. Second, the information must be delivered in a timely manner so that the educator has an opportunity to intervene with a given student or group of students. Third, the information must be specific enough to be actionable for the teacher or the student (Black & Wiliam, 1998a, 1998b).

Today, there are many computer-based tools that can be used to collect information about student learning. Unless that information, however, is closely aligned with, and collected in proximity to, learning goals (for the current or next lesson), it does not meet the definition of formative assessment. For this reason, periodic tests given to monitor progress toward broad learning objectives do not fall within the definition of formative assessment. Instead, these periodic assessments are considered interim assessments. Similarly, while the results from summative assessments can be used to identify topics and skills that students appear to have mastered or that need further development, the gap between the receipt of summative information and the next opportunity to further develop specific knowledge and skills precludes this use of summative tests as a form of formative assessment.

In the context of this chapter, a computer-based technology is defined as any device that relies on computer-based algorithms to record, process, and present information. This includes such tools as desktop and laptop computers, handheld computers (e.g., PalmPilots), student response devices, web-based applications, and/or state-of-the-art cell phones that enable web-based communications (e.g., iPhones). Any and all of these devices can be integrated into a DTP to support formative assessment. While there are many ways in which computer-based technologies can be used to support formative assessment, this chapter limits its focus to three promising uses. These uses include cognitive diagnostic assessment, playback of interactive items, and outsourcing scoring or coding of student work samples. These examples are followed by a brief reflection on the role of formative assessment in DTPs and the importance of considering the validity of formative assessments.

COGNITIVE DIAGNOSTIC ASSESSMENT

For many decades, teachers and test developers have attempted to examine student responses in order to identify errors that are made while solving mathematical problems. In most cases, error analyses focused on the misapplication of common algorithms used to solve a class of problems. By helping to correct an error that occurs when a problem-solving algorithm is employed, it was thought that students would develop stronger skills in a given area of mathematics. It was also believed that as the presence of student errors decreased, conceptual understanding had improved. One shortcoming of error analysis, however, is that it typically focuses on the accuracy with which a student follows a given procedure for solving problems, rather than on the student's conceptual understanding. While error analysis is effective for identifying where in the application of a problem-solving strategy a student is prone to error, it is unable to identify persistent and systematic conceptual errors or misunderstandings.

Rather than focusing on steps students follow when solving a problem, diagnostic assessments focus on the cognitive understanding a student applies when solving a problem. Cognitive understanding is specific to the construct being measured, and the assessments of cognitive processes that flow from that understanding are based on cognitive theory specific to that construct. Recognizing that the application of misconceptions and underdeveloped reasoning is inconsistent when students are first exposed to a new concept, statistical models can be applied to estimate the presence of misconceptions or underdeveloped understanding across multiple instances rather than just a single item. Thus, diagnostic assessments point teachers to instructional activities that focus on conceptual understanding rather than activities that target a specific step in solving a problem.

The Diagnostic Algebra and Geometry Assessment Projects

The Diagnostic Algebra Assessment (DAA) and the Diagnostic Geometry Assessment (DGA) are examples of diagnostic assessments designed to help teachers to identify students who are performing poorly in a given area of algebra and geometry, as well as to identify *why* they are performing poorly. Consistent with the processes of a DTP, for students who are identified with a specific misconception, the DAA and DGA link teachers and students to instructional resources that focus on that misconception. These instructional resources focus on explaining the theory behind the misconception and providing instructional strategies to target the misconception in the classroom. In this way, the DAA and DGA take a systems approach that includes collecting information about a student's current state of understanding, returning that information in an efficient and informative manner, linking teachers and students to instructional and learning resources specific to a given misconception, and providing opportunities for teachers to assess changes in student understanding. It is also important to emphasize that, as in a DTP and unlike some computer-based learning or tutorial systems, the DAA and DGA depend on active participation of the teacher in the student's learning process.

Before instruction begins, teachers should assess pre-existing beliefs and conceptions harbored by students, investigate the thinking behind these beliefs and conceptions, and then design appropriate instruction based on the findings. Because students do not enter the classroom as blank slates, teachers need to elicit initial understandings in order to build upon or refine those understandings (Airasian, 1991; Bransford & Vye, 1989; Bruer, 1993; Fennema & Franke, 1992; Fisher & Lipson, 1986; Mestre, 1987; Popham, 1995; Resnick, 1983; Wittrock, 1986). This basic belief that, because of the the prior knowledge of students, assessment needs to be administered before instruction begins is the foundation of the DAA and DGA.

The DAA and DGA apply findings from a large body of cognitive research that focuses on identifying existing misconceptions in algebra and geometry. The initial versions of the DAA and DGA focused on the following misconceptions: concept of a variable, equality, graphing, shape properties, transformations, and measurement.

Developing the Tests. Two short tests, each containing 10 to 12 items, were developed for each misconception. The intent for each test was to provide teachers with one test that could be used early in the instructional process to identify students who may operate with the targeted misconception, and a second test that could be used later in the instructional process to examine whether the student's conceptual understanding had changed. Each test was designed to simultaneously estimate the student's level of understanding of the targeted concept and the extent to which the student applied the targeted misconception.

The first step in developing these tests involved creating multiple item sets, each focusing on a specific misconception. This process is similar to that employed by Confrey and Maloney (see Chapter 8, this volume), with the exception that the focus was on specific misconceptions rather than current location within a learning trajectory. In future development efforts, it would be valuable to combine Confrey and Maloney's approach of placing a student within a learning trajectory, and our approach of identifying a specific misconception associated with the current location that may be impeding a student's progress through the trajectory.

Test items were designed based on existing cognitive research. Each test item contained the correct answer, an answer option likely to be selected if the student applied the targeted misconception, and additional distracter answer choices that were unrelated to the targeted misconception. These tests were pilot-tested and a subset of items from each test was selected to form the most reliable and unidimensional scale.

Cognitive Validation Studies. After the new tests were created from the best-performing items, cognitive validation studies were conducted to examine the extent to which the scale provided information about a specific misconception. Messick's model of validity was used (1989). In this model, validity is defined as a unified concept comprised of four aspects: content-related, construct-related, criterion-related, and consequential-related.

Content-related validity is the extent to which an assessment adequately and representatively samples the domain of interest. Content-related validity was evaluated by comparing the test items to the domain of algebra as defined by the United States' National Council of Teachers of Mathematics Standards.

Construct-related validity is the extent to which an assessment requires an examinee to apply the construct of interest without also applying additional constructs that are not of direct interest (i.e., Is the test measuring what it purports to measure?). Construct validity was assessed by using intervention studies, conducting statistical analysis that focused on the internal structure of each scale, and examining the consistency of classifications based on multiple sets of diagnostic items that measured a given concept and associated misconception.

Criterion-related validity is the extent to which an assessment provides information that is consistent with other information about the examinee with respect to the construct of interest. Criterion-related validity was assessed by comparing results of the DAA to teacher assessments based on each student's classroom work.

Consequential-related validity is the extent to which the use of information provided by an assessment leads to positive and desired consequences and limits undesirable or negative consequences. Consequential-related validity was evaluated by conducting a pilot efficacy study that used a four-group cluster randomized control trial design.

Executing the Tests. Teachers were randomly assigned to one of four groups: a control group receiving only traditional feedback from the DAA (the percentage of correct responses and item-level correct/incorrect information), a group that received traditional feedback and diagnostic feedback that focused on student misconceptions, a group that received traditional feedback and the package of instructional resources, and a group that received both the diagnostic feedback and the instructional resources (the full intervention). Multiple groups were used to separate the effects of the instructional resources from the effects of the diagnostic feedback.

Forty-four teachers completed all requirements for the pilot study. These teachers administered the DAA pre- and post-tests to 905 students. After administering the pre-test, teachers were provided with traditional or diagnostic feedback (depending on their group assignment). Teachers in groups that received the instructional resources were then directed to use those resources over a period of 3 weeks. Finally, teachers in all groups administered a post-test. The pre- and post-tests each contained 34 items (10 to 12 items for each misconception) and were matched by content and difficulty.

The results of the construct-related and criterion-related validity studies for the DAA provide preliminary evidence that the DAA is an effective assessment of the targeted algebraic misconceptions. Specifically, the DAA consistently classified high performers and students operating under a targeted misconception. Classification consistency ranged from .73 to .87, depending on the misconception.

After the initial validity studies were complete, the pilot efficacy study was conducted. This study found that 14% of students operated under the concept of a variable misconception, 12% operated under the graphing misconception, and 11% operated under the equality misconception.

The differences among the pre-test scores of the four groups were also analyzed. Statistical analyses indicated that the full-intervention had a large, significant effect on ability scores compared to the three other interventions (the effect sizes ranged from 0.76 to 0.91 standard deviations). These results indicate that students in the full-intervention group had higher ability scores on the post-test than students in the three comparison groups (Russell, O'Dwyer, & Miranda, 2009).

Similar results were found when the items were scored for whether they indicated a student was operating under the misconception. The standardized mean of the full-intervention group was 0.72, 0.63, and 0.80 standard deviations lower than the control group, the group that received diagnostic misconception reports without instructional resources, and the group that received instructional resources without diagnostic misconception reports, respectively. These differences indicate that students in the full-intervention group had lower misconception scores on the post-test than students in the three comparison groups. Both these misconception results and the ability results represent moderate to large effect sizes. Additional multilevel regression models used to estimate the treatment effect revealed the same pattern of results as the effect size analysis (Russell et al., 2009).

Impact of the DAA and DGA Tests. The DAA has demonstrated success in identifying student misconceptions and assisting teachers in targeting those misconceptions. It has also shown far-reaching effects: Approximately 84 teachers and 2,000 students across 26 states participated in the pilot and validity testing. An additional 44 teachers and nearly 1,000 students participated in the initial pilot efficacy study. In addition, the DAA served as a springboard for research conducted in collaboration with the Maine, New Hampshire, Rhode Island, and Vermont state assessment directors to examine the feasibility and utility of building an adaptive diagnostic component into their state assessments (Russell & Famularo, 2008).

While there is still considerable work to be done to fully develop diagnostic assessment systems for algebra and geometry, the initial success of these projects demonstrates that educational tests can do more than estimate student ability. The work conducted to date provides evidence that well-constructed response options can be developed to simultaneously measure cognitive understanding and the presence of a specific misconception. Moreover, the validity work conducted to date provides evidence that students who have a strongly developed understanding of a given concept consistently select response options that represent the accurate application of that conceptual understanding. Similarly, evidence shows that students who hold a given misconception apply that misconception consistently across a sample of test items designed to measure a given concept. Finally, results of the pilot efficacy study indicate that when instructional activities designed to help correct a given misconception are employed, the misconception is corrected and conceptual understanding improves.

Looking to the future, the DAA and DGA have the potential to serve as models for a new approach to classroom assessment, consistent with the processes of DTPs, that focuses both on student achievement and on reasons for poor achievement. Although the development of diagnostic items and associated instructional activities is labor-intensive and requires a substantial investment of time, the techniques employed for the DAA and DGA are applicable to a wide range of scientific and mathematical concepts. Further, because the resulting measures are relatively short but provide immediate feedback to teachers, these assessments can be easily incorporated into DTPs and other forms of classroom instruction. It is important to note that the active involvement of the teacher in the feedback and instructional effort to address a misconception is consistent with the second loop within the Digital Teaching Platform described in Chapter 1 of this volume.

INTERACTIVE ITEM PLAYBACK

Computer-based delivery of formative assessments provides important opportunities to employ interactive item types in order to assess students' current state of understanding and problem-solving processes. Traditional assessments often rely on multiple-choice items or short, text-based responses. These item types provide efficiencies, both in terms of item development and item scoring. Absent, however, is insight into the steps students take when solving a problem.

Interactive items, however, provide opportunities to document the steps students take as they solve a problem. Interactive items generally begin by presenting students with a problem situation. Students are then provided tools with which to solve the problem. In some cases, the tools allow students to conduct simulated experiments. As an example, the National Assessment of Educational Progress (NAEP) Technology-Rich Science task asks students to explore the relationship among volume of a balloon, the mass of a payload, and the height to which the balloon is able to lift the payload. Students are provided tools that allow them to conduct a series of simulated experiments in which they are able to alter the balloon's volume and the mass of the payload. Students are also provided with tools to measure the balloon's altitude and record information in a table. Through these tools, students are able to conduct a series of experiments to collect data that they are then expected to analyze in order to explore the relationship among the volume, payload mass, and lift. Chapter 7 of this volume describes how immersive interfaces can provide even richer student experiences for assessing what they do and do not know.

Other interactive items present students with objects that they are expected to manipulate to demonstrate understanding of a concept. Figure 9.1 shows a screen shot of an interactive item for the shapes misconception discussed briefly above. For this item, students can move the line segments to form rectangles. Lines can be moved anywhere within the workspace, manipulated in any order, and repositioned at any time. This item also asks students to make a definite statement about the number of rectangles they create and to explain why some line segments could not be used. A similar interactive item developed for the measurement misconception requires students to exhibit their thought processes about *how* they structure space to measure area. Students are asked to manipulate objects (in this case a square tile) to determine the area of the rectangle. Students must also provide a numerical response indicating their estimate of the area and an explanation of how they found the area using the tiles.

For both of these items, the students' numerical response can be analyzed to estimate their level of understanding. Additional information, however, can be acquired by examining the steps taken prior to producing the numerical response. In the case of the item in Figure 9.1, automated scoring algorithms could also be applied to classify students' manipulations of the line segments into two or more score categories. In fact, for this item, procedures were developed to classify students' responses into three categories: full understanding, underdeveloped understanding, and limited understanding. For full understanding, students' line manipulations resulted in three rectangles, one positioned with the long sides horizontally, one vertically, and one on a diagonal. For underdeveloped understanding, students are able to produce the horizontally and vertically oriented rectangles, but not the diagonal. For limited understanding, no rectangles or only a vertical or horizontal rectangle is produced. To score responses automatically, an algorithm examines the distance between line segments and compares the pattern of distances for a given response to the pattern of distances for a set of responses originally scored by two human raters.

Figure 9.1. Screen shot of shapes hybrid item.

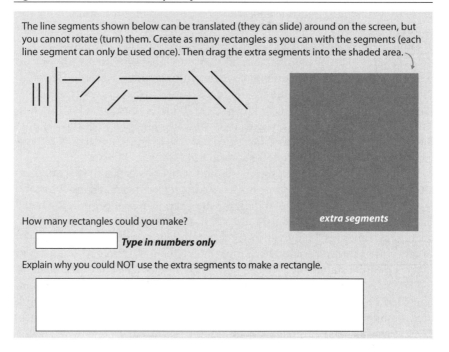

The line segments shown below can be translated (they can slide) around on the screen, but you cannot rotate (turn) them. Create as many rectangles as you can with the segments (each line segment can only be used once). Then drag the extra segments into the shaded area.

extra segments

How many rectangles could you make?

Type in numbers only

Explain why you could NOT use the extra segments to make a rectangle.

Regardless of whether the manipulation and/or the numerical response is employed to classify students, a potentially powerful use of these types of items is playback of student procedures. For students who are categorized as "misconceivers" or as students with underdeveloped understanding, playback of their performances can provide teachers with important insight into the procedures students employ when solving a problem. For the line segment problem depicted in Figure 9.1, playback displays each manipulation the student made while solving the problem. To save time, the playback occurs as a sequence of manipulations without time between each one. In this way, a teacher can identify which line segments students attempted to manipulate, the order of manipulations, and possible confusion students encountered while manipulating certain line segments.

Similarly, an item designed to measure students' understanding of area asks students to manipulate tiles of various shapes to estimate the area of an object. For these area problems, playback allows the teacher to view each step a student took and provides insight into whether a student attempted to fill the area to count the number of tiles that fit into the shape, applied a given algorithm (e.g., length x width), confused area with perimeter, or employed a different strategy. This playback can be very rich in its data, as described in Chapter 7 of this volume. When playback is shared with other students through a gallery (as described in Chapters 6, 8, and 10), teachers can use student responses to engage the class in discussion about the concept, different strategies for solving a problem, and a specific misconception. The capturing, analysis, and display of feedback is a major potential strength of DTPs.

In our work, the use of playback has not yet been examined in a classroom setting. However, we believe that the combination of automated scoring, feedback on classification of students' current understanding, and playback of student procedures holds promise to provide teachers with deeper insight into student thinking and problem-solving procedures. In addition, playback may provide opportunities for teachers to identify students in need of help and talk through their thinking while watching the playback together.

OUTSOURCING

Great emphasis has been placed on data-based decision making in education. Within the confines of the classroom, teachers often collect a substantial amount of data about student learning but struggle to make good use of that data.

To further increase the efficiency of collecting student data, outsourcing may be useful. For some people, the word *outsourcing* has a negative connotation. Many people confuse outsourcing with relocation, which involves the transfer of jobs from the United States to another nation where labor is less expensive. Outsourcing, however, is more complex than simply moving jobs from one place to another. Outsourcing involves transferring one part of an organization to another organization. When done thoughtfully, this transfer focuses on lower-level, mundane aspects of an organization, the removal of which frees up time and resources for the organization to focus on more challenging and profitable aspects of their work.

As an example, consider a tax preparation firm that handles both simple tax returns and complex tax returns. Rather than invest internal resources to process simple returns, a firm may opt to expend its expertise on complex returns. To do so efficiently, but without declining the business of simple returns, the firm may either establish a branch that employs accountants with lower levels of expertise to process simple returns, or it might outsource those returns to a separate organization that is established to process simple returns efficiently. In either case, rather than investing the time of well-trained accountants into working on many fairly simple returns, the firm outsources those returns so that they can apply their extensive knowledge to a larger number of more complicated returns.

Outsourcing with Reading Assessments

In the field of education, there are some aspects of assessment that might be performed more efficiently by someone outside the classroom. As an example, reading records require a considerable investment of time for a teacher to listen to and code. While teachers learn important information about specific aspects of a student's reading while listening to them read, outsourcing the careful coding of reading records could free up time for teachers to engage in other activities.

In many early elementary classrooms, teachers use frequently collected "running" reading records to monitor students' progress in developing reading skills. Running records require teachers to observe an individual student as the student reads a passage aloud. Traditionally, the teacher has a paper-based copy of the same passage and marks portions that are mispronounced, skipped, repeated, corrected, or otherwise present the student with a challenge. Once the student finishes reading, the teacher typically tallies categories of errors and records the tallies in a notebook. Over a period of time, these records provide evidence that the teacher can use to assess the development of a student's reading skills.

Although reading records are used in thousands of elementary classrooms, the process of documenting, tracking, and reporting progress using paper-based records is cumbersome and limiting. Too often, the wealth of data provided by reading records sits in a file cabinet and is used only to make gross assessments of reading progress. Because of their detailed nature, however, reading records have the potential to provide fine-grained assessments of specific challenges students encounter when reading.

To enhance the efficiency and utility of reading records, Wireless Generation developed mCLASS:Reading, a palm-based application that allows teachers to capture information about students' reading skills electronically. (For a better understanding of this application, see http://www.wirelessgeneration.com/assessment/mclass-reading3d/overview/.) The application allows teachers to create profiles for each student in their classrooms. It displays an electronic copy of the text that a student reads aloud. As the student reads, the teacher records errors directly on the PalmPilot or other mobile device. Upon completion of the passage, mCLASS automatically tallies the number of marks recorded for each error type. Teachers then upload the student's new record to a database on their computer.

Once uploaded, the teacher may examine the student's record using a variety of visual displays. One visual allows the teacher to view the frequency with which a specific type of error occurs over a period of observations. Another display allows the teacher to examine the change in a student's reading level over a period of time. A different display allows the teacher to compare a given student to his or her peers in order to identify peers who are having similar challenges or are at a similar reading level. Using these visuals, a teacher is able to make more informed decisions about small-group instruction or reading partners. The software also allows teachers to identify books that are aligned with a student's current reading level and challenges.

By collecting data electronically, uploading that data to a central database, and providing several tools for exploring the results of reading records, mCLASS:Reading can enable formative assessment. It does so by simplifying the assessment of student reading skills in three ways. First, the application has a large number of commonly read texts built into its database. When a student selects a text to read for his or her reading record, the teacher does not need to access a paper copy of the text. Instead, the teacher can access the text and record all errors directly on a PalmPilot. This reduces the preparation required prior to conducting a reading record.

Second, rather than tabulating the number and type of reading errors on paper and then transferring this record to a database, mCLASS:Reading performs these tasks automatically. Automatic tabulation saves time and assures the data are available in a timely manner to make informed decisions about instructional practices. Finally, the data are presented using numeric and graphic displays. Reports summarizing a single running record, multiple running records for a specific student, or a synthesis of all students in the class are generated. These reports simplify the process of analyzing data collected across multiple observations and from several students to make informed decisions about classroom instruction. In comparison to traditional paper-based records, computer-based tools like mCLASS:Reading can streamline the assessment process and provide rich data in an easy-to-interpret format. This application also illustrates the ways in which handheld devices can complement larger computers in a DTP.

Recognizing the potential for electronic data collection and analysis to improve the efficiency and utility of formative assessment, Center for Applied Special Technology (CAST) has a computer-based tool, Thinking Reader, that allows teachers to collect electronic samples of students' oral reading. Teachers can then access these electronic reading samples for coding. Once coded, the teacher can examine scores to identify strengths and weaknesses for each student, as well as to document change over time.

Tools such as mCLASS and Thinking Reader capitalize on technology to improve the efficiency of how student work samples are collected and coded. These tools also provide teachers with electronic tools that allow them more easily to analyze assessment data in order to identify skills on which students need further support, and to examine changes in performance over time. These tools, however, still require considerable time and effort on the part of the teacher to code student responses before the benefits of assessment can be realized.

In this example, outsourcing the analysis of student reading could be performed by a computer-based program with speech recognition capabilities, or by a human located outside of the classroom. Results could then be returned rapidly, allowing the teacher to modify instruction accordingly. By maintaining electronic copies of student readings, teachers could access summaries of student results and then selectively listen to samples for students with targeted problems.

In essence, this efficiency is similar to that provided by the DAA and DGA, which identify students who are believed to be operating with a misconception, allow teachers to selectively view playback of some student work samples, and link the teacher with instructional resources that are specific to the student's current state of knowledge. DTPs enable a data infrastructure that seamlessly allows for various forms of outsourcing that can help teachers be more focused and effective.

Other Educational Uses of Outsourcing

The notion of outsourcing might be applied to other areas of assessment, such as grading. For many teachers, grading papers and problem sets is tedious. The vast majority of problems a teacher grades are done correctly. It is only those students who are struggling on many problems who really need the teacher's attention. Yet teachers spend most of their time looking at problems that are done correctly. Outsourcing grading would send work samples to someone outside of the classroom who analyzes those samples, grades the work, and returns a summary of performance to the teacher. Summary information could focus on student performance, common issues one or more students had, a list of students who performed very poorly along with possible reasons why, and samples of their work. Rather than spending time grading, teachers could acquire similar information in substantially less time, freeing them to focus on other aspects of teaching. The same could occur for written assignments. Rather than reading and commenting on every written assignment, some of this work could be outsourced to educators who specialize in providing feedback on writing. Students would still receive preliminary feedback, and teachers would still see students' final products, but teachers would have more time to work individually with more students rather than reading drafts from all students. Through outsourcing, the DTP extends beyond the individual classroom to distant resources that can empower teacher effectiveness.

VALIDITY

Test validity focuses on the inferences and subsequent decisions one makes based on a test score. Given the relationship among test scores, inferences, and decision making, it is important to place questions of test validity in the context of an assessment's purpose. As discussed, the primary purpose of a formative assessment is to collect information about students' current state of knowledge and understanding in order to inform instruction. Given this purpose, the aspects of test validity that are more pertinent to formative assessment focus on the extent to which information provided by a test is related to the knowledge and skills of interest, the degree to which that information is provided in a manner that is interpretable and timely, and the degree to which teachers are able to use that information to tailor instruction based on one or more students' current state of knowledge or understanding. In addition, given that the stakes associated with the instructional decisions are relatively low, the need for highly reliable information may be relaxed.

The examples presented above provide interesting opportunities to consider issues of test validity that may be most relevant for formative assessment. As explained previously, diagnostic assessments are developed to measure very specific constructs and associated misconceptions. Mis-specifying the construct of interest, employing answer options that are inaccurate representations of a targeted misconception, or inappropriately classifying a response as a misconception will decrease the quality of information provided by the assessment. When decreased quality of information leads to misclassifying a student, two outcomes may result. In the first case, a student who would benefit from instruction designed to "correct" a misconception may be denied, resulting in the student persisting with the misconception. In the second case, a student who does not hold the misconception may receive instruction that does not meet his or her current learning needs. In the second case, the instruction is unlikely to impede the student's conceptual development, but may delay more appropriate learning opportunities. The first case may result in harmful instructional practices. To limit the detection of a false positive, diagnostic assessments might be designed to be administered multiple times, which is easy to do within the infrastructure of a DTP. In fact, this is one reason why the DAA and DGA provide teachers with two versions of each diagnostic test.

The two other examples explored above also raise important validity issues. Specifically, playback of student interactions with items can provide powerful insight into students' problem-solving strategies and procedures. However, to capitalize on this potential, teachers must be trained to associate observed behaviors with a specific strategy or procedure. Similarly, to capitalize on the potential utility of outsourcing, professionals who reside outside of the classroom must be trained to identify errors, misconceptions, and underdeveloped knowledge that is reflected in student work samples. Methods for efficiently conveying this information back to the teacher, such that the information is interpreted appropriately, are also required. Once accomplished, the potential benefits of outsourcing must be weighed against the potential loss of information incurred when teachers are not directly involved in the analysis of their students' work products. This is an important issue for research in DTPs.

THE FUTURE OF DIGITAL TEACHING PLATFORMS

Formative assessment should play an important role in informing classroom instruction. To maximize the positive effects that formative assessment can have on student learning, it is important that these assessments collect information that is closely linked to instructional goals, provides insight into students' cognitive understanding and processes, and is returned to teachers in a timely and easy-to-interpret manner.

The examples explored in this chapter demonstrate how computer-based technologies can assist with each of these steps. Diagnostic assessments can be used to efficiently pinpoint students' current understanding and identify misconceptions that are interfering with the development of that understanding. Playback of students' interactions in digital environments can provide valuable insight into students' cognitive processes. Outsourcing can provide rapid return of information without requiring teachers to invest instructional time analyzing every detail of student work. By integrating these and other digital solutions into a DTP, formative assessment can become a seamless component of classroom instruction.

REFERENCES

Airasian, P. W. (1991). *Classroom assessment.* New York: McGraw-Hill.

Black, P., & Wiliam, D. (1998a). Assessment and classroom learning. *Assessment in Education, 5*(1), 7–74.

Black, P., & Wiliam, D. (1998b). Inside the black box: Raising standards through classroom assessment. *Phi Delta Kappan, 80*(2), 139–148.

Bransford, J. D., & Vye, N. J. (1989). A perspective on cognitive research and its implications for instruction. In L. Resnick & L. Klopfer (Eds.), *Toward the thinking curriculum: Current cognitive research* (1989 ASCD Yearbook) (pp. 173–205). Alexandria, VA: Association for Supervision and Curriculum Development.

Bruer, J. T. (1993*). Schools for thought: A science for learning in the classroom.* Cambridge, MA: MIT Press.

Fennema, E., & Franke, M. L. (1992). Teachers' knowledge and its impact. In D. Grouws (Ed.), *The handbook of research on mathematics teaching and learning* (pp. 147–164). New York: Macmillan.

Fisher, K. M., & Lipson, J. I. (1986). Twenty questions about student errors. *Journal of Research in Science Teaching, 23,* 783–803.

Messick, S. (1989). Personality consistencies in cognition and creativity. In S. Messick and Associates (Eds.), *Individuality in learning* (pp. 4–22). San Francisco: Jossey-Bass.

Mestre, J. (1987). Why should mathematics and science teachers be interested in cognitive research findings? *Academic Connections* (pp. 3–5, 8–11). New York: The College Board.

Popham, W. J. (1995). *Classroom assessment: What teachers need to know.* Needham Heights, MA: Allyn & Bacon.

Resnick, L. B. (1983). Mathematics and science learning: A new conception. *Science, 220,* 477–478.

Russell, M., & Famularo, L. (2008). Testing what students in the gap can do. *Journal of Applied Testing Technology, 9*(4), 1–28.

Russell, M., O'Dwyer, L. M., & Miranda, H. (2009). Diagnosing students' misconceptions in algebra: Results from an experimental pilot study. *Behavior Research Methods, 41,* 414–424.

Wittrock, M. C. (1986). Students' thought processes. In M. C. Wittrock (Ed.), *Handbook of research on teaching* (3rd ed). New York: Macmillan.

IMPLEMENTATION

Part IV examines particular implementations of the Time To Know curriculum and DTP in schools in the Dallas, Texas, area and New York City.

Chapter 10 describes how Time To Know is designed to empower the classroom teacher, and why professional development is critical to the success of this transformative technology. According to this paradigm, educational technology in the classroom is no longer a partial project but a holistic system that supports, not replaces, the teacher. Time To Know consists of five components that create a holistic solution: infrastructure, interactive core curriculum, Digital Teaching Platform, pedagogical support, and technical support.

Chapter 11 provides preliminary results of the initial implementations of the Time To Know DTP in Texas. The chapter revolves around three core issues: fidelity of implementation versus variation of implementation for evaluation, customization of technology to fit teaching practices, and how the Digital Teaching Platform can lead to stronger academic outcomes for students. Through interviews and the Retrospective Pedagogy Matrix (RPM), the authors find that the flexibility of the Time To Know resources and their adaptability permit teachers to customize instruction to match their approach to the content and to meet the needs of their students. The Digital Teaching Platform provides teachers with the scaffolding and the freedom to remove themselves from the sage-on-the-stage role. Time to Know changes the conversation from discussions about ubiquitous computing and the use of computers to improve student performance to that of teaching and strategies for getting the most from their students.

Chapter 12 synthesizes the ideas presented in the book into an overall summary about the current state of Digital Teaching Platforms. The evolution of DTPs from design-based research to practical, scalable classroom implementations is a work in progress. From research, practice, and policy perspectives, the authors articulate next steps in the evolution of Digital Teaching Platforms. They relate the potential role of DTPs to current contextual initiatives, such as the Common Core Standards, Race to the Top, and the 2010 National Educational Technology Plan. They also summarize the conditions for success, both in context and in infrastructure, for DTPs.

CHAPTER 10

The Instructional Design of Time To Know's Teaching and Learning Environment

Dovi Weiss
Becky Bordelon

This chapter describes an innovative approach to leveraging 1:1 educational technology that embeds an interactive, comprehensive curriculum in a Digital Teaching Platform. This combination creates a teaching and learning environment designed to empower–not replace–the teacher.

THE PEDAGOGICAL VISION OF TIME TO KNOW

When teachers enter a typical classroom, they confront three major obstacles to job success: differentiation, student perception of traditional teaching methods, and feedback. Table 10.1 describes these challenges and demonstrates how Time To Know (T2K) addresses each of them.

Time To Know's Digital Teaching Platform creates a partnership between the teacher and the technology that takes advantage of the strengths of both.

Background: The Time To Know Solution

The T2K teaching and learning environment consists of the following five components:

- *Infrastructure.* The environment includes a 1:1 networked laptop for each student and a networked desktop workstation for each teacher, as well as a projector and a whiteboard in each classroom.
- *Interactive Comprehensive Curriculum.* There is a recommended sequence of interactive learning activities that are aligned with state standards. Teachers can modify these sequences by uploading

their own best practice materials directly into the lesson flow, rearranging lessons, or rearranging parts of lessons. Curriculum has been developed for 4th- and 5th-grade reading/language arts and mathematics.

- *Digital Teaching Platform.* This platform enables the teacher to conduct and plan lessons, receive assessment reports, add their own content, adjust the interactive learning activities to their teaching needs, and display and showcase student work.
- *Pedagogical Support.* Ongoing, high-quality professional learning experiences are designed to empower 21st-century teaching strategies and support teachers through the change process.
- *Technical Support.* Personnel and a support call center are provided to support full implementation of the DTP and the comprehensive curriculum.

When combined, they create a holistic solution that combines personalized technology, student support, and curricular assessments.

Supporting Differentiation of Students

Unique differentiation strategies are built into the lesson flow and permit students to offer their insights and perspectives during the learning process. The teacher functions as mediator and guide, leading the group toward

Table 10.1. Time To Know solutions to the obstacles teachers face today.

Obstacle	T2K Solution
Differentiation	
How can one teacher answer the curricular needs of 25-35 students who all differ from one another?	Turn diversity into an opportunity. By providing lesson activities that are differentiated by ability and learning styles, all students are set up for success.
Traditional Teaching	
How can the teacher interest and engage digital-native students who do not readily respond to traditional chalkboard lectures?	Create meaningful learning experiences. Time To Know engages students in relevant activities and learning opportunities geared to 21st-century teaching and learning.
Providing Feedback	
How can a teacher give timely feedback and support to ever-increasing numbers of students?	Time to Know integrates assessment and real-time feedback into teaching and learning process.

creating a shared product or jointly solving a problem. Differentiation is a cornerstone of the math and English/language arts curriculum. Students are supported in their learning with materials that present the same concepts to everyone but that are modified where needed in lexile complexity, differentiated vocabulary, and varying levels of background knowledge. In mathematics, students are allowed to discover conceptual understandings through a series of activities focused at their individual learning levels.

Differentiation also occurs through the use of open-ended questions that promote rigorous discussion and the opportunity to learn from peers as alternative approaches emerge. Students who are struggling are provided access to scaffolded hints that meticulously support them and become less frequent as students gain skills. All students have the opportunity to experience success and move to higher levels of achievement.

The curricular activities include a set of scaffolding tools containing contextual hints that systematically move students toward the solution of a problem. Reference materials, a set of discipline-focused *applets*, and links to web-based locations provide the student with a broader understanding of the activity and assist in problem solving. Each student is responsible for selecting tools, determining how to use them, and incorporating those tools into an activity. For example, while trying to solve mathematical multiplication equations, the student can choose to use the multiplication applet, which represents the equation in a visual way. As an alternative, other students may choose to use a spreadsheet that provides a visual, step-by-step algorithm for solving equation problems.

The Digital Teaching Platform is designed to present differentiated materials to different groups simultaneously and to support diverse learning levels for the same topic. If the teacher desires, the class may be divided into homogenous groups of students with similar mastery levels on a given topic. For example, when teaching mathematics, the teacher can divide the class into three mastery levels. In this case, the students in each group would work on an assignment appropriate for their current level of proficiency. Only the degree of difficulty among the levels is affected, not the context or the required standard that needs to be achieved.

Similarly, in language arts, the teacher can divide the class into pre-level, on-level, or above-level groups. The students then receive an assignment to compare texts. While the themes and the context are the same for all of the levels, in each group there will be lexical differences that provide easier vocabulary or different syntax. After finishing the assignment, all of the students send their work into a communal gallery where responses are discussed.

Adaptive acquirement of vocabulary and mathematical skills is promoted by incorporating a Practice and Learning (PAL) mechanism consisting of three components:

- *Knowledge-Level Test.* This is a test performed by the student that creates a snapshot of the learner's current knowledge map. At this point, the teacher can generate a student report or class-specific report reflecting the current knowledge maps on a given topic.
- *General Knowledge Acquisition.* Based on the Knowledge Level Test, the student is required to practice a vocabulary set or math exercise focused on skills not demonstrated during the test phase. After completing these tasks, the student's knowledge map is updated within the system, allowing the teacher to receive a report about the increase in the student's knowledge as a result of the learning process.
- *Retaining Games.* Students are presented with additional practice of the skills acquired in a game-based environment in order to increase retention and consolidation of the knowledge in the learner's long-term memory.

The Time To Know platform supports an adapted learning pace for the students in numerous ways. First, the teacher can control the exposure rate of different learning activities during the lesson, and students can progress at their own pace through different questions and screens. This allows students to maintain their self-esteem while engaged in the program, and, as discussed in Chapter 4 of this volume, all students are able to expand their challenge zones. In addition, advanced students who finish the assignment before their peers can easily access engaging, game-based activities. When performing computerized assessment, the teacher can allocate extra time for students if needed. The curriculum is built to provide extra materials on various levels for different learning needs. For example, in mathematics, the curriculum includes enrichment materials, practice materials for each specific lesson, and intervention materials. The teacher can allocate those materials to different students according to their specific needs and learning pace.

Creating Meaningful Learning Experiences

The lesson flow is based on guided social constructivist pedagogy. Each teacher-guided lesson progresses through a cycle of engaging exploration, experimentation, and discussion. This promotes deeper understanding of the materials by the students and the learning of new concepts. The lesson cycle is demonstrated in Figure 10.1. Learning activities one through four compose the guided learning part of the lesson that the teacher facilitates. Students then move into independent learning activities that are differentiated and assigned based on their needs. The lesson also includes *extras*, where both remediation and acceleration activities are located.

Figure 10.1. The lesson flow moves from guided learning to independent learning.

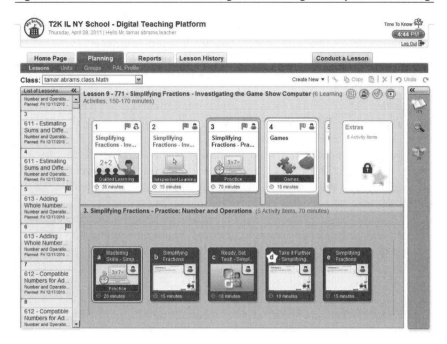

For example, in mathematics, the teacher opens the lesson with an animation, which is used as a trigger for a specific learning topic, such as fractions. Next, a class discussion on the topic increases the curiosity of the students, who then explore the topic and perform guided experiments individually using the fraction applet. The students then submit their work to the class gallery, where the teacher projects the work and engages the students in a discussion that leads learners to concept generalization.

Open-ended applets provide an explorative and discovery environment. The student can engage and manipulate applets and multiple representations for a deeper exploration of a given task or problem. For example, in language arts, the student is required to read and analyze a given text. The student can use tools in the live text applet to explore the written text by highlighting and emphasizing different parts, such as words and paragraphs. The student can review pre-defined *hot words* to access additional explanations or information about those words.

Throughout the entire lesson, the student is provided a coherent, creative story line that functions as a contextual environment to promote the constructivist principles of solving problems in the real world. One 5th-grade teacher at Whitt Elementary School in Grand Prairie Independent School

District (ISD) commented that while she has always been able to teach skills in isolation, "I could never plan the integrated units that are available to me in the Time To Know curriculum" (Personal communication, April 2010). One example of this skill development through integrated units is a mathematics lesson that begins with a story about a theme park, including different railroad-based arcades. Students use the geoboard applet to plan a new railroad for the park according to specific geometric principles. This challenges the students and promotes curiosity and fantasy, thus making the work more fun and engaging, motivating the students and promoting the application of a concept to real-world problems.

The gallery functions as a public sharing space where students post and review their work. The teacher projects the gallery on the class board to compare and contrast activities and encourage modeling and learning from peers. The students can use the gallery commenting tools to provide peer comments and reviews that contribute to others' ideas and promote social learning. This type of public display and common discourse is a significant tool for improving student achievement (see Chapter 5, this volume).

The multi-user activity items are designed to promote collaboration in pairs or groups. The students gather as a team, register their names within the activity item, and perform a group collaborative activity. With the teacher guiding the students to ensure effective collaboration, they work together, share knowledge, and construct a mutual product. Collaborative products are then sent to the gallery by each team for class discussion and review.

Teacher and student folders provide a storage tool for external curricular materials, such as web pages and multimedia files. This feature allows the teacher and students to gather authentic and relevant materials, store them in their private spaces, and later share them with the entire class using the class folder. This functions as an infrastructure for storing research materials and provides additional authenticity to the learning.

Students can store materials and collaborate with one another using Web 2.0-based tools, which creates a mutual knowledge base on different topics. For example, the students can use the Time To Know wiki feature to create a shared class glossary. As shown by Parker and Chao (2007), wikis promote flexible collaboration. They can be used for developing research projects, building collaborative and annotated bibliographies, building concept maps, and group authoring. They also show that wikis stimulate the writing process, function as a communication and collaboration tool, and promote reading and revision (Parker & Chao, 2007). Flexibility for teachers to personalize the program allows them to maintain their professionalism and ensure that best practice initiatives that have been honed over their careers can be included in their daily work.

Integrating Assessment into Teaching and Learning

Several features of the Time To Know DTP offer meaningful feedback to students. The automatic feedback is instructionally designed to be content and context specific. This feedback is sensitive to possible misconceptions and provides each student with unique assistance based on their inputs; it challenges students and supports them in reaching conclusions. All feedback is provided in a multimodal method, involving auditory, textual, and visual channels, thus ensuring the message is consistent and reaches all students regardless of their learning style. For example, in language arts, the student may be required to locate all of the words in the text that indicate positive emotions. The student selects some, but not all, of the emotions and clicks the check button. A feedback window is opened that says, "You have found some of the positive emotions, but there are more positive emotions in the text. Try to locate them by focusing on the highlighted paragraph in the text." At this point, as part of the feedback, a specific paragraph inside the text becomes highlighted, aiding the student in locating the emotions. Azevedo and Hadwin (2005) showed that this type of adaptive scaffolding was effective for moving students toward more sophisticated mental models, for increasing declarative knowledge, and for promoting self-regulated learning strategies.

The Time To Know DTP provides both formative (ongoing) and summative assessment to the teacher. The curriculum includes long-term assignments and projects for which ongoing assessments are provided as a means of continuous evaluation during different phases of an assignment. For example, in language arts, the students are given a writing assignment. They select a topic and write a first draft. The teacher reviews it and provides feedback based upon a set of rubrics. The students improve their work and create a second draft. This draft is sent to the gallery to undergo peer review, with additional feedback from the teacher. The students make one more set of revisions and deliver their final work to the teacher. The teacher then uses a scoring guide and provides the students with a summative assessment along with a final, verbal formative assessment of their work.

The Time To Know DTP functions as a holistic environment where the student can retrieve data and information (using curricular activities, references, and web tools), process the data (using word processing capabilities, spreadsheets, unique applets, etc.), store the data (using the student's folder), publish the data, receive feedback, and be evaluated by the teacher and peers. Sadler (1989) showed that improvement of performance relies on students' ability to know how they are progressing. Information should be provided not only by the teacher, but also by the students themselves, allowing the students to acquire evaluative expertise. The ability for students to comment on others' works-in-progress promotes higher-order thinking skills and hones specific skills such as editing.

The performance task applet provides an opportunity for alternative assessment. The students are required to produce a creative product, such as a website template or a magazine page. The students utilize different features provided in the task, such as choosing a background, placing objects in their proper location, and writing descriptive texts. The teacher can decide to review and evaluate this task using rubrics, promote class evaluation of the work using the gallery, or promote peer assessment by asking the students to write comments on their peers' work. The DTP guides the student through the different steps of the task and provides scaffolding when needed. For example, students can use the *sentence bank* to get ideas for their writing.

The Time To Know DTP includes an assessment environment that allows the teacher to quickly and easily review student work. The teacher can sort student work vertically (checking the entire question set for each student) or horizontally (checking and comparing a specific question across all students). This environment provides the teacher with rubrics for each assessment activity where automatically checkable questions (such as multiple-choice questions) receive an automatic score by the computer. The teacher can then modify the automatically assigned score and use the rubrics to assign a score for the open-ended questions. The teacher can easily provide the student with verbal feedback for any question in the assessment activity.

After the teacher has finished assessing, the results and the feedback are released to the students and can be printed out as a report by the teacher. When necessary, the teacher can decide to provide a correction cycle for the students, allowing them to improve their results and undergo another assessment.

Real-time classroom monitoring provides the teacher with an instant snapshot of ongoing class performance. The monitor presents the teacher with a view of class progress and allows the teacher to drill down and explore the specific progress of each student. The monitor alerts the teacher when a student is making multiple mistakes or is not keeping up with the rest of the class. This *dashboard*, as pictured in Figure 10.2, can also indicate when a student is progressing well and is ahead of his or her peers. The monitor emphasizes when a specific activity is not understood by the majority of the class, thus allowing the teacher to automatically stop the lesson and provide additional explanation for the group. The teacher is able to assess and understand the status of each student in real time and, as a result, can provide assistance, intervention, or additional materials throughout the ongoing flow of the lesson. Studies have shown that frequent feedback to students about their learning produces learning gains (Black & Wiliam, 1998).

The report mechanism indicates class and student status for the teacher and supports the data-driven decision-making process. The reports provide

Figure 10.2. Real-time class monitoring provided on the dashboard for teachers to monitor students.

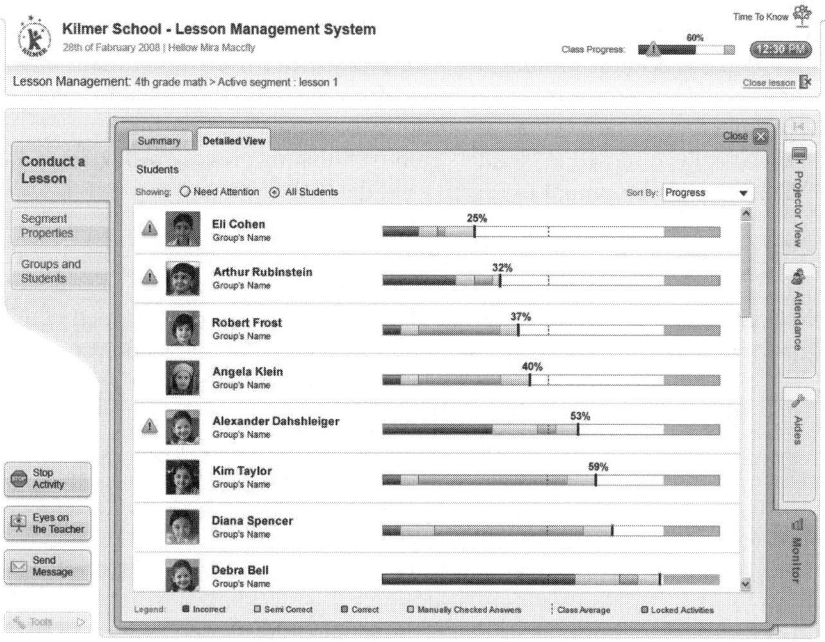

information on different levels: class level, student-specific level, and even specific activity level (comparing students' performances for a specific activity). The teacher can see an overview of the students' progress across curricular content and standards, and explore the specific level of achievement in each activity. As a result of the trends visible in the reports, the teacher can decide which additional activities should be allocated to different students.

The teacher can provide the students with a self-achievement report, promoting self-reflection. The fact that the technology is fully integrated into the class curriculum provides a significant enhancement to the evaluation process. All of the lesson data, including students' progress, levels of success, content coverage, time spent on an activity, test scores, and feedback are recorded, so the teacher has easy access to an understanding of the learning process.

BRINGING 21ST-CENTURY SKILLS INTO THE CLASSROOM

Twenty-first-century skills—critical thinking and problem solving, communication, collaboration, and creativity and innovation—are integrated into the curriculum. The curriculum includes a wide range of idea creation techniques (e.g., open-ended questions and problems), which promote brainstorming and present many possible solutions. The Time to Know Digital Teaching Platform creates a social atmosphere in which learners feel secure enough to play with ideas.

The project environment is an infrastructure for creative, team-based assignments focused on problem solving in the context of real and relevant subject matters. Tools such as the graphic organizer and performance tasks are specifically designed to facilitate creative thinking processes, development of ideas, and development of creative products.

Critical Thinking and Problem Solving

Games incorporated in the curricular materials promote inductive and deductive reasoning. For example, in the Knight game, the student is asked to assist the knight to cross the bridges on the way to his castle. On each bridge, the student is provided with a rule and is required to fill the bridge with objects that comply with the given rule. As another illustration, in the Science Lab game, the student meets a scientist who asks the student to eliminate objects that comply with specific changing criteria until discovering the rule behind the combination of all the given criteria.

Open-ended applet tools, such as the place value applet shown in Figure 10.3, provide additional support and scaffolding in solving unfamiliar problems in both conventional and innovative ways. For example, the student can solve mathematical equations by using the calculator tool or can use the multiplication applet in order to represent the equation in a graphical fashion.

Communication and Collaboration

The curriculum includes activities in which different students are provided with assignments that have differing contexts but cover the same content. One student is required to build a graph representing information from an animation. Another student builds a graph based on a different set of information. The students exchange their products using the gallery, review one another's work, and assist one another when necessary. Multi-user activity items and the teacher's ability to divide the students into groups quickly and easily promote working in diverse teams and sharing responsibility for the collaborative products.

Student folders allow students to bring different media files into the class (photos, audio, video, animations, and web pages), which can be shared and reviewed by their peers and the teacher. The students can learn how to assess the impact and the effectiveness of different media channels.

Figure 10.3. Place Value Chart is one of the applets available in the program.

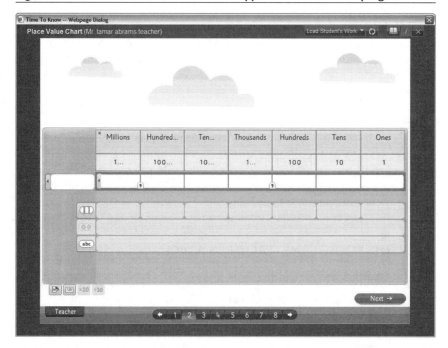

The project environment allows the teacher to easily guide different groups to perform explorative research projects. The teacher and the team members are able to value and assess the individual contribution of each member to the project, along with the evaluation of the group work as a whole.

Information Media and Technology Skills

Students work in a fully computerized environment with access to local and web-based tools and materials, which supports the development of information and technology literacy. Students have access to various sources of information during the learning process, including reference materials in the tools area, the Internet, and extra materials provided in the lesson flow.

Students learn the rules of proper usage of the gallery feedback mechanism. Individual learning leads to class discussion on the topic of proper and ethical behavior in information technologies. The performance task is designed and focused to promote easy creation of media products, which can later be presented and evaluated by the teacher and the class.

Life and Career Skills

The additional materials located in the curriculum promote efficient utilization of time and workload by teaching students how to manage their time and by increasing students' awareness of the capabilities provided by a technology-rich environment. The project environment promotes productivity and accountability by teaching the student to set goals, manage priorities, and perform planning sessions in order to achieve desired results.

Students are required to be flexible and adapt to changes. They play different roles during a lesson, such as switching between being an active participant and a listener in a discussion, or by working as an individual, then with a partner, and finally in a collaborative learning group. Students learn to incorporate feedback by receiving constructive feedback both from teacher and from peers throughout the lesson.

THE ROLE OF THE TEACHER IN A DIGITAL CLASSROOM

Time To Know is committed to ensuring that all teachers are prepared to work in the new, 21st-century classroom. Teachers are systematically supported by an instructional coach. These well-trained subject-matter experts assist teachers as they tackle the challenge of creating a climate for student-centered learning. This is done by providing ongoing support to teachers and administrators. There is intensive support for teachers before they begin using the system. They learn how to use the program features and how to manage a classroom environment that incorporates 1:1 technology components. Once the school year starts, instructional coaches work directly with teachers to assist them in planning lessons, integrating their personal best-practices strategies, and providing modeling and mentoring in the classroom environment. Continued content growth is fostered through a series of pedagogical tutorials that are integrated into the content as well as by providing continuous access to a professional learning portal that provides virtual support to teachers through a library of videos and other support materials. Ongoing webinars engage participants in exploring aspects of the system as well as in-depth pedagogy instruction.

Retooling Lesson Planning and Learning in the DTP

In this new learning environment, instructional planning takes on a fresh meaning. Teachers review student assessment data and determine which lessons will be placed on their digital bookshelf based on student needs, program scope, and sequence. Additional instructional resources that support the lesson flow, such as videos, websites, Power Point presentations, and graphic organizers, are selected from among the teachers' best practices and uploaded onto the DTP. Students are placed into appropriate, dynamic learning groups so that activities can be differentiated as needed. Multiple teaching and learning modalities are accommodated as the teacher determines how each part of the lesson will be delivered.

Teachers encourage students to discover and construct meaning while continuously monitoring the lessons through real-time alerts provided in the program. After checking the student alerts on the teacher station, circulating around the room to encourage students and to check for understanding becomes the norm for the effective teacher.

The implementation of a Time To Know DTP and the integration of online curricula present classroom management challenges for teachers. To remedy this, the teacher and coach discuss lesson planning and effective instructional strategies. With early monitoring and appropriate adjustments, teachers can quickly master the tasks of setting up computers and starting lessons with minimum disruption. The blended instruction approach of the curriculum requires that teachers practice routines with their students, so loss of instructional time is minimized as students transition from on- and off-computer activities. Collaborative group work is alternated with individual work, and teachers need to learn to welcome a certain amount of the noise and movement that accompany an interactive learning environment.

Embracing lifelong learning is yet another role that teachers confront as they become more fluent with digital technology in the classroom. While the curriculum can be utilized as is, knowledgeable teachers will quickly want to utilize the many platform features that allow them to incorporate best practice materials and strategies into the prescribed lesson flow. In regular conferences with coaches and peers, teachers can expand the horizons of the system. Participating in professional learning experiences promotes skill building and creativity. The 21st-century student is not afraid to "jump in the deep end" and try new technologies; teachers must be willing to do the same.

Teachers fluent in utilizing the DTP will also take on roles as change agents, both for themselves and their students. The biggest obstacle to changing how we deliver education to our students is the status quo. Some educators have not embraced the 21st-century skills necessary to ensure that our students are productive workers and citizens. As our teachers become masters of utilizing a Digital Teaching Platform, they need to be advocates who promote the benefits of this new era in teaching and learning. When asked about her experiences with the platform, one grade 5 teacher in Grand Prairie ISD stated that she could not even imagine working in a district that did not use Time To Know.

Implementing Pedagogical Change

The most significant implementation change is a shift in focus from teacher-run classrooms to environments where students are encouraged to construct their own learning. Teachers continue to play a critical role as guides and facilitators, but the emphasis is on creating a learning environment where students grow as independent thinkers. In order to foster this atmosphere, both district and campus leadership roles must focus on a student-centered vision.

District leadership must examine priorities in order to direct resources. Teachers must be afforded the time to learn new practices and plan student-centered instruction. District leaders must rethink how technology resources are allocated. There must be a transition from thinking about technology as a "subject," such as word processing, to conceptualizing a platform and tools that foster multiple forms of learning. Students need access to up-to-date technology at all times, so teachers must transition in and out of the platform resources required of a blended learning approach.

District Level. At the district level, transformation to an authentic digital teaching and learning environment requires support but can reap substantial benefits. By utilizing a teaching and learning platform that will grow with the district, sustainability becomes a significant gain. New, district-selected best practice strategies can easily be incorporated into the system.

District administrators are encouraged, through leadership opportunities, to examine initiatives and ensure that they are aligned with their vision. Strategic processes are encouraged that monitor and support the learning and teaching platform within the framework of the district plan. District leaders have immediate access to the many reports available on the system, which provide real-time information on the effectiveness of the program as well as on the progress of schools, classes, and individual students. Having 24/7 access to the T2K virtual support site allows all constituents the ability to access, not only the curriculum, but also the many resources that support a true community of learners. Educators expand their skills as they participate in site components such as blogs and wikis, which encourage collegial sharing of best practices and implementation strategies.

School Level. At the school level, the shared vision promotes a coherent focus on effective instructional practices, such as increased on-task student and teacher behaviors, and on ensuring that student progress is monitored. As the school implements the system, instructional time is restructured and resources are aligned to effectively support teaching and learning. School and district leaders play a critical role in encouraging teachers to value and successfully implement the program. Monitoring and assessing the effectiveness of this innovative way to teach and learn is required. Communication tools promote the expansion of a true community of learners including administrators, teachers, staff, students, and parents. Allowing students and parents to access the program from home promotes the successful use of instructional tools in a way that is motivating to today's learner. Parents become real partners in their child's learning experience as they access the reports and curriculum.

Impact on the classroom can be seen both through rigorous curriculum and teaching strategies, and via a decrease in disruptive student behaviors. Students engaged in motivational, self-created projects and activities increase their instructional on-task time and their willingness to participate in valid learning activities. Classroom resources become increasingly available to all students as teachers transition to the DTP tools.

Teacher Level. Increased teacher effectiveness is another significant advantage of the DTP. Once teachers are prepared to use the platform, they are exposed to consistently rigorous curriculum content and have many additional resources instantly available. The sustained professional learning provided to the teachers by the coaches ensures that all teachers, regardless of their current skill level, are able to effectively utilize the platform and master the content. A diligent focus on instruction has been shown to have a positive impact on both teacher effectiveness and student learning.

Teachers who champion the shift toward the Time To Know DTP are rewarded with access to the support and tools afforded to many other professions that have already embraced 21st-century technology. Teachers are no longer required to spend countless hours creating their own teaching materials or chasing down resources. Today's teacher can conveniently retrieve materials and resources, as well as have access to the thoughts, ideas, and best practices of their colleagues. Not only do teachers have up-to-the-minute tools at their command, but they learn to be first-rate mentors for 21st-century skills.

Such a transformation from traditional methods of instruction requires support. The sustained professional learning experiences provided by instructional coaches guide districts, campuses, and teachers on this journey. Planning and needs assessment occur before instruction begins. Along with this support from T2K staff, district and school administrators examine needs and expectations that are documented and addressed. An implementation and professional learning plan is developed, followed by the identification of implementation roles and responsibilities. Once participants are skilled in using the DTP, instructional coaches provide ongoing support through a coaching, mentoring, and modeling process. Teachers receive initial guidance in the planning of lessons, in effective classroom management strategies, and in modeling blended learning lessons. Additional assistance is made available to ensure that teachers and administrators effectively use student achievement data to guide instruction. Teachers are afforded opportunities to discuss and practice ways to encourage student-constructed learning. As teachers gain new 21st-century skills, opportunities for teacher leadership emerge. These teacher leaders become the cornerstone of expansion opportunities for the school and district.

THE FUTURE OF DIGITAL TEACHING PLATFORMS

To discover why it is critical that we adopt Digital Teaching Platforms, take a look at how children live their lives right now. They are not waiting to become digital–they are digital. Today's children are creating a narrative for their lives that is connected to the global reality of life. Today's children construct learning–they do not just memorize facts. Children already know how to find, validate, and synthesize information. They can leverage, collaborate, communicate, and problem-solve. The only time they sit and wait for learning to happen is when they are in the classroom.

The fundamental constructs of current pedagogy are grounded in the practices of the last century, but today's reality must be embraced now for classroom instruction to remain relevant in the digital age. Today's teacher must be willing and able to use the power of technology to transform knowledge and instruction into products, solutions, and new information. It is indeed an exciting time for learning. We must create the learning environment that we want our own children to have. If we know that students need to be able to think, create, analyze, and evaluate, we must start by ensuring that our teachers have the tools to do the same. This is the vision and mission of Time To Know.

ACKNOWLEDGMENTS

The writers would like to thank to Danny Livshitz and Adi Kidron and Catherine Page from Time To Know for their assistance.

REFERENCES

Azevedo, R., & Hadwin, A. F. (2005). Scaffolding self-regulated learning and meta-cognition. Implications for the design of computer-based scaffolds. *Instructional Science, 33*, 367–379.

Black, P., & Wiliam, D. (1998). Assessment and classroom learning. *Assessment in Education, 5*, 7–71.

Parker, K. R., & Chao, J. T. (2007). Wiki as a teaching tool. *Interdisciplinary Journal of Knowledge and Learning Objects, 3*, 57–72.

Sadler, D. (1989). Formative assessment and the design of instructional systems. *Instructional Science, 18*, 119–144.

CHAPTER 11

Evaluating Time To Know
Research Concepts and Practical Decisions

Saul Rockman
Brianna Scott

Educators have been concerned and curious about teaching and learning with technology for more than 50 years. Enthusiasts have promoted the advances in learning that would certainly occur with its presence in the classroom. Researchers have sought to link the use of various technologies with changes in classroom behavior, thinking processes, and academic performance. Teachers have been frightened by the thought of technology, and Larry Cuban (2001) has forcefully argued that this is because they do not know how to use it and are reluctant to learn. Everybody–parents, teachers, school administrators, board members, policy makers, and state and federal government officials–has been curious about whether children learn from and with technology, and how to pay for it. Is it a waste of time? Could it improve test scores? Would students learn new skills and develop capabilities they would not otherwise?

It has not mattered which technology was in the public eye; researchers, educators, and parents have been asking if it could be harnessed to provide or improve teaching and learning. Encouraging evidence has accumulated, whether it is acceptable to policy makers or not, that students of any or all ages can learn from technology. This evidence supports the notion that technology can be used effectively for teaching and that students can learn by using it on their own or by teachers using it in the classroom. More than 40 years ago, Chu and Schramm (1967), in their compilation of research on learning from television–and they could have been writing about any technology–noted that the question is "no longer whether students learn from it, but rather (1) does the situation call for it? and (2) how, in a given situation, can it be used effectively?" (p. 98).

The question of whether or not students learn from technology has been asked—and continues to be asked—about each new and emerging technology. Now that Digital Teaching Platforms (DTPs) can bring together multiple media under the management and control of the classroom teacher, we are beginning to have the ability to conduct research on the more important questions of appropriateness (does the situation call for it?) and effectiveness (how, in a given situation, can it be used effectively?). Time To Know has provided the opportunity to explore these questions in classrooms; our pilot project takes a first step to provide answers.

This chapter follows two narratives. The first provides a historical perspective; the second is more functional. One situates Time To Know in the context of school reform initiatives that focus on leveraging technology for change; the other seeks to answer questions raised within the marketplace of education.

IDEATION OF TIME TO KNOW

Let us begin with a perspective on the more recent lineage of Time To Know (T2K). In the past 2 decades, computer-based technologies have been central to many initiatives designed to change the way we teach and learn.

In the technology-based school reform movement of the 1990s and early 2000s, a series of solutions for improving teaching and learning were postulated—often based on hope and constructivist theory, rather than substantive research. One-to-one computing focused on the use of technology for individual and small-group work; technology-supported collaborative learning offered chances for classrooms to change; web-focused research tasks encouraged the development of new skills for the next generation of students. All of these approaches explored how to change the nature of instruction and learning. All considered the role of the teacher moving from the *sage on the stage* to the *guide on the side* (e.g, Duffy & Cunningham, 1996; King, 1993)—a change in the structure of teaching that was not necessarily appealing to all who worked in the classroom. These approaches also consider the teacher less important than interactions among students, and this belief led to more initiatives. Constructivism (students building their own knowledge rather than assimilating information) was supported by the evidence that computer technology could provide an environment for students to learn independently and differently.

At the same time, frequent assessments and the carrots-and-sticks approach of No Child Left Behind placed more responsibility on the teacher to provide curriculum coverage and improve test scores. Teachers and their principals became the ultimate middle managers: pushed by forces from above that they could not influence, and responsible for students whose out-of-school technology experiences were much more engaging and personally productive than their experience at school.

One of the issues examined in research on technology-supported school reform in the last 2 decades was the role of technology as the critical element in teaching and learning. This focus on technology was in the context of a larger shift: Teacher professional development was altered to encourage guided learning rather than a firm control of the instructional process. These changes were neither universally desired nor accepted by teachers. Options to use technology were flatly rejected by some; others assessed the incentives and disincentives for using technology in their classrooms and elected to go with what they knew best. Only a few teachers took full advantage of what students could do with technology.

The natural tendency of teachers is to apply what works, not to take an absolute position on pedagogy and technology. Curriculum developers, pressed to create instructional materials that could boost test scores, became more and more prescriptive about what should be done in the classroom. They created technology-based classroom resources, with the expectation that these materials would be administered exactly as designed. They identified sequences of applications, rubrics for assessment, and even scripts for teachers to follow. Thus, fidelity of implementation became a central part of research on school reform, since the outcomes of instruction needed to be linked closely to the technology-supported treatment. Measuring an intervention in a valid and reliable manner depends on the fidelity of that intervention's implementation across classrooms (O'Donnell, 2008).

Time To Know takes a different approach when compared to the technology-focused school reform initiatives we have been studying over the past 15 years (see Chapter 10, this volume). While Time To Know includes ubiquitous computing, constructivist approaches, 21st-century skills, integrated formative assessments, and multimedia, the critical difference is the increased control of the teaching-learning process by the classroom teacher. The technology-supported tools and pedagogical options are under the management of the teacher, which leads to greater teacher buy-in and greater integration and use of technology in the classroom. As discussed in Chapter 1 of this volume, this is the hallmark of a Digital Teaching Platform.

Time To Know brings together many of the elements in technology-supported school reform that researchers have studied over the past decades, and provides an opportunity for an integrated research and evaluation program. However, this platform's option for alignment with one's own teaching style creates a few problems for evaluation, both conceptually and practically.

Although there are clear learning objectives for T2K, as well as the curriculum and curriculum materials to help reach those objectives, teachers have the power to choose different paths for their classrooms to take. The teachers can also customize the content and strategies to match their students' needs and abilities, while keeping in mind the demands of state assessments and mandated instructional practice.

There is no single treatment; no two classrooms are doing the same things, even though they may be trying to reach the same outcomes. Consequently, there is no expectation for fidelity of implementation. No two students may have the same experiences, since the opportunity for teacher-directed customization is ever-present. *Fidelity of implementation* becomes *variation of implementation*, since each teacher is responsive to his or her students within the range of his or her best judgments about appropriate pedagogy. Yes, teacher training and other professional development offerings may reduce the variance somewhat; but when class is in session, the teacher is in control.

EVALUATION OF TIME TO KNOW

This brings us to the second, more practical, narrative thread, the one that deals with the questions raised in the marketplace.

Rockman et al (REA), an independent research and evaluation group headquartered in San Francisco, conducted an evaluation of Time To Know during its first year of implementation in the United States. Given its limited distribution and a series of constraints, the organization saw this effort as a pilot to explore some of the elements integrated in a DTP. While we examined a range of implementation issues and outcomes (Rockman et al (REA), 2010), this chapter focuses on issues that relate to specific problems in fidelity of implementation.

A theory-of-change model of evaluation emphasizes the relationship between implementation and outcomes: To what extent has a program been implemented as intended and how does the degree of implementation (i.e., dosage) influence outcomes? What happens, then, when no single model of implementation exists, when it can vary for each teacher, student, and classroom? This is the challenge faced in evaluating Time To Know. Rather than chase the moving target of implementation with a very small sample, we chose to evaluate teacher and student outcomes—but not processes—using a quasi-experimental design (Weston & Bain, 2010). We were interested in knowing the aggregate impact of exposure to Time To Know versus a business-as-usual model. This case describes our experiences with an outcomes-only evaluation and reflects on the quality of information gathered to describe program efficacy.

Parameters of the Time To Know Study

Our resources forced us to make decisions that we would like not to have made in a more perfect world; but that is always the case. There are real-world limitations in short-term research projects, a fact of life outside of the laboratory. Below, we discuss how we dealt with the limitations, the outcomes and impacts we studied, and specific findings from the Rockman et al pilot study.

Two Dallas-area school districts were recruited by the Time To Know staff to participate in the pilot study. Four control schools were purposively sampled to "match" the four T2K schools on the basis of known demographics (e.g., neighborhood, teacher, and student characteristics).

Teachers were nominated by their principals and were given the option to participate. In the summer of 2009, T2K teachers were provided with 60 to 70 hours of professional development to help prepare for the integration of the program into their classrooms in the fall of 2009. Control teachers did not receive the Time To Know professional development, but were likely to have participated in other summer programs. Eight T2K teachers and eight control teachers ultimately participated in the evaluation. In order to obtain truthful and open feedback regarding student performance, teaching practices, and T2K products and operations, we promised all teachers complete anonymity in any internal or published reports/chapters. Thus, no names or specific citations are used in association with quotes, but individual's roles are noted. All 353 of the participating teachers' students had parental permission to be part of the study. Most had a home computer and were connected to the Internet.

Research Design

Our basic research task was to document and assess the overall implementation of the Time To Know math and language arts materials in 4th-grade classrooms, and to relate consistency and variation in implementation strategy to academic outcomes. While we conducted a series of studies, for the purposes of this chapter, we report only a sample of the findings as they relate to the issue of fidelity of implementation versus variability of implementation.

We took a mixed methods approach, which, as Creswell and Plano Clark (2007) point out, provides more reliable data than any single method. In other words, we had the opportunity to use the qualitative data to inform the quantitative data and vice versa. Given the inherent constraints of this pilot study described earlier, REA collected as much data as possible to best triangulate the results. Data, for the purposes of this chapter, includes interviews, the Retrospective Pedagogy Matrix, surveys, and informal observations.

Evaluation Tools

Due to budgetary constraints, we could not make site visits or conduct structured observations on a regular basis. Consequently, we developed a substitute that we hoped would capture a sufficient amount of information about classroom processes for both treatment and control classrooms. REA created the Retrospective Pedagogy Matrix (RPM) in order to assess the frequency of teaching practices in English/language arts and mathematics classes over a designated period of time (the previous school year for the pre-survey and the previous 2 weeks for each follow-up survey).

The survey consisted of two different types of items. First, teachers were asked to estimate the amount of time they spent *each day* teaching the subject in question, using different activities and grouping structures (e.g., direct instruction, work with pairs of students or small groups, and use of authentic tasks and problems). Teachers were shown a scale marked in 15-minute intervals from 0 to 135 minutes. They checked the interval that best reflected the time spent on a given activity. Because the activity categories were broad and likely to occur on a daily basis, it was expected that teachers would be able to identify the amount of time in which they and their students engaged in that activity.

Second, REA wanted to know about instructional activities that might not occur every day, but might occur in blocks of time throughout the week (for instance, taking quizzes, writing in journals, or using mathematical manipulatives). To assess the frequency of these activities, researchers asked teachers to indicate the amount of time *per week* devoted to specific instructional and assessment practices. Teachers responded using a scale from "None" to "Some" (11% to 25% of instructional time for the week) to "Considerable" (more than 50% of instructional time for the week). The scale and many of the instructional practices were taken from the Council of Chief State School Officers' Surveys of Enacted Curriculum (2009).

The RPM facilitated the collection of time-series data through an online survey interface that recorded at which time point each teacher completed the matrix. Teachers were contacted via email with a reminder to participate in the survey process. In total, a previous-year RPM and five current RPMs were completed. In addition to retrospective measures of classroom processes, REA interviewed teachers and administrators near the beginning and end of the school year in order to dig deeper into teachers' instructional philosophies, perceptions of school climate, and expectations of how Time To Know would make a difference in their pedagogy and for their students.

Academic Outcome Measure

This chapter focuses mainly on teaching and learning mathematics, due to the discrete timeline and content studied. The math assessment was narrowly focused on a short-term bar graph unit that was taught in both the control and T2K classrooms. Thus, the assessment was most similar to a unit test, but the items were drawn from statewide standardized tests from New York, Virginia, and Texas. The open-ended items, which measured critical thinking skills, were developed by both the Time To Know math experts and REA staff. The math assessment was a post-only test because the unit was short; thus, showing movement on an assessment was unlikely. Students' 3rd-grade and current math scores on the Texas Assessment of Knowledge and Skills (TAKS) were collected from the individual schools and school districts for use as both control and outcome variables.

INITIAL FINDINGS FROM THE TIME TO KNOW PILOT PROJECT

All of the results presented here are based on the evaluation report for Time To Know by REA (2010). It is important to recognize the tentative nature of the findings of the pilot project evaluation. The critical concern is the small number of treatment and control classrooms and teachers.

Teacher Control: Technology-Supported Tools and Pedagogical Options

At the start of the semester, Time To Know teachers in the pilot study described their role in the classroom as facilitators or guides. Further, teachers stated they were there to "help the children grow," and one reported that her style was being "always on [her] feet, in the middle of the class." Another teacher emphasized her use of visual and hands-on approaches with her students. Yet another Time To Know teacher avoided using *facilitator* or *guide* in describing her role in the classroom. Instead, she said she was "a mentor, a role model, a leader." This teacher reported that sometimes she used a lecture style of teaching, and she believed teachers must be authoritative: "It's what kids need."

Of the control teachers in the pilot study, five described their role as a facilitator. The sixth teacher, with 39 years of teaching experience, had a slightly different response: "I drive everything. It's only as good as I make it." This teacher explained that she mostly used direct instruction with students "because I'm comfortable and successful with it."

REA researchers conducted intermittent informal observations of three Time To Know classrooms, focusing on four areas: student-teacher interaction, student engagement, student-computer interaction, and issues with technology.

The Time To Know lessons seemed to have three main components: a teacher-led pre-lesson with videos displayed on the whiteboard, an independent practice period, and a debrief and review of independent work. During the pre-lesson, students interacted with teachers by raising their hands to respond to teacher questions. Teachers called on students randomly, and answers were shared out loud. During this time, no students received individual attention unless they had a login problem.

During the independent practice period, levels of student-teacher interaction varied by group. In one math class, the teacher circulated throughout the room, interacted with several students about the content being worked on, and answered questions. In another math class, the teacher walked around the room but interacted with only a few children. At other times, she was observing the class as a whole or working at her desk. In the English/language arts class observed, the teacher took one student aside and worked one-on-one with her while the other students worked independently. The teacher did not have contact with other students during that time. This illustrates the variation of approaches that makes discussing fidelity of instruction inherently difficult. However difficult this is for evaluation, the variation of implementation makes for stronger teacher buy-in and customization; the teachers can utilize the program in multiple ways while maintaining their own teaching style.

Mathematics: Teaching Strategies

A different approach to capturing classroom processes was the Retrospective Pedagogy Matrix (RPM). As described above, the RPM was a survey that all participating teachers had the opportunity to complete at six different time points. One note regarding the following analysis: each 15-minute increment is equated to a score of 1. That is, 1 to 15 minutes is equal to 1 in the analysis; 16 to 30 minutes is equal to a score of 2, and so on. This allowed us to examine mean time spent and compare across groups. For example, if Time To Know teachers had a mean score of 2.67 at a particular time point, this equates to approximately 40 minutes.

We saw a pattern of increased ability-level grouping with T2K math classes. Math control teachers, however, decreased the amount of time spent grouping students by ability level from last year to this year. At the second time point, three out of four control teachers reported spending 1 to 15 minutes teaching with students grouped by ability level, while two out of three T2K teachers reported spending 76 to 90 minutes with students grouped by ability. At time period 5, control teachers' mean time spent in ability-level groups was 1.50, a

.50 decrease from the year before, and T2K teachers reported a mean time of 2.67, an increase of 1.92 over the prior year. One teacher explained how Time To Know helped her to work with students grouped at different levels:

> As I am moving around the room during [independent] work on T2K, I check on the lower students frequently while the higher level students continue on quickly through many activities.

Later in the year, this teacher elaborated how Time To Know lessons allowed her to differentiate instruction for different levels of students:

> The entire [Time To Know] lesson allowed students to work at their own level. Many higher-level students were able to complete all segments of the lesson plus answer the open-ended questions with ease whereas the lower level students were able to use the narration and hints so they would understand exactly what was being asked of them in the segments. They moved through at a slower pace.

While T2K teachers reported using authentic tasks and problems less than control teachers in the previous year, by the end of the pilot year, T2K and control teachers reported spending the same amount of time using authentic tasks and problems (Figure 11.1). In addition, there was great variation over time for the T2K teachers, while the control teachers stayed fairly consistent

Figure 11.1. Math: Time spent teaching using authentic tasks and problems.

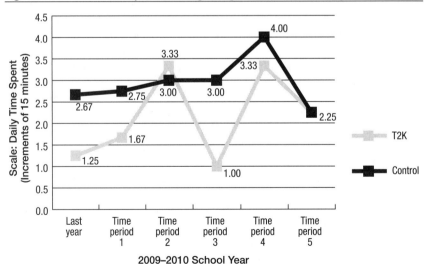

over the school year, providing more evidence for greater variation of implementation within the Time To Know classrooms.

Qualitative data reveal that T2K teachers may have spent less time than control teachers preparing real-life examples because of the integration of these illustrations into Time To Know curricula. For the previous year, one T2K teacher noted that it was "time consuming to find real-life examples." The same teacher also commented at time period 1 about the use of authentic examples in the Time To Know curriculum: "The T2K lesson had several real-life problems blended in to the fraction lessons. The students seemed to enjoy the challenge of solving them."

A control teacher stated that she tried to make "all of [her] lessons authentic," while at the same time, a T2K teacher stated, "They were simple to use—disbursed throughout the Time To Know lesson." A T2K teacher also found the unit problems to be "very creative and differentiated [Time To Know] problems."

Given the difficulties teachers face in gathering authentic problems for students to work on and the great benefit they offer both students and teachers, the Time To Know curriculum seems to offer the double benefit of effectively engaging students while minimizing preparation time for teachers.

From the 2008–2009 academic year to 2009–2010, T2K students increased the amount of time spent on extended response items (for which students must explain or justify their answers), while control students decreased the amount of time spent on this task. This represented a shift from 2008–2009 in which T2K students spent less time than control students on these problems (see Figure 11.2). Again, the T2K teachers showed greater variability in their approach than the control teachers. The Time To Know program, it seems, provides greater opportunity for flexibility and personal agency in the teaching practices.

Of the teachers who commented on this aspect of their teaching ($n = 19$), T2K teachers ($n = 10$) were more descriptive and effusive than control teachers ($n = 9$) in describing the success they felt using this strategy with the Time To Know curriculum. By contrast, control teachers provided short feedback (e.g., "good") or mentioned they spent the majority of time "preparing for" the Texas high-stakes test. One T2K teacher wrote that:

[T]he hands-on approach where the students manipulate and answer problems on the computer is amazing. We have large class discussions as I have never had before because they all want to contribute.

Another teacher emphasized other features of the T2K classroom:

I love the Wrap it Up sections that require the students to respond in complete sentences. It brings great reflection to the lesson. They enjoyed the lesson where we measured each other's height. Those types of hands-on activities bring a nice variety to the lessons. Also, I am constantly making student observations of their learning as I monitor the room.

Similarly, other T2K teachers reported increasing amounts of time spent systematically observing students. On the other hand, control teachers decreased the amount of time spent observing students throughout the year. It is possible that the format of Time To Know, in which students can work independently on their own computers, allows teachers more time for systematic observation of students as they work.

THE FUTURE OF DIGITAL TEACHING PLATFORMS

The data collected as a part of this evaluation have begun to paint a picture of success on several levels. First, although it proves somewhat difficult for evaluation, there is no one standard way of implementing Time To Know in the classroom. The teachers still have control over their classrooms and feel empowered by the added resources and engaging materials provided by Time To Know. Most teachers (control and T2K) believe that they play the role of facilitator or guide in the classroom. The T2K teachers have a DTP that provides them with some scaffolding and the freedom to remove themselves from the sage-on-the-stage role.

Figure 11.2. Math: Students' time spent with extended response items for which they must justify their answer.

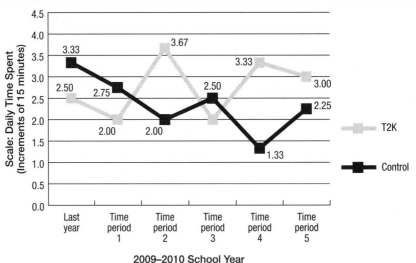

Fidelity of implementation is difficult to measure because of this level of individualization. Are the teachers using Time To Know as expected? The answer would have to be a resounding "Yes," because teachers can implement Time To Know in a way that fits with their particular classroom and the approach that they feel would be most successful. The data obtained from this evaluation can begin to inform the consistent areas of implementation that could be measured easily as the program grows. That is, there may be best practice strategies for using Time To Know in the classroom that can be shared with like-minded teachers and propagated to new schools and districts.

Time To Know changes the conversation about technology in education from discussions about ubiquitous computing and the use of computers to improve student performance, to that of teaching and instructional strategies for getting the most from students. The individualization offered by this Digital Teaching Platform seems to be most useful at the teacher level. Teachers are not replaced by the technology; instead, the technology affords the teachers the opportunity to enhance and/or change their own teaching style. Consequently, the focus in a DTP shifts from fidelity of implementation and "teacher-proofing" curriculum and technology to purposeful variation of implementation and empowerment of teachers to use their experience and personal pedagogy to augment the use of technology in the classroom.

In fact, despite the variation in implementation, the Time To Know students still outperformed the comparison students on content assessments (e.g., mathematics multiple-choice tests and critical thinking assessments) designed for evaluation, as well as on the math standardized test scores. Thus, strict adherence to a single method of teaching and learning is not the only, or necessarily the best, way to achieve learning gains, even on high-stakes standardized tests. The DTP Time To Know is beginning to demonstrate that individualized instruction, teacher experience enhanced by technology, and student engagement with content and technology can be a winning combination.

Like Weston and Bain (2010), we hope to reframe the conversation about how researchers and educators—and especially advocates—consider the implementation of ubiquitous computer programs in schools. Once the technology fades into the background, pedagogy and curriculum become the critical features in the classroom; these are under the control of the teacher, not the technology. By using a DTP, teachers have greater control over both pedagogy and curriculum, and can offer a range of strategies and materials to their students. Commonality of implementation disappears, and greater individualization emerges. Therefore, implementation variation means that each student gets greater access to a personalized experience in school.

REFERENCES

Council of Chief State School Officers. (2009). *Survey of Instructional Practices and Content for English, Language Arts, and Reading* [Survey]. Retrieved from http://seconline.wceruw.org/Reference/K12ELARSurvey.pdf.

Chu, G. C., & Schramm, W. (1967). *Learning from television: What the research says.* Stanford, CA: Institute for Communication Research.

Creswell, J. W., & Plano Clark, V. L. (2007). *Designing and conducting mixed methods research.* Thousand Oaks, CA: Sage.

Cuban, Larry. (2001). *Oversold and underused: Computers in the classroom.* Cambridge, MA: Harvard University Press.

Duffy, T. M., & Cunningham, D. J. (1996). Constructivism: Implications for the design and delivery of instruction. In D. Jonassen (Ed.), *Handbook of research for educational communications and technology* (pp. 170–198). New York: Simon and Schuster Macmillan.

King, A. (1993). From sage on the stage to guide on the side. *College Teaching, 41,* 30–35.

O'Donnell, C. L. (2008). Defining, conceptualizing, and measuring fidelity of implementation and its relationship to outcomes in K-12 curriculum intervention research. *Review of Educational Research, 78,* 33–84.

Rockman et al (REA). (2010). Time To Know: Program evaluation of a digital teaching platform. Unpublished manuscript.

Weston, M. E., & Bain, A. (2010). The end of techno-critique: The naked truth about 1:1 laptop initiatives and educational change. *Journal of Technology, Learning, and Assessment, 9*(6), 5–25. Retrieved from http://www.jtla.org.

CHAPTER 12

The Evolution of
Digital Teaching Platforms
Synthesis and Next Steps

Chris Dede
John Richards

This book presents various aspects of Digital Teaching Platforms (DTPs). The picture that emerges looks like a jigsaw puzzle; each group articulates several pieces of what a DTP needs for success. In conclusion, we ask questions such as: If one were to put the puzzle together, is everything necessary to complete a sophisticated, mature DTP currently available, or are pieces still missing? What are the challenges in integrating the various aspects of DTPs described? How do DTPs fit into the larger context of the 2010 National Education Technology Plan (U.S. Department of Education, 2010)?

ARTICULATING THE DIMENSIONS OF A DTP

Chapter 1 describes three characteristics that together define a DTP. First, the DTP is a completely realized networked digital environment that includes interactive interfaces for both teachers and students. Teachers use the administrative tools of this digital environment to create lessons, assign them to students, and manage the work the students return. Second, the DTP digitally provides the content of the curriculum and assessment for teaching and learning. Third, the DTP supports real-time, teacher-directed interaction in the classroom.

The authors delineate eight features that should be part of any system for a 21st-century classroom: an interactive digital environment, teacher administrative tools, student tools, course authoring tools, curriculum content, assessment content, classroom support, and pedagogical support. Subsequent chapters describe some aspects of DTPs related to these eight features.

Content and Pedagogy

Chapter 3 focuses on teacher-led personalized learning as exemplified in the Web-based Inquiry Science Environment (WISE) project. The WISE pedagogical model centers on inquiry activities informed by a knowledge integration framework. The WISE pedagogy is based on a learning progression that involves four knowledge integration processes: eliciting ideas, adding ideas, distinguishing ideas, and sorting out ideas. Overall, evaluations have shown the superiority of the personalized WISE approach over conventional curriculum.

Chapter 4 describes a variety of technologies that support reading instruction in the context of DTPs. The authors discuss how computer tools for analyzing texts at multiple levels can provide rich feedback to students and teachers. This feedback then can guide technology-based interventions for reading instruction, complementing customized instruction by the teacher. Acting in consort, all these supports can help students make the shift from learning-to-read to reading-to-learn. The next challenge becomes providing assistance to students in developing causal mental models of content, such as the immersive learning environments described in Chapter 7 and the visualizations and virtual experiments developed by Linn in Chapter 3.

Chapter 5 describes ASSISTments, a web-based system that provides tutoring based on student responses, as well as diagnostic results to both students and teachers. Teachers can use ASSISTments in a variety of ways, including as a distributed DTP that provides its part of student instruction outside of school.

The DTP provides tools that help teachers to elicit student thinking and evaluate its quality. Teachers can use various aspects of ASSISTments for lesson planning, delivery, and evaluation, as well as homework support. Case studies illustrating these types of usage are delineated in the chapter, demonstrating the flexibility and teacher control of this DTP. Overall, ASSISTments is a focused DTP that, for the type of instruction it supports, is very adaptable to different teaching styles.

Chapter 6 is centered on three aspects of implementing DTPs: the connectivity used in classrooms, the curriculum, and the interactions between students and teachers. The authors discuss how modern digital infrastructures support new forms of classroom communication that are richly social. They argue that in mathematics, to induce deep learning, the meaning and usage of various types of presentations can prompt rich, sustained interactions among students and teachers.

Work with SimCalc MathWorlds is used to illustrate these points. They show that a DTP is a synergistic integration of software affordances and participatory-infused curriculum, which yields highly adaptable interactive instruction. This enables each student to articulate and to challenge ideas in ways not possible without the DTP. Overall, the authors posit that DTPs can support personalization through individualized, participatory learning under the guidance of the teacher.

Personalization

Chapter 7 describes immersive learning environments. The author delineates how multiuser virtual environments (MUVEs) enable technology-intensive educational experiences that draw on a powerful pedagogy: situated learning with authentic contexts, activities, and assessment coupled with guidance from expert modeling and mentoring. This type of learning is important in fostering transfer from classroom settings to real-world performance.

If added to the instructional repertoire of DTPs, immersive environments can deepen the engagement of students, can enable customized learning experiences, and can provide detailed, rich feedback for both formative and summative assessment.

Chapter 8 focuses on three key functions of classroom assessment: curricular monitoring, formative or embedded assessment, and diagnostic assessments. They identify the design elements DTPs must have to support each of these functions. Overall, their work provides rich examples of various dimensions along which DTPs can foster increased personalization of learning.

Chapter 9 describes three characteristics of formative assessment central for DTPs: First, the information provided to educators must be linked to current learning goals. Second, the information must be delivered in a timely manner so that the educator has an opportunity to intervene with a given student or group of students. Third, the information must be specific enough to be actionable for the teacher or the student.

The chapter also describes how interactive items provide opportunities to document the steps students take as they solve a problem. In summary, the chapter illustrates a variety of formative assessment strategies from which DTPs can benefit.

How do the various aspects of DTPs discussed by all the authors summarized thus far relate to the eight features of the 21st-century classroom articulated in Chapter 1? Overall, every aspect of these features is described in one form or another by the work of the research teams above. Content, pedagogy, and personalization emerge as hallmarks in emerging capabilities for DTPs. But are real-world examples available of how all these features can be integrated and implemented at scale?

SYNTHESIZING AND INTEGRATING
THE DIMENSIONS OF A DTP

Chapter 2, describes the historical evolution of technology-intensive classrooms, culminating in one-student-per-device implementations gradually growing over the last decade. The key difference between schools succeeding with one-to-one computing and those that are not is nine implementation factors. The issue is not finances, but lack of knowledge about how to be effective in managing this infrastructure not just technically, but in ways that realize its educational potential.

The chapter further argues that striving for second-order educational change is crucial for success. This entails moving from teaching-by-telling to full-personalized, student-centered pedagogy focused on various forms of active and collaborative learning that one-to-one access enables. The author describes how Digital Teaching Platforms fulfill this instructional vision and are structured to include the nine implementation factors crucial for success. Over time, he sees DTPs as the future of one-to-one computing.

Chapter 10 highlights ways in which the Time To Know DTP has realized all the features laid out in Chapter 1. The authors show how Time To Know integrates a comprehensive curriculum into a networked infrastructure that provides tools enabling teachers to customize students' learning experiences. Both pedagogical and technical supports are provided for teachers. The emphasis of Time To Know is on differentiation of instruction, with students receiving various types of support from the instructional system, from peers, and from the teacher. Different types of embedded assessment are provided by the Time To Know system both formatively and summatively.

Studies of this unique, first-generation DTP show considerable promise, as described in Chapter 11. Most of the teachers involved in the Time To Know pilot in Texas implemented the curriculum with fidelity to its facilitator/guide pedagogical model, a tribute to the effectiveness of Time To Know's professional development component. They confirmed that this DTP allowed greater differentiation of instruction and more relating of content to authentic real-world issues than did the standard curriculum. Teachers described that they had more time to work with students individually. Students performed higher on the high-stakes standardized tests with the Time To Know DTP than with the standard curriculum.

Yet Chapter 11 also describes the challenges involved in evaluating DTPs such as Time To Know. Because each student receives a differentiated learning experience, determining whether the mix of interventions that students collectively receive is as powerful as possible is very difficult. In contrast, when students are given "one size fits all" instruction, the measurement challenges in determining whether some variant might be more effective are much easier. However, without the customization of learning experiences to each student that DTPs provide, that the unitary model of teaching would be better is unlikely. The issue is less proving which overall approach is better, and more finding ways to improve DTPs when the learning process is so complex and variegated. The WISE refinement studies discussed in Chapter 3 provide an illustration of how this type of improvement might be achieved for DTPs such as Time To Know.

THE RELATIONSHIP OF DTPs TO THE
2010 NATIONAL EDUCATION TECHNOLOGY PLAN

This volume parallels the suggestions of the National Education Technology Plan (NETP) released by the U.S. Department of Education (2010). The first three sections of the NETP appropriately center not on technology, but on learning, assessment, and teaching. Below, we use the discussion of these themes in the NETP as a framework to examine the promise of DTPs.

Learning: Engage and Empower

DTPs combine a social constructivist model of learning with embedded assessment and practice. Their inherent personalization is designed to meet students where they are, and engage students with challenging material. This is consistent with the assertion in the NETP that

> engaging and effective learning experiences can be individualized or differentiated for particular learners (either paced or tailored to fit their learning needs) or personalized, which combines paced and tailored learning with flexibility in content or theme designed to fit the interests and prior experience of each learner. (pp. 11–12)

Also, the digital environment of a DTP classroom matches the connected and multimedia world external to the classroom. This accords with the statement in the NETP that all learning experiences should be based on three principles for universal design:

- Provide multiple and flexible methods of presentation of information and knowledge. . . .
- Provide multiple and flexible means of expression with alternatives for students to demonstrate what they have learned. . . .
- Provide multiple and flexible means of engagement to tap in to diverse learners' interests, challenge them appropriately, and motivate them to learn. (p. 19)

Further, the NETP calls for "learning resources that use technology to embody design principles from the learning sciences" (USDE, p. 23). As demonstrated in this book, the concept of a DTP is emerging from the laboratories of the learning sciences and related research to scale in district implementations.

Assessment: Measure What Matters

The NETP provides two statements about 21st-century assessment that speak directly to the strengths of DTPs:

> Through multimedia, interactivity, and connectivity it is possible to assess competencies that we believe are important and that are aspects of thinking highlighted in cognitive research. It also is possible to directly assess problem-solving skills; make visible sequences of actions taken by learners in simulated environments; model complex reasoning tasks; and do it all within the contexts of relevant societal issues and problems that people care about in everyday life. (p. 27)

As discussed throughout the book, DTPs have the potential to monitor and collect data on sophisticated individual and group tasks, and developments in the learning sciences can be incorporated because of the infrastructure. In addition, DTPs provide continuous formative assessment for each child and ongoing reporting to the student, teacher, administrators, and parents. This is consistent with the vision of assessment presented in the Plan:

> When students are learning online, there are multiple opportunities to exploit the power of technology for formative assessment. The same technology that supports learning activities gathers data in the course of learning that can be used for assessment. . . . As students work, the system can capture their inputs and collect evidence of their problem-solving sequences, knowledge, and strategy use, as reflected by the information each student selects or inputs, the number of attempts they make, the number of hints and feedback given, and the time allocation across parts of the problem. (pp. 29–30)

Thus, DTPs embody core principles of 21st-century assessment.

Teaching: Prepare and Connect

One strength of a DTP is that it is designed to provide ongoing support for the teacher in the classroom. Too often technologists rely on a digital solution and try to "teacher-proof" the technology and the curriculum. From our perspective the teacher is now and will remain the most critical contributor to a student's learning. The DTP provides tools that assist the teacher in preparing lessons, support in the teaching of the curriculum, assistance in classroom management, and ongoing feedback of student performance.

These characteristics of DTPs are consistent with the discussion of teaching for personalization found in the NETP:

> Connected teaching offers a vast array of opportunities to personalize learning. Many simulations and models for use in science, history, and other subject areas are now available online, including immersive virtual and augmented reality environments that encourage students to explore and make meaning in complex simulated situations (Dede, 2009). To deeply engage their students, educators need to know about their students' goals and interests and have knowledge of learning resources and systems that can help students plan sets of learning experiences that are personally meaningful. . . . Although using technology to personalize learning is a boost to effective teaching, teaching is fundamentally a social and emotional enterprise. The most effective educators connect to young people's developing social and emotional core (Ladson-Billings, 2009; Villegas and Lucas, 2002) by offering opportunities for creativity and self-expression. Technology provides an assist here as well. . . . Digital authoring tools for creating multimedia projects and online communities for sharing them with the world offer students outlets for social and emotional connections with educators, peers, communities, and the world at large. Educators can encourage students to do this within the context of learning activities, gaining further insights into what motivates and engages students—information they can use to encourage students to stay in school. (pp. 41–42)

Putting the teacher at the center of the instructional process and creating tools that can make more teachers great is critical for achieving the improvements in learning and performance crucial for 21st-century education.

NEXT STEPS IN THE EVOLUTION OF DTPs

The ongoing evolution and validation of the Digital Teaching Platform rises to the level of a grand challenge in the sense that the Plan suggests (see NETP, pp. 77). In our judgment, an important grand challenge is bringing the DTP to scale and validating the various aspects of the design. This requires addressing the comprehensive nature of the DTP: as an integrated system providing real-time access to learning experiences that, through embedded assessments, are tuned to the levels of difficulty and assistance that optimize learning for all learners; as a curriculum that integrates common core educational content and 21st-century skills; and, perhaps most challenging, provides real-time support for the teacher in the planning, teaching, and managing of today's often chaotic classroom settings.

The financial exigencies schools are encountering underscore the importance of this grand challenge and the key role DTPs will play in education's future. We believe educational transformation is coming not only because of the increasing ineffectiveness of schools in meeting society's needs–though that is certainly a good reason–but even more due to the growing unaffordability of the current classroom model. Events of the last few years, and projections of our nation's economic future, paint a bleak picture of the financial viability of schools as we know them; we can no longer support an educational system based on inefficient use of expensive human labor. Some districts are now moving to high school classrooms with 45 or even 60 students per teacher. Without the power of DTPs to assist them, educators cannot succeed with these levels of students. In contrast, with DTPs, educational effectiveness may increase to the point that society is persuaded to invest more resources in this model, which combines the power of technology with the irreplaceable qualities of human insight into instruction.

REFERENCES

Dede, C. (2009). Immersive interfaces for engagement and learning. *Science, 323*(5910), 66–69.

Ladson-Billings, G. (2009). *The dreamkeepers: Successful teachers of African American children.* San Francisco: Wiley.

U.S. Department of Education, Office of Education Technology. (2010). *National education technology plan 2010: Transforming American education: Learning powered by technology.* Washington, DC: U.S. Government Printing Office.

Villegas, A. M., & Lucas, T. (2002). Preparing culturally responsive teachers. *Journal of Teacher Education, 53*(1), 20–32.

About the Editors and Contributors

Chris Dede, EdD, is Timothy E. Wirth Professor in Learning Technologies at Harvard Graduate School of Education. Dede's fields of scholarship include emerging technologies, policy, and leadership. His funded research includes four grants from the National Science Foundation and the U.S. Department of Education Institute of Education Sciences to explore immersive simulations and transformed social interactions as means of student engagement, learning, and assessment. In 2007, he was honored by Harvard University as an outstanding teacher, and in 2011 he was named a Fellow of the American Educational Research Association. Dede has served as a member of the National Academy of Sciences Committee on Foundations of Educational and Psychological Assessment and a member of the 2010 National Educational Technology Plan Technical Working Group. He serves on advisory boards and commissions for PBS TeacherLine, the Partnership for 21st Century Skills, the Pittsburgh Science of Learning Center, and several federal research grants. He co-edited *Scaling Up Success: Lessons Learned from Technology-based Educational Improvement* (2005) and edited *Online Professional Development for Teachers: Emerging Models and Methods* (2006).

John Richards, PhD, is founder and president of Consulting Services for Education Inc. (CS4Ed) and adjunct professor at Harvard Graduate School of Education. Richards is a senior executive in education, technology, and media with extensive experience in business development, strategic planning, market research, and developing and launching award-winning products. CS4Ed (www.cs4ed.com) works with publishers, developers, and educational organizations as they negotiate the rapidly changing education marketplace to improve business-planning processes, find funding to help schools purchase products and services, and to develop, evaluate, and refine products and services. Richards has held senior-level positions at several companies including The JASON Foundation for Education, Turner Learning, the educational arm of Turner Broadcasting, and Educational Technologies at BBN Systems and Technologies. He has served on boards for a variety of education groups including NECC, Cable in the Classroom, Software Information Industry Association (SIIA), Education Market section, and Association of Educational Publishers (AEP). John's projects have won numerous awards including two Golden Lamps and several CODIEs, as well as several Emmy nominations. He is an internationally recognized leader in merging media and technology with educational needs and has taught at MIT and the University of Georgia. Richards is a respected keynote speaker, has authored or edited three books and more than 80 articles, and has been responsible for the publication of over 1,000 educational products.

Becky Bordelon, MEd, is director of instruction and learning at Time To Know, Inc. Bordelon worked in public education for over 25 years as a teacher and as a campus and district administrator. Bordelon has taught grades 1 to 8, worked in 5 states, and has teaching and administrative certifications in 6 states. Bordelon worked in the online technology industry for 14 years before joining Time To Know.

Jere Confrey, PhD, is Joseph D. Moore Distinguished Professor of Mathematics Education at North Carolina State University and a senior research fellow at the William and Ida Friday Institute for Educational Innovation. Confrey is a member of the Validation Committee for the Common Core State Standards and the Research Committee of the National Council of Teachers of Mathematics.

Michele Bennett Decoteau is a grant writer and academic editor specializing in science, education, and environmental topics. Michele studied neuroscience and behavior at Florida State University and the University of Massachusetts at Amherst.

Arthur C. Graesser, PhD, is professor of psychology and co-director of the Institute for Intelligent Systems at the University of Memphis. He is the editor of *Journal of Educational Psychology* (2009-2014), and was formerly editor of *Discourse Processes* (1996–2005). He is author of a dozen books (including *Handbook of Discourse Processes*) and has developed intelligent software in learning, language, and discourse technologies, including AutoTutor, Coh-Metrix, Operation ARIES, Question Understanding Aid, QUEST, and Point&Query.

Thomas Greaves is founder of The Greaves Group and cofounder of NetSchools. Greaves holds multiple patents and patent disclosures for student computing. He is the Software Information Industry Association (SIIA) Mobile Computing Trends Watch Report Editor. Greaves's recent work is highlighted by the 2006 and 2008 America's Digital Schools surveys, which have extensive coverage of 1:1 computing devices and implementations.

Cristina L. Heffernan, MA, is co-founder of ASSISTments and chief teacher trainer at Worcester Polytechnic Institute. Heffernan has taught in public and private schools and coached teachers as a consultant in Boston's Connected Math Project curriculum.

Neil T. Heffernan, PhD, is director of ASSISTments, associate professor, and co-director of the PhD Program in Learning Sciences and Technologies at Worcester Polytechnic Institute. Heffernan has published more than 24 peer-reviewed publications in the learning sciences and technologies area.

Stephen J. Hegedus, PhD, is director of the James J. Kaput Center for Research and Innovation in STEM Education and Professor of Mathematics at the University of Massachusetts Dartmouth. Hegedus is the PI/Co-PI of various NSF-funded and U.S. Department of Education (IES)-funded projects. He was awarded the prestigious UMass Dartmouth Scholar of the Year award in 2009.

Marcia C. Linn, PhD, is professor of development and cognition specializing in education in mathematics, science, and technology in the Graduate School of Education at the University of California, Berkeley. Linn has served as chair of the AAAS Education Section and as president of the International Society of the Learning Sciences. She directs the NSF-funded Technology-enhanced Learning in Science (TELS) center.

Alan Maloney, PhD, is senior research fellow at the William and Ida Friday Institute for Educational Innovation and extension associate professor, North Carolina State University. He has co-designed mathematics educational software, including the applications Graphs N Glyphs and Function Probe. He serves as research coordinator for the DELTA and LPPSync projects at North Carolina State University.

Danielle S. McNamara, PhD, is a member of both the Cognitive Program and the Institute for Intelligent Systems at the University of Memphis. McNamara's work has been funded by the Institute of Education Sciences, the National Science Foundation, and the McDonnell Foundation. She serves on review panels for the Institute of Education Sciences, the National Science Foundation, and the National Institute of Health.

Matthew Militello, MEd, PhD, is assistant professor of Leadership, Policy, and Adult and Higher Education at North Carolina State University. Militello is co-author of two books: *Leading with Inquiry and Action* (2009) and *Principals*

Teaching the Law (2010). He is currently an evaluator for a National Science Foundation (GK–12) grant that uses an intelligent tutoring system.

Saul Rockman is president of Rockman et al, an independent evaluation, research, and consulting firm headquartered in San Francisco. The company, now in its 20th year, works with preschool, K–12, postsecondary, and adult educational institutions in formal education, as well as with informal education projects having a wide community or consumer audience.

Jeremy Roschelle, PhD, is director of the Center for Technology and Learning, SRI. He also consults on innovative technologies in education for companies such as Texas Instruments, Apple, and Scholastic. Roschelle serves on the editorial boards of five leading journals.

Michael Russell, PhD, is an associate professor in the Lynch School of Education, directs the Nimble Innovation Lab and is vice president of innovation for Measured Progress. He developed a universally designed computer-based test delivery system and works with several state testing programs. Russell is the founder and chief editor of the *Journal of Technology, Learning, and Assessment.* He has also been affiliated with the Center for the Study of Testing, Evaluation, and Educational Policy (CSTEEP) since 1994.

Brianna Scott, PhD, is a senior researcher at Rockman et al. Prior to joining the REA team, Scott worked for the National Collegiate Athletic Association (NCAA) managing a wide range of research projects and performing high-level statistical modeling of college student-athletes' academic performance in order to inform national policies.

Joseph Walters, EdD, is vice president for research at Consulting Services for Education, Inc. Previously, Walters was director of assessment and evaluation at Riverdeep: The Learning Company; was senior scientist at TERC; and worked at Project Zero at the Harvard Graduate School of Education (HGSE). He has written more than 50 proposals and directed 20 grant-funded research and development projects.

Dovi Weiss, MEd, MBA, PhD candidate, is chief pedagogical officer and co-founder, Time To Know, Inc. Previously, Weiss served as CEO at e-nnovate; head of high tech innovation at SIT Ltd.; and head of interactive training and learning products at Onyx Interactive. In 2010, Weiss was chosen to be among the top 50 influential Israeli people in education.

Index

Page numbers followed by *f* or *t* indicate figures and tables, respectively.